The Northern Question

The Northern Question

A History of a Divided Country

Tom Hazeldine

VERSO

London • New York

First published by Verso 2020
© Tom Hazeldine 2020
An earlier version of Chapter 9 appeared as 'Revolt of the Rustbelt',
New Left Review 105, May–June 2017

1 3 5 7 9 10 8 6 4 2

Verso
UK: 6 Meard Street, London W1F 0EG
US: 20 Jay Street, Suite 1010, Brooklyn, NY 11201
versobooks.com

Verso is the imprint of New Left Books

ISBN-13: 978-1-78663-406-1
ISBN-13: 978-1-78663-408-5 (US EBK)
ISBN-13: 978-1-78663-407-8 (UK EBK)

British Library Cataloguing in Publication Data
A catalogue record for this book is available from the British Library

Library of Congress Cataloging-in-Publication Data
A catalog record for this book is available from the Library of Congress
Library of Congress Control Number: 2020941831

Typeset in Sabon by MJ & N Gavan, Truro, Cornwall
Printed in the UK by CPI Group (UK) Ltd, Croydon CR0 4YY

For Anton, my Londoner

The lamented 'growing abyss' between North and South should not really be a subject for mere figures, nor for moral outrage, nor for futile retreads of Westminster-inspired 'modernisation': it can't be tackled within the existing State, because it is the existing State, the dominance of the Crown (or 'anti-industrial') culture, the thriving pseudo-nationalism of the Old Regime.

Tom Nairn, *The Enchanted Glass* (1988)

Contents

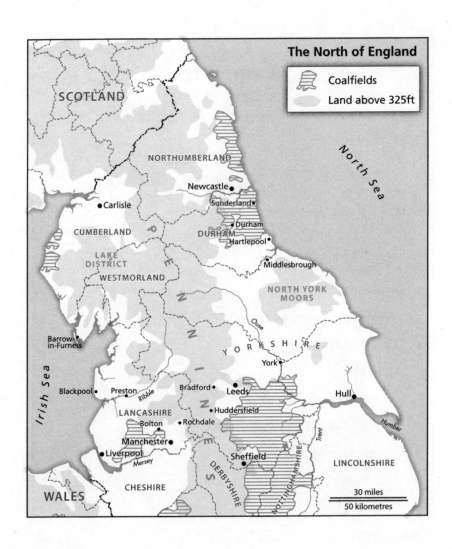

The North of England

Coalfields
Land above 325ft

SCOTLAND

NORTHUMBERLAND

North Sea

Newcastle
•Carlisle
Sunderland•
CUMBERLAND
Durham•
DURHAM
Hartlepool•
LAKE
DISTRICT
Middlesbrough•
WESTMORLAND

NORTH YORK
MOORS

P
E
N
N
I
N
E
S

Ouse

Barrow-
in-Furness

YORKSHIRE

York•

Irish Sea

Blackpool•   Preston•   Bradford• •Leeds
Ribble
LANCASHIRE   •Huddersfield
Bolton•   •Rochdale
Hull•

Humber

Manchester•
•Liverpool
Mersey

Sheffield•

Trent

N
O
T
T
I
N
G
H
A
M
S
H
I
R
E

LINCOLNSHIRE

WALES   CHESHIRE

D
E
R
B
Y
S
H
I
R
E

30 miles
50 kilometres

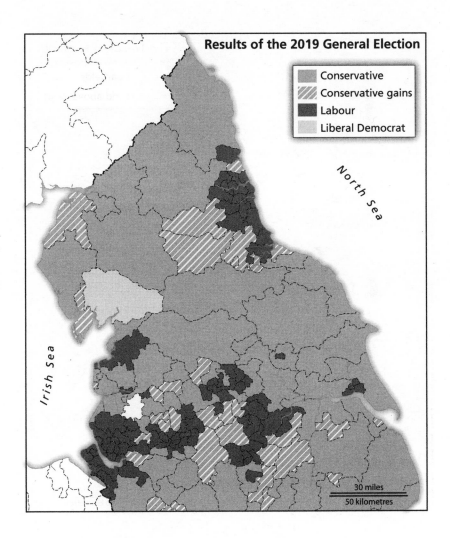

Results of the 2019 General Election

Conservative
Conservative gains
Labour
Liberal Democrat

North Sea

Irish Sea

30 miles
50 kilometres

Preface

How to get a handle on the politics of an out-of-kilter country like Britain? In *The Northern Question* I wager that it requires an approach to the problem of regional division. There was a brief period in the late 2010s when this became something of a commonplace. Nothing else could account for the topsy-turvy quality of the pre-pandemic years, when, as the *Financial Times* put it, 'a new national appetite for upheaval' turned Britain into 'the Western world's box of surprises'.[1]

The political temperature in the capital gave a misleading impression of where the crisis over Brexit was headed. Opinion in Westminster and the City was, for the most part, dead-set against leaving the EU. Fleet Street was more divided but just as flummoxed by the referendum result. The *FT* awoke with a start to a 'roar of rage from alienated voters' that toppled the prime minister, jeopardised the Union, diminished the UK's international standing and destabilised the currency and bond markets, sending the pound to a thirty-year low. 'Intense volatility was inevitable given how far prices had been bid up in anticipation of a Remain vote,' it regretted.[2] Ordinary Londoners voted Remain in 2016 and Labour in 2017 and 2019; whoever was in charge through this period, it wasn't them.[3]

Among the 'devolved nations', parliamentary arithmetic and the logistics of cross-border trade gave the Unionist majority in Belfast special leverage over the Theresa May government, but as beneficiary of the crisis on the mainland not prime mover. Scottish politics had stabilised after Labour's 2015 implosion, while the Cardiff administration continued to be all but invisible.

It was instead northern England that propelled itself to the foreground of national attention, for the first time since the socio-economic crisis of the Thatcher years. Wasted by Whitehall spending cuts, the North voted down the Cameron government in the referendum, then declined to fall into line with Theresa May's pro-Brexit but also pro-austerity administration at the subsequent general election, helping to land the Conservatives – against all expectations – in a hung Parliament. Following that debacle, I wrote a draft article for *New Left Review* arguing that Britain's ruling institutions, having shot the industrial North dead on behalf of the conflicting policy requirements of the City of London, all of sudden found a northern albatross lying heavy around their necks. Editors at the journal objected to the metaphor of a dead bird, but otherwise kept the image. The weight of the North bore down on Westminster, imperilling any attempt to forestall the impending farewell from Brussels through the ruse of a second referendum.

Saying this much isn't to figure rustbelt discontent as the sole dynamic in play. The pressure on Conservative seats from UKIP that edged Cameron towards the precipice of a Remain/Leave referendum, and the July 2019 election of Johnson as party leader on a hard-Brexit platform by a Tory membership concentrated in the Home Counties, suggest otherwise. The trumping of material predictors of a Remain position by an ideological adherence to Leave – call it 'reassertion of ex-imperial national identity' – was strongest in affluent Berkshire, Buckinghamshire and Oxfordshire.[4] The South contributed a lower surplus of 'Out' ballots than the Midlands or the North, where the objective conditions for a protest vote were stronger, but it exercised a leading influence over the Conservatives' path into and through the crisis.

That Johnson was ultimately able to drag his party and government clear of the Brexit morass, however, relied on the lifeline thrown him by traditionally Labour-voting constituencies in the North's former industrial monotowns and coalfield communities. For the geographer Doreen Massey, writing after a second resounding election victory for Thatcher in 1987, Labour's strongholds in the North, Scotland and Wales constituted the 'heartlands of defeat'.[5] If history repeats itself, its variations never fail to surprise. In 2019, support for Labour in the heads of the Valleys and West Wales dropped, the SNP consolidated its local hegemony north of the Border, and most strikingly of all, northern England powered the governing Conservatives to national victory. A section of the deracinated northern working class reeling from forty years of Thatcherism had 'lent' its support to a Tory administration first hoisted into power by John Bull pensioners in the southern shires.

Whatever one thinks of these proceedings – and exiting the European Union caught some on the left in no man's land between Bennite Euroscepticism and hostility towards the Powellite Leave campaign mounted by Farage – a fuller contextualisation is needed for the protest votes that upended politics-as-usual before ushering in a restoration under a Conservative government whose distinctive mixture of late-Thatcherism, public-school amateurism and electoral populism will determine our passage through the more profound dislocations of the current decade.

The North held on to its unusual political prominence until the March 2020 budget, after which Westminster was overwhelmed by the coronavirus. The pandemic has placed new stresses on the UK's territoriality: devolved administrations going their own way over how and when to unwind the spring lockdown; new metro mayors popping up on national media threatening to do likewise, though in reality powerless to manage the contagion; the more consequential tier of local authorities below them frustrating the government's early reopening of English schools. But in spite of these irritants, the failure to control the coronavirus is a failure of the centralised, neoliberalised British state – one that, as I write, has delegated responsibility for post-lockdown contact tracing to the FTSE listed outsourcing firm Serco, routinely rated 'piss poor' by *Private Eye*, in preference to municipal directors of public health.

In theory, the non-metropolitan North ought to enjoy exceptional prominence ahead of the next election, due by 2024, the strategic calculations of Johnson's Downing Street pivoting on the wants and needs of small-town rustbelt areas previously consigned to the political margins. But our present problems are so overwhelming, and so general, that Beltway politics is going to have its hands full. Britain-without-London, to adapt a term used by Anthony Barnett, may have to make do with Jubilee festivities and all the other rigmaroles of national togetherness – 'one nation, indivisible', as the republican tradition in France and America has it; 'Better Together' is all that the local bourgeoisie has recently come up with.[6] Neither a modicum of capital investment nor a cushioning of the next round of cuts to revenue expenditure will close the regional gap. Nor, in all likelihood, will the collateral damage from the virus.

I won't pretend that the North–South divide explains all the problems of English (still less, British) history. Yet by looking at the interaction between nation-state, social class and geographical region, we can let some light in through several windows. What follows isn't comprehensive, but should contribute to (and if necessary, restart) an important debate. Whitehall's long abandonment of the North needs to be explained, not merely deplored.

1

North and South

The rise and fall of northern England as an industrial power is one of the signal processes in modern British history: something to set alongside the rise and rise of the City of London. Its pioneering Industrial Revolution has a stronger case for priority in the world-historical reckoning than anything the rest of the country can boast; only London as capital of empire and high finance will bear the comparison. In the immediate aftermath of the First World War, the economies of the South East (including London) and the North were roughly on level pegging, accounting for 35 and 30 per cent of British gross domestic product respectively. By the end of the twentieth century, the South East's share had risen to 40 while the North's had dropped to 21 per cent. From a position near parity, the regions had so diverged in their fortunes that the output of one was twice that of the other. Through boom and bust, London then increased its share by another 5 percentage points between 1997 and 2017.[1]

Regional disparities grounded in successive rounds of uneven development and the biases of official policy are not peculiar to Britain. As David Harvey has written, 'Capitalism *is* uneven geographical development' – and, if anything, becoming more so. The era of neoliberal globalisation multiplied opportunities for 'the uneven insertion of different territories and social formations into the capitalist world market'.[2] As regulatory powers are stripped away, wealth is becoming more and more concentrated in the hands of the opulent few. The Organisation for Economic Co-operation and Development, a mouthpiece for free-market economies, notes that 'while gaps in GDP per capita across OECD countries have narrowed over the last two decades, within their own borders countries are witnessing increasing income gaps among regions, cities and people'.[3]

If this is the common pattern, Britain is nevertheless a special case in a European context: more lopsided economically than Italy, despite its notoriously incomplete Risorgimento; than Spain, with its historic polarity of Catalan–Basque industry and Andalusian *latifundia*; than Germany, where a quarter of a century after reunification GDP per head in the East was still only two-thirds of that in the West; than France, enshadowed by a metropolis great enough to warrant comparison with its cross-Channel neighbour. At the time of Cameron's Brexit referendum, output per head was eight times higher in inner west London than in West Wales and the Valleys, the largest difference to be found in any EU member state from Bantry Bay to the Dniester.[4] So it is that a former regional-policy adviser at the European Commission could observe that 'the economic geography of the UK nowadays increasingly reflects the patterns typically observed in developing or former-transition economies rather than in other advanced economies'. In several peripheral states – Ireland and Portugal in the far west; the Czech Republic, Hungary, Poland, Romania and Slovakia to the east – only the capital city region achieves output per capita above the EU average.[5] The UK is richer, but aside from the intermezzo of the Industrial Revolution, its development has been similarly monocentric.

The enmeshing of low-wage Asian and east European economies in Western capitalist supply chains in the last quarter of the twentieth century caused the manufacturing bases of all West European and North American countries to contract to some degree. But northern England has tumbled from a unique pedestal, that of the world's first industrial region, and fallen further than the world-economic conjuncture demanded. The contribution of manufacturing to national output in the UK has flatlined at just 10 per cent since 2007, barely a third of the figure for Germany and a smaller proportion also than for other comparable economies.[6]

One would have struggled to get a sense, however, from pane-gyrics to the North – whether by writers in residence or those exiled in London – of any sort of regional crisis brewing. According to Martin Wainwright's *True North* (2009), published toward the end of the New Labour period, the region has it all: breath-taking countryside, the Sellafield nuclear complex, fish and chips.[7] Through all their ups and downs, northerners have retained their inventiveness and independence of mind. Derelict industrial sites have found new life as heritage parks, leisure attractions and loft conversions. Manchester has been 'utterly, wonderfully trans-formed' since an IRA bombing in 1996 blasted away the city's declinist mentality. Likewise, Liverpool is an 'astonishingly dif-ferent' place to the decaying, demoralised hulk of the eighties. The credit for the latter's revival belongs to Michael Heseltine, Thatcher's minister for Merseyside, whose diagnosis of the city's ills – sidelined and demoralised local leadership, weak corporate management and belligerent trade unions – was 'spot on'.[7] Forget, for a moment, that Liverpool still had one of the worst real unem-ployment rates in Britain, and that Manchester suffered the largest decrease in gross disposable household income per head, relative to the UK average, of any local area under New Labour and the Cameron coalition.[8]

In language reminiscent of Thatcher's diatribe about 'moaning minnies' when challenged by a Tyne Tees reporter about high unemployment in the North East, Wainwright warns about a victim mentality spreading out from coalfields: a misplaced sus-picion that London will never play fair by the region. It would be much better, in his view, to accentuate the positive. 'I know there is a downside to life up here, just as there is everywhere in the world. But we really don't need to go on about it.' Northern editor of what was once the *Manchester Guardian*, Wainwright would probably agree that the North has a reputation for plain speaking: it warrants sharper treatment than this.[9]

Part of the problem in writing about the North is how to charac-terise a region which constitutionally doesn't exist. For as long as it lasts, the United Kingdom is a unitary, not a federal, state: *political power* is focussed on the golden triangle of Whitehall, Westminster and St James's – a West End counterpart to the concentration of *financial* power within the Square Mile. Devolved parliaments and assemblies in the Celtic fringe exist purely at Westminster's pleasure, as periodic reversions to direct rule over Northern Ireland attest. Delegation of executive functions from London to the English regions is officially countenanced only in contingency planning for a nuclear attack or – almost as bad – large-scale trade-union strike action.[10] There *used* to be a Northern region running along the Scottish border until the Major government, tinkering with the structure as it looked to draw in EU funding, reassigned Cumbria to the North West and created a North East region out of the remainder. So much for the official North: no more than a caprice of the Whitehall mind.

If the North isn't a hand-me-down from the UK's archaic constitutional arrangements, nor is it a product of simple geography. The old riverine markers – Defoe likened his foray beyond the Trent to crossing the Rubicon – weren't clinching facts even in feudal times. According to a recent appraisal, the medieval North could be said to have comprised the five and a half counties above the Humber, Ouse and Ribble; the eight counties north of the Humber, Trent and Mersey; or these eight together with Cheshire and Lincolnshire.[11]

Does the North announce itself with any clarity? A sense of cultural belonging certainly exists, but it's low-wattage compared to the nationalist imaginaries of the Basque Country and Catalonia, with their separatist movements, distinctive languages and jealously guarded autonomies. Unlike Spain, regional identities in England have been levelled out by a millennium of centralised rule and the modern impress of powerful institutions like the Fleet Street of old and the BBC. The British state may have independence movements to contend with in Northern Ireland and Scotland but there is no prospect of the English core coming unstuck. Despite a regional inflection to voting patterns, the English choose between national political parties and consume the same news. The *Northern Echo*, self-styled 'Great Daily of the North', has a circulation of just 23,000 spread across County Durham, north Yorkshire and Teesside. Another 'national newspaper for the North', called 24, launched in Carlisle in 2016 only to close within a few weeks, squeezed out by the Fleet Street dailies. Three northern regionalist parties emerged either side of the 2014 European Parliament elections, beginning with Yorkshire First, founded by an expat Holmfirth businessman, but it would require the introduction of regional assemblies elected by proportional representation to give such groups a foothold, and the Holyrood model looks increasingly foolhardy from a Whitehall perspective – devolution is 'a dangerous game to play', says Blair – so there will be no significant loosening of centralist shackles.[12] Taken together, the current North East, North West and Yorkshire–Humber regions are two-and-a-half times the size of Scotland in terms of population and economic output, apparently without meriting any relaxation of direct rule from London.

In academic literature, 'a consensus emerges that northern consciousness is both extremely fragile and generally secondary to other systems of identification.'[13] Even smaller regional groupings struggle to overcome local particularities. The North East is 'incoherent and barely self-conscious'; Lancashire 'more a geographical expression than a cultural unity'; Yorkshire the butt of Conservative jokes on account of infighting between its municipal elites.[14] Simon Green, co-editor of the *Northern History* journal at the University of Leeds, concedes that

> England's historic regions seldom enjoyed much more than the trappings of independent government. As a result, they always wanted, and now self-evidently lack, many of the most important political dimensions of modern regionalism. That institutional poverty had inevitable cultural implications too. Put bluntly, English regionalism was and is comparatively weak.[15]

Remarkably, *Northern History* nevertheless managed to pull together a working model of the North in short order. When it launched in 1966, the journal defined its target region, without further ado, in terms of 'the six northern counties': Cumberland, Durham, Lancashire, Northumberland, Westmorland and Yorkshire. Six shortly became seven with the surreptitious addition of Cheshire at the behest of editorial committee member Arthur Taylor. 'The change was not only silent, it was unexplained in private as well as in public sources. It remains, largely, unexplained,'

comments Green quizzically.[16] The selection may apparently serve
as its own justification.

Northern History grew out of a campus study group established in Leeds in the late fifties by Asa Briggs, liberal historian of
Victorian Britain, just as fresh ideas like new social history were
emerging onto the academic scene. 'Professional historians have
begun to pull apart "nation", "economy" and "society" and to
examine the nature and significance of local differentiation,' wrote
Briggs. His edited volume *Chartist Studies*, a set of area-based
studies, dates to this period. Outside the academy, public agencies
and private-sector developers were combining to transform the
face of the North – slums and smokestacks giving way to high-
rise flats, industrial estates, shopping precincts, ring roads and
motorways. 'The North of England is changing so rapidly,' Briggs
observed, 'that now is the time to clarify some issues in its history
which it may be difficult to sort out in the future.'[17] The idea of the
region was also in political vogue. Macmillan appointed a minister
for the North East; Wilson pledged to create economic planning
machinery in every region.[18]

In *Northern History*'s inaugural issue, Briggs urged contrib-
utors to keep away from the parish-pump, antiquarian school
of local history. 'Outward-looking rather than inward-looking
northern history is what is most needed, the kind of history which
sets out to compare.' But he was writing from a new billet at the
University of Sussex, and founder editor Gordon Forster instead
aimed for a balance between comparative analysis and more
conventional town and county history. Forster's own interests
were weighted towards the latter: he contributed well-rounded
pieces on early modern Beverley, Hull and York to the famously
antiquarian *Victoria County History* series.[19] In the event, *Northern History*'s publication record has favoured local and discrete
studies – the evolution of the Doncaster corn market, burial practices in the northern Danelaw – over wide-angled or unorthodox
perspectives. Comparative pieces tend to be confined to northern
territory: the strength of Methodism in three contrasting areas
of the Durham coalfield; Second World War civilian morale in
Hull, Liverpool and Manchester. On Green's count, the proportion of articles taking up a general regional theme has risen over

time from a quarter to closer to a third. A 2013 retrospective by Sheffield historian David Hey to mark the publication of *Northern History*'s fiftieth volume jettisoned the 'old tradition' of a North–South divide on the ground that the sheer diversity of the North, amply demonstrated in the journal's pages, defied generalisation. The journal has accumulated a rich storehouse of scholarly work, but as an intellectual project it amounts to northern history virtually without a North.[20]

The only serious general history of the North has been Frank Musgrove's *The North of England: A History from Roman Times to the Present* (1990), which originated outside the history faculty – as does this present venture. Musgrove was a professor of education at the University of Manchester and a headstrong, combustible writer inflected with the libertarian impulses of the New Right. He had taught in schools on the Nottinghamshire coalfield and in colonial Uganda (the British 'certainly left Africa far too early').[21] A Nottingham grammar school boy, he became a trenchant critic of the move under Wilson and Heath to all-ability comprehensive education. Mass schooling of adolescents was a disaster. It was up to society, not overworked teachers, to solve 'the already serious problem of massive surpluses of human beings in post-industrial states'.[22] Evincing a patrician disgust for the sordid business of electoral politics, he endorsed the Maastricht Treaty on the unorthodox ground that 'when a significant amount of our political life has been displaced across the Channel we may at last devote appropriate time, talent and resources to other vital areas of our national life like philosophy, science, literature, industry and technology'.[23]

These conservative reflexes are evident in his history of the North, which highlights 'four periods of particular northern distinction, importance and power': Roman times, including York's brief fame as an imperial capital; the Northumbrian renaissance of the seventh and eighth centuries; the Wars of the Roses; and the Industrial Revolution. The principal dynamic is the ebb and flow of power between centre and circumference. In Musgrove's telling, the North has not so much been transformed through its history as periodically set free. Instances of government neglect, whether of medieval border defences or today's inner cities, ought to be occasions for provincial flourishing. 'The essential conflict of the later twentieth century is not against a dominant "class" but against a dominant and over-extended centre.' Thatcher's sell-offs of public corporations heralded a welcome new phase of decentralisation. He makes no mention of privatisation's corporate beneficiaries or of the Conservatives' simultaneous assault on local-government freedoms. Instead the book closes with a broadside against the 1984–5 miners' strike, condemned as an outrageous example of regional sectionalism. The pits were a drain on the Exchequer and had to go.[24] While the strike was on, Musgrove exploited his academic credentials to denigrate the miners in the Murdoch press as ill-educated dupes, 'diluted human residues', whose 'conceptual range does not extend much beyond "scab"'.[25]

The North was due a historian but hardly deserved becoming a target of this wretched social Darwinism. Nevertheless, frothing *obiter dicta* don't lessen the significance of Musgrove's book; indeed, one could fairly say it towers over the rest of what is available, if only because it offers a historical take on the North in a *longue durée* going back to Roman times; is consistently class-focussed; sets the region in a context wider than just the South – above all its relation to Scotland, but also Europe; and integrates the intellectual–cultural aspects of the region fully along with the economic and political dimensions. Criticism, in a case like this, can never be simple dismissal.

Within the academy, though, *The North of England* was out of step with the cultural turn overtaking northern studies in this period. Musgrove's colleague at Manchester Patrick Joyce indicates the postmodern mood of the times in *Visions of the People* (1991), an anti-Marxist polemic wrapped up in an account of mass culture in industrial Lancashire between the decline of Chartism and the First World War. Class consciousness, argues Joyce – 'the term has indeed an antiquated ring to it' – was not strongly in evidence outside the factory and trade-union chapel. In other settings, non-economic and populist conceptions of the social order prevailed. Of course, Joyce was hardly the first to remark on the 'essentially bourgeois ideas and viewpoints' of English workers.[26]

One of the better books to come out of the cultural-studies

complex, Dave Russell's *Looking North: Northern England and the National Imagination* (2004), examines the amount of cultural autonomy enjoyed by the North in fields ranging from dialect literature to the big screen. 'The North has never been able to enjoy a sustained or broad-based cultural leadership,' Russell observes. English national culture 'has always been largely constructed from within London and its immediate environs'. Breakthrough moments for the region – the industrial novels of the 1840s, the Wigan Pier era, the kitchen-sink dramas of the late fifties and early sixties, post-industrial Manchester's music scene – were flash-in-the-pan affairs, even if Factory Records still enjoys plenty of cachet.[27]

DJ Dave Haslam and NME writer Paul Morley have each hazarded Hacienda-tinged reflections on the historical personality of 'Madchester'.[28] Morley's euphoric place-memoir and montage book *The North (and Almost Everything in It)* (2013) venerates 'a North packed with intrepid people handing on the North, as they see it, all that history, and nature, and difference. A North, all on its own.' There isn't much concession to London-centrism here. As an exercise in style and rhetoric, Morley's offering is ambitious. It alternates between localized, micro-Stockport reminiscence/self-presentation and a collage of decontextualized figures, from or connected to, the North – comedians, writers, musicians, artists, scientists, politicians – plus chronological oddments going back to the Middle Ages. The method, according to the author, is a combination of *Tristram Shandy* and trawling the internet. Morley's lead hero, because he comes from Oldham, is Labour frontbencher J. R. Clynes, best known for his ignominious role in helping to break the General Strike (the year 1926 is conspicuously missing from Morley's chronological landmarks). There is a reverent tribute to Clynes's refusal to fight the class war from David Miliband, while another former New Labour minister praises Barbara Castle for her valiant effort to tighten industrial-relations law. Harold Wilson, meanwhile, is converted into 'one of the outstanding scholars of his generation'. A hymn to the 'brilliance of the North' and its 'twenty-first-century Renaissance', *The North (and Almost Everything in It)* is, in its own account, 'hallucination, not history'. In this excitable company, literary critic Terry Eagleton, also formerly of Manchester University, is probably right to caution that 'there's no need to get too misty-eyed about the region'.[29]

Let's instead pick up the trail laid down by George Orwell in *The Road to Wigan Pier* (1937), when he observes that 'it was the industrialisation of the North that gave the North–South antithesis its peculiar slant.'[30] The proliferation of cotton mills, coalmines and shipyards in a hitherto backwater region lent British capitalism an unusual dual character. During the factory capitalism of the long nineteenth century, stretching from the Napoleonic Wars to 1914, England was split between older capitalist sectors in the South – commerce, finance, agriculture – and leading-edge industrial concerns upcountry.[31] The small traditional manufactories of southern counties were driven out of business; in consequence, the shires were turned over more fully to the agricultural and leisured classes. 'London was once the very focus of national thought and industry, surrounded on every side by the most flourishing parts of the country,' the *Cornhill Magazine*, a bastion of the metropolitan literati, wistfully remarked in 1881. But the South had been reduced to 'a succession of quiet rural districts', while the Great Wen depended for continued greatness upon its traditional administrative functions, its enormous number of inhabitants, its centrality in the national transport network and its unrivalled amenities for high society.[32]

Surveying the pattern of party affiliation shortly afterwards, in the Edwardian period, the liberal economist J. A. Hobson noted a hardening electoral divide between a Unionist, non-industrial South and an industrial North which voted Liberal or Labour. Each bloc had a distinct pattern of money making, lifestyle and culture. They amounted, in these matters, to separate countries:

> One England in which the well-to-do classes, from their numbers, wealth, leisure and influence, mould the external character of the civilisation and determine the habits, feelings and opinions of the people, the other England in which the structure and activities of large organised industries, carried on by great associated masses of artisans, factory hands and miners, are the dominating facts and forces.[33]

The distinction between an industrial North and genteel–commercial South persisted in the interwar period. Even though the South East had by this point amassed more manufacturing jobs than the North West, as new consumer industries clustered around the enormous London market, there still wasn't much of an industrial stamp about the Home Counties, which continued to function as a pleasure park for the moneyed classes despite the wealth-sapping effects of the war and a bumpy world economy. 'There is at least a tinge of truth in that picture of southern England as one enormous Brighton inhabited by lounge-lizards,' commented Orwell.

> For climatic reasons the parasitic dividend-drawing class tend to settle in the South. In a Lancashire cotton-town you could probably go for months on end without once hearing an 'educated' accent, whereas there can hardly be a town in the South of England where you could throw a brick without hitting the niece of a bishop.

The North, by contrast, remained home to most of the coal industry and other Victorian staples, and therefore also to 'the most typical section of the English working class'. The region had become a byword, however, not for earnest industry – Hobson's phrase – but for mass industrial unemployment. 'To study unemployment and its effects you have got to go to the industrial areas,' wrote Orwell. 'In the South unemployment exists, but it is scattered and queerly unobtrusive. There are plenty of rural districts where a man out of work is almost unheard-of, and you don't anywhere see the spectacle of whole blocks of cities living on the dole and the [Public Assistance Committee].'[34]

The North reflated during the Second World War, but in the post-1945 period its smokestack industries were no match for the newer manufacturing plant and bustling service economy of the South, which soon began to pull away again. To deflect criticism over this discrepancy, Labour and the Conservatives between them extended a modest state-aid regime across the whole of northern England, Scotland and Wales. Private-sector manufacturers were cajoled, but not directed, into siting overspill plant in the former depressed areas. 'To the southerner, the North, like the poor, is "always with us": and to assist the unluckier half of this island is a work of expensive charity,' observed Neil Ascherson in 1962.[35] Drifting into difficulty a decade later, British capitalism threw the burden of provincial manufacturing overboard. The real value of regional industrial assistance fell by two-thirds between 1975 and 1985.[36]

Industrial decline, retrenchment of the state's social functions and, latterly, market-driven urban redevelopment have combined to blight large swathes of the North. 'Staring out the window, the strangest thing I saw was how desolate and empty the streets are now. We would drive for minutes without seeing anyone,' remarked journalist Stephen Armstrong, surveying the legacy of New Labour's urban-regeneration programme in bulldozed east Manchester in 2011. 'Instead of dirty, closely packed housing there were acres and acres of desolate ground all grassed over. You could still see the outline of streets, where houses used to be – but now, nothing. It was as if the Triffids had arrived.' Armstrong's previous work, *The Super-Rich Shall Inherit the Earth* (2010), had given an ambivalent assessment of the doings of the global economic elite on the British scene. The UK had become 'a kind of damp Monte Carlo', the world-financial hub of London attracting billionaires from around the world on account of its money-laundering facilities, property portfolios and enviable lifestyle options. Just as J. A. Hobson had written a century earlier, south-east England remains, for the privileged classes, 'a place of residence and a playground'.[37]

Deindustrialisation has meant that contemporary regional disparities are characterised less by industry versus finance than by the positional superiority of London in a services-dominated national economic space – the northern rustbelt acting, in effect, as senior representative of left-behind England. However, since the North has never achieved the escape velocity needed to free itself from its industrial past, we may have licence to approach the region by way of the original sites of the manufacturing revolution, in order to see how they have fared. So defined, the North centres on the old Lancashire–Yorkshire textile belt, flanked by the ports of Liverpool and Hull; the former heavy-industrial zones of west Lancashire, west Cumberland, south Yorkshire and the

North East coast; and the abandoned coalfields these conurbations grew up on and around. This North encompasses the major urban areas of the official North East, North West and Yorkshire–Humber regions while also taking in High Peak textile towns such as Glossop and New Mills as well as the north Derbyshire coalfield, which 'looked to Sheffield as a natural centre'.[38]

On a statistical basis, much more of the Midlands belongs on the northern side of the regional divide. The aggregated socio-economic indicators point to a fissure running east to west between the Humber and Severn estuaries, stranding not just the northern regions but also the West Midlands except Warwickshire and the East Midland counties of Derbyshire and Nottinghamshire in the zone of relative economic disadvantage.[39] In the aftermath of the deep industrial recession inflicted by the first Thatcher administration, Beatrix Campbell penned *Wigan Pier Revisited* (1984) in dialogue with Orwell's original commentary. 'The crisis of the eighties occasions a return visit,' she explained. But Wigan, shorn of its cotton and coal, was now a town 'much like anywhere else, with a bit of light engineering and service industries'. Campbell therefore extended her remit to the recession-blighted West Midlands. Its auto trade had been one of the twentieth century's major growth industries; the car worker, not the coal miner, was 'the modern paradigm of the working class'. When this industry hit the buffers in the seventies, it supplanted Lancashire cotton as the emblem of British manufacturing decline. To study mass unemployment and its effects, you didn't any more need to travel further north than Coventry, where 'on whole housing estates half the population are on the dole.'[40]

Crucially, though, the Midlands arrived at this sorry pass via a different route. Until the eighteenth century it had been

bound into a nexus of economic and social values which connected it to the prevailing county interests of the South. Anglican, Tory, protectionist, this 'estate' culture was inimical even to the pre-industrial values of the less heavily 'countified' North ... Later, the eclipse of the [rural] Warwickshire interest and the rise of industry in the Midland towns appears to re-centre the region in the general scheme of things, bringing its character (if not its exact structure) more into line with the North and causing some renegotiation of its currency.[41]

Closer to the North, but still structurally distinct, the Midlands hosted some notable early experiments in factory production: Boulton's Soho manufactory near Birmingham, Coalbrookdale in Shropshire, Wedgwood's Staffordshire pottery works. But once Manchester had cornered the steam-powered cotton trade, the East Midlands was relegated to also-ran status – busy in the manufacture of hosiery and lace, boots and shoes, and subsequently also of locomotives, but no industrial behemoth – while Birmingham and the Black Country met the booming demand for a miscellany of domestic metal goods (pots and pans, locks, light arms, etc.) by multiplying the number of workshops and sweatshops instead of concentrating production in big factories. What the Industrial Revolution required, wrote Hobsbawm, was 'the special kind of expansion which produced Manchester rather than Birmingham'.[42] When J. A. Hobson in 1910 accused Birmingham of severing itself from the bulk of industrial Britain through its defection from Liberalism to Unionism, he explained this shift not only in terms of the charisma and political machine of former mayor Joseph Chamberlain, but also by reference to the city's peculiar industrial structure: 'small factories or workshops which do not favour effective trade unionism, and are engaged in making goods which are exposed to close foreign competition, to an unusual extent'.[43] An artisanal centre slow to switch over to the factory system, Birmingham followed its own distinct trajectory; it has a different story to tell.[44]

Such are the *objective* coordinates that have historically differentiated England's North, Midlands and South. On the other side of the coin is the question of when, and in what ways, the North became a *subjective* category of widely received social or political significance. What were the stages and markers of this process? Once again, the answer appears to lie in the industrial era. Although Helen Jewell's book *The North–South Divide* (1994), subtitled *The Origin of Northern Consciousness in England*, purports to track regional self-consciousness back to Northumbrian times, what emerges from her trawl of the archives is instead the cultural othering of a backwater region – in her rendering, 'ferocious, obstinate and unyielding' – within the upper ranks of southern English society. In other words, it shows the all but complete absence of regional self-consciousness in the period she covers, roughly 600–1750. What at the end she does concede, to her credit, is that in so far as there were conceptions of the 'North' as a separate region/culture within England, these came from the South, not the North itself. But they were themselves at most casual and sporadic.[45]

Genuine crystallisation of a systematic identification of the North as a region seems to date only from the 1850s, the moment of Elizabeth Gaskell's novel. For Raymond Williams, 'the mood of England in the Industrial Revolution is a mood of contrasts'. *North and South* captured it best of all the industrial novels. The book is an adventure in binaries: town and country, Anglicanism and Dissent, rich and poor, paternalism and laissez-faire, even a little pride and prejudice.[46] It is also the strongest dramatisation of the changed regional equation resulting from the spatial concentration of the factory system. Gaskell's protagonist, Margaret Hale, is a young gentlewoman from Hampshire with London tastes cultivated during visits to an aunt in Harley Street. When her clerical father has Doubts, the family must relocate to Milton-Northern, a fictionalised Manchester. Unfortunately, Margaret has 'almost a detestation for all she had ever heard of the North of England'. The Hales travel to Milton via London, where Margaret's mother rhapsodises about the fine carriages and vast plate-glass shop windows. On arriving at Milton, a different cityscape confronts them:

> Long, straight, hopeless streets of regularly built houses, all small and of brick. Here and there a great oblong many-windowed factory stood up, like a hen among her chickens, puffing out black 'unparliamentary' smoke, and sufficiently accounting for the cloud which Margaret had taken to foretell rain. As they drove through the larger and wider streets, from the station to the hotel, they had to stop constantly; great loaded lorries blocked up the not over-wide thoroughfares. Margaret had now

and then been into the city [of London] in her drives with her aunt. But there the heavy lumbering vehicles seemed various in their purposes and intent; here every van, every wagon and truck, bore cotton, either in the raw shape in bags, or the woven shape in bales of calico. People thronged the footpaths, most of them well-dressed as regarded the material, but with a slovenly looseness which struck Margaret as different from the shabby, threadbare smartness of a similar class in London.[47]

Manchester versus London: a smoke-ridden monoculture dealing in a single commodity, juxtaposed with the varied commercial life of the capital, its high-end retail outlets and better-turned-out common folk. While it is possible to match up certain functionally equivalent towns on either side of the North–South divide – cathedral cities Canterbury and York; spa towns Bath and Harrogate; the ports of Bristol and Newcastle – there are no southern counterparts to the great industrial cities of the North. As Gaskell puts it, 'Milton is a much more smoky, dirty town than you will ever meet with in the South.'[48]

Margaret's impression of a difference in social mores in her new home is soon vindicated. The factory hands are brassy; the mill owners bluff. 'One had need to learn a different language, and measure by a different standard, up here in Milton.' Disagreements multiply about social ethics and standards of living. Margaret is appalled by the poisonous industrial relations in the town. Her paternalistic instincts are perhaps in keeping with the Hale family's accustomed milieu of clergymen and country squires; they may also reflect Gaskell's reading of Thomas Carlyle. But in Milton they run up against the hard-faced Manchester school of self-help. This from cotton magnate John Thornton:

I value my own independence so highly that I fancy no degradation greater than that of having another man perpetually directing and advising and lecturing me, or even planning too closely in any way about my actions. He might be the wisest of men, or the most powerful – I should equally rebel and resent his interference. I imagine this is a stronger feeling in the North of England than in the South.[49]

Margaret defends the southern way against Thornton but changes tack when quizzed by careworn factory hands about a land where, according to her wistful remembrances, 'food is cheap and wages good, and all the folk, rich and poor, master and man, friendly like'. No, she insists, the South would not suit them:

> You would not bear the dullness of the life; you don't know what it is; it would eat you away like rust. Those that have lived there all their lives, are used to soaking in the stagnant waters. They labour on, from day to day, in the great solitude of steaming fields – never speaking or lifting up their poor, bent, downcast heads ... You could not stir them up into any companionship, which you get in a town as plentiful as the air you breathe, whether it be good or bad.

This overcooked passage ignores a tradition of agricultural protest, most conspicuously the Swing riots of 1830–31, but serves its purpose of bringing England's two halves back into essential balance. One of Margaret's interlocutors obligingly concludes, 'North an' South have each getten their own troubles. If work's sure and steady theer, labour's paid at starvation prices; while here we'n rucks o' money coming in one quarter, and ne'er a farthing th' next.'[50]

Identification of the North as a society composed of just two classes, industrialists and factory workers, neither of whom existed in the South, underwent two subsequent, crucial modifications. Next came the moment when, the industrial bourgeoisie having so completely either fused with capital or the ruling class at large or just faded away, the North became identified essentially solely with the working class that remained *in situ*, forming anyway the great majority of the population. This wasn't necessarily at all a negative projection. It dates from a century later, between the late 1950s and the arrival of the Beatles in 1962 – the years of Richard Hoggart's *The Uses of Literacy*, kitchen-sink dramas such as *A Taste of Honey* and *Room at the Top*, and the beginnings of Granada television in Lancashire and Yorkshire, whose success would force BBC output onto northern terrain (*The Likely Lads*, *Z Cars*).[51] For a brief period, this heady brew took the character of a creative insurgency against the southern citadels of cultural complacency. Arguably it was ultimately incorporated (a first wave of corporate 'diversity') into the renewal/déclassement of the London cultural–intellectual establishment, but the work of northern novelists, film directors and television writers, as well as the music scene, asserted a preponderantly positive image of the region's post-war working class.

Then came, in a sharp twist, crystallisation of the North's – unequivocally negative – identity as the loser in the divide between two regions. This happened in the Thatcher years, and ironically succeeded a prior phase in which identification of the North with popular life and working-class culture in a positive regis-ter actually peaked.[52] The recession of the early 1980s afforded the backdrop for Alan Bleasdale's *Boys from the Blackstuff* in high-unemployment Liverpool, with its 'Gizza job' refrain, com-plemented later in the decade by Harry Enfield's 'Loadsamoney' persona on *Saturday Live*, a satire of the self-made Essex man.

Moral indignation at this turn of events, of the sort articulated in Mark Herman's film *Brassed Off* (1996), set in a south York-shire colliery slated for closure, was drowned out by the feel-good musicals of the New Labour boom (*The Full Monty* and Herman's follow-up *Little Voice*), termed by the critic Owen Hatherley the 'dance, prole, dance' genre.[53] On the small screen, Peter Flannery's keynote saga *Our Friends in the North* (also 1996) – contrast-ing sixties working-class Newcastle and seedy swinging London, united by the endemic corruption of public life – concluded with two of its Geordie protagonists edging towards the New Labour law-and-order establishment, the third flourishing as an entre-preneur, the fourth a down-and-out but urged not to follow the example of John Osborne's play of 1956, *Look Back in Anger*. The past is history, just so much water under the Tyne Bridge. A depoliticised, bepuzzled North entered the new millennium a basket case of eccentric small-town traditionals (Count Arthur Strong, *League of Gentlemen*) and council estate 'chavs' (*Shame-less* or, in a more affectionate register, *The Royle Family*), with some room afforded for bohemian enclaves in the major cities (*Queer as Folk*).

☙

If these are the rough historical outlines of England's socio-cultural regional divide, what is the question such a mapping exercise sets us on the way to answering? Italian Marxist Antonio Gramsci's approach to Italy's 'Southern Question', from which the title of this book takes its cue, offers some pointers. His thinking on the subject went through three iterations. The first appeared on 5 January 1920 in the pages of *L'Ordine Nuovo*, journal of Socialist Party leftists in Turin shortly to break away to form the Italian Communist Party. Gramsci had enrolled at Turin University following a youth spent on the impoverished island of Sardinia, where separatist feeling ran high. Its school-yard rendering, in his recollection, was 'Throw the mainlanders into the sea!'[54] The move to Turin set him down among these very mainlanders. The Piedmontese capital had lain at the centre of the Italian national project for several decades either side of the Risorgimento of 1861, and had gone on to become the beating heart of the country's late-developing manufacturing sector. Immersion in its industrial politics modified Gramsci's insular political formation, bringing the dynamics of region and class into productive tension.

As he penned his article on 'Workers and peasants', the Bolshevik revolution still belonged to the realm of current affairs and the road seemingly lay open for communist advances in Italy as well as across the Alps in the defeated Central Powers. Gramsci set out the strategic imperative of ranging both northern factory worker and southern agricultural labourer against Giolitti's faltering liberal–bourgeois state. 'The northern bourgeoisie has subjugated the South of Italy and the Islands, and reduced them to exploit-able colonies,' he protested. Parliamentary reformism was never going to set them free. Only a proletarian state could do that, liberating the peasant masses from the yoke of northern banking and industrial giants. In turn, it was in the interests of the Turin militants – this was the essential burden of his argument – to enlist the support of the peasantry, not least to avoid the Mezzogiorno becoming a safe-house for counterrevolutionary forces.[55]

To this theme he returned in 'Notes on the southern problem', an essay written in the weeks preceding his arrest by Mussolini's Fascists on 8 November 1926 and prompted by a mischaracterisation of his views on agrarian policy by an upstart socialist publication in Milan. The Turin communists, he insisted, had correctly identified the Southern Question as 'one of the essential problems of the national politics of the revolutionary proletariat'. In a country like Italy, where industrial workers were largely confined to a triangle of northern cities – Turin, Milan, Genoa – they could only hope to become hegemonic ('leading and dominant') through a system of class alliances to organise the consent of the immiserated population living further down the peninsula. Bourgeois-derived prejudices against the South as 'a ball and chain that prevents a more rapid progress in the civil development of Italy' had to be broken to prevent a retreat into the cul-de-sac of regional particularism.[56]

During his decade of incarceration, writing under the censor's scrutiny, the Southern Question underwent a change of time span and of protagonist. From the looked-for proletarian revolution on the horizon, Gramsci switched his gaze to its truncated bourgeois predecessor of 1861, in a reconstruction of Italian political development reaching deep into the past. The medieval bourgeoisie, he observed, created 'molecular' urban communes in the North – Bologna, Genoa, Milan, Padua and so on – without ever cohering around a national-popular programme. Intellectuals instead assumed a cosmopolitan character, modelled after the resident Catholic Church. (The Holy Roman Empire exercised a similar retarding influence on German national development.) Machiavelli's hopes for a nation state capable of resisting foreign domination during the Renaissance were dashed. Formal unification, when it came in the nineteenth century, completely failed to create any kind of genuine peninsular unity, which required popular integration of the masses in North and South alike into the new state, of the kind that had been achieved in Revolutionary France. The prime minister of Piedmont, Count Cavour, carried the North and Centre with a minimum of popular engagement. Garibaldi's Expedition of the Thousand toppled the dilapidated structure of Bourbon rule in Sicily and Naples at a stroke, only to hand the South over to the Piedmontese monarchy and its Mezzogiorno latifundist associates. Garibaldi was too much in thrall to the House of Savoy to raise the peasantry as part of a rival liberal-national republican formation. (The French Jacobins, binding rural France to the hegemony of Paris, had shown how this was to be done.) Instead, Italy's rulers held the South by an admixture of military force – the war against brigandage – fiscal imposition and public–payroll clientelism. The tasks this historical inheritance posed the revolutionary movement of Gramsci's own time were those he had been adumbrating since 1920. 'Any organization of national popular will is impossible, unless the great mass of peasant farmers bursts simultaneously into political life.'[57]

If the feebleness of Italian nationhood called forth, from Gramsci's pen, an unmatched working-through of the geographical complexity of social stratification under 'real' historical conditions, what relevance can this have to England, one of the strongest national formations of all? There is at least a family resemblance between chauvinist disparagement of the Mezzogiorno and the condescension of London intellectuals towards unfashionable outlying stretches of the UK. The *Spectator* judged Shelagh Delaney's *A Taste of Honey* 'the inside story of a savage culture observed by a genuine cannibal', while the present century has seen a libertarian think tank in Westminster describe north-east England as one of 'Whitehall's last colonies', a sink of welfare dependency that ought to be cut adrift of state aid.[58]

More than parallelism, however, Gramsci's writing provides the occasion for contrastive reflection. In the nineteenth century, southern Italy and northern England occupied inverse positions in their national orders: respectively, those of an overwhelmingly rural economy and a thriving modern industrial zone. Upon unification, Cavour imposed Piedmont's liberalised commercial arrangements on the rest of the peninsula in short order, killing off petty workshops in the Mezzogiorno previously sheltered by high tariffs. The industrialists of Lancashire, on the other hand, were Britain's foremost champions of free trade, secure for the time being in their commercial superiority over foreign competitors. The economic backwardness of southern Italy persisted through the twentieth century, even as modern industry thrived in the North. In Britain, meanwhile, a fallen industrial North was reduced to pleading for state rescue, only to be given short shrift by London governments in thrall to a flourishing financial and commercial South. From different starting positions, the two regions had fallen into distinct but analogous states of ill fortune.

In some ways, the North–South divide in Britain is more qualified than in Italy. The Midlands is an intermediate zone of greater weight than Lazio/Romagna, and there is also the looming presence of Scotland as a much more distinct part of the UK than northern England, with a long past of previous statehood. Northern identity in England is weaker than the insular southern identity in Italy, due to the prior centuries of differential statehoods in the Mezzogiorno, as against the lack of any of these beyond the Trent.

But whereas the South in Britain is defined above all by possession of London, in Italy the capital isn't in the North, and Rome in cultural connection and character is closer to the South, qualifying the polarity in counterbalancing fashion. Southerners have played a much greater modern role in the political class and bureaucracy of united Italy than northerners have in Britain. As Gramsci observed, while the urbanised society of northern Italy produced industrial technicians, the southern rural bourgeoisie sent forth state officials and professionals.[59] Since his time, the South has supplied as many Italian prime ministers as the North, not to mention the two most recent heads of state, whereas in postwar Britain, London and the Home Counties have accounted for ten prime ministers, the North only two, Eden and Wilson, both of whom had drifted away from the region by early adulthood.[60] Italy, for all its fissures, is a modern nation state with considerable provincial autonomies. The UK is the opposite: a hyper-centralised administration set within a pre-modern, composite kingdom – 'not really a national state', argued Tom Nairn, but rather 'a southern-lowland hegemonic bloc uniting a hereditary elite to the central processing unit of commercial and financial capital'.[61]

This text, far too long in the making, began life immediately preceding the 2008 financial crisis, when left politics was in the doldrums. It made sense, at the time, to follow the precedent of Gramsci's third and final iteration of the Southern Question, in the *Prison Notebooks*, and shift the burden of the regional question from the revolutionary left to the liberal-conservative centre. The overarching problematic was conceived like this: what challenges did the rise and fall of the industrial North present to a remote and unsympathetic British state, and how have policy decisions taken in London – rarely for the best of motives – guided the region's economic parabola from manufacturing powerhouse to twenty-first-century also-ran?

The crash of 2008 put paid to the New Labour 'economic miracle' against which the book polemicises, but the 2016 Brexit vote then threw the regional question into high relief. Although the northern economy was in worse shape than before, a mass protest vote had made it politically salient again. This prompted fresh considerations. What roles has the North, and the social groups within it, played within the social-power configurations of the British Isles? Only in fits and starts have social classes within the region threatened to become 'leading and dominant' on the national stage. It is unusual, of course, for a historically less populous and less wealthy region to hegemonise a richer and better-located one: Prussia's rule over the Rhineland was gifted by outside powers, in a conjuncture that prized military over economic strength. The North of England may not have Scotland's power of secession, but it's always exerted pressure, from a subaltern position, on the affairs of state, in ways particular to the historical moment: the ructions of a medieval borderland, its magnates wont to tread on kings, aren't those of a precocious industrial society or subsiding post-industrial one, where different social forces are in motion. In this sense, what's been termed the 'problem of the North' changes from one era to the next.[62]

Retreating into a pure form of regional history would provide few answers to any of these points. Northern questions aren't resolved on home territory: sovereign power and political accountability lie elsewhere. So we delve into the politics of Westminster and Whitehall, observing these proceedings from a northern perspective, to see what English history looks like when stood upon its head.

2

Badlands

The first question of all is how the middle swathe of Britain ended up as the unloved ward of an English state whose centre of operations lay 200 miles to the south, the perambulations of its kings and queens rarely straying beyond Watling Street in all the years until the territory they ruled over had so increased its domestic extent that Victoria and Albert could withdraw to the seclusion of Balmoral in Aberdeenshire.[1] England and Scotland are both so long in the tooth, as political structures go, that state formation on this European outcrop dates back to the Early Middle Ages, superimposed on yet older rounds of uneven cultural development usually operating to the advantage of the island's southern climes. The greatest Iron Age monumental landscapes lie within walking distance of one another in the Wiltshire countryside, while the civic life of Roman Bath, London and St Albans was leagues ahead of the garrison economy of the border country beyond Chester and York.

True, the more or less complete collapse of social organisation following the legions' withdrawal in the fifth century temporarily upended this regional hierarchy. A meeting-point of the Saxon and Celtic worlds, the Anglo-Saxon kingdom of Northumbria fused together their cultural elements to light up the Dark Ages and make a signal contribution to the revival of art and letters in the Latin West. The monks of Jarrow and Lindisfarne produced the foundational text in the history of the English peoples and some of the finest decorative manuscripts in the Hiberno-Saxon style, while York's cathedral school furnished the template for the palace school at Aachen, where Alcuin of York marshalled the Carolingian Renaissance. Alcuin's paean to 'York's famed city' describes how his own tutor, Ælberht, sought out books in foreign lands, building a library of 'priceless treasures'.[2]

But a long North Sea flank exposed Northumbria to the Scandinavian invasions of the eighth and ninth centuries which destroyed Ælberht's celebrated library and swallowed up York into the Viking world. By a process of elimination, it was left to the kingdom of Wessex at Britain's southern limit, the only Anglo-Saxon polity to withstand the Norsemen's advance, to act as nucleus for the English state. Æthelstan of Wessex, self-styled 'king of all Britain', seized control of the kingdom of York in 927. After a period of confusion, York's last Norwegian ruler was felled at Stainmore in the Pennines, at a stroke reducing it from a Viking statelet to an English provincial town.[3]

Æthelstan's Anglo-Saxons never fully assimilated their Northumbrian annexe, however, entrusting its governance to resident Anglo-Scandinavian earls. Yorkshire was an unwieldy addition to the Wessex shire system, more than twice the size of any other county. There were no royal sheriffs in the country to its north, nor would the Domesday survey be hazarded in these parts. In Cumbria, an obscure Celtic polity lingered under Scottish lordship for a quarter of a century after the Norman Conquest. Circumstances dictated, therefore, that the prospects for Norman rule in the North wouldn't be decided by a distant battle at Hastings.

Bending with the wind, the last Anglo-Saxon Archbishop of York crowned William of Normandy at Westminster on Christmas Day 1066. The *Anglo-Saxon Chronicle* relates that Ealdred prised an oath from the Conqueror to 'hold this nation as well as the best of any kings before him did'. Ealdred's stricture was given short shrift by the king's lieutenants, Odo of Bayeux and William fitz Osbern, who 'built castles widely throughout this nation, and oppressed the wretched people; and afterwards it always grew very much worse'.[4] They brought the ecclesiastical province of York under Canterbury's sway and initiated a tenurial revolution in the shadows of the fortresses bemoaned by the *Anglo-Saxon Chronicle*. The Domesday survey shows a couple of dozen Continental barons in receipt of more than 90 per cent of Yorkshire manors.[5] The land was parcelled out into territorially compact baronies, very unlike the jumbling of fiefs in more securely held southern counties. One of Odo's retainers, Ilbert de Lacy, administered an enormous cluster of confiscated estates in the West Riding from the Norman castle town of Pontefract, which guarded an entrance into the Vale of York and crossing points over the Aire river.

The biggest of the myriad challenges to the onset of Norman rule arose in the North East, among a people accustomed to running their own affairs. According to the Wiltshire chronicler William of Malmesbury, southern England's nearest equivalent to Bede, the Northumbrians 'had been taught by their ancestors either to be free or to die'.[6] The Conqueror initially went down the West Saxon route of appointing native strongmen to the earldom of Northumbria, but his original candidate was no sooner in place than murdered by a member of the house of Bamburgh, and his replacement – Cospatric, a kinsmen of the assailant – absconded to join the party of Edgar Ætheling, English claimant to the throne, affronts which brought a change of tack. William despatched one of his own attendants, Robert Cumin, to the tiny monastic town of Durham with 700 knights. Writing thirty years later a Durham Benedictine monk alleged that Cumin 'allowed his men to ravage the countryside by pillaging and killing'. Symeon took care to attribute the ensuing revolt not to the Durham townsfolk but to the people north of the Tyne, 'united in one accord not to submit to a foreign lord'. Early one January morning in 1069, they 'burst in together through all the gates and rushed through the whole town killing the earl's companions'. The mob set the bishop's house ablaze and settled accounts with Cumin as he fled the flames.[7]

The indigenous rebellion spread to York, the only appreciable urban settlement beyond Chester, as forces under Edgar and Cospatric combined with a newly landed Danish army to overwhelm its garrison and capture the sheriff. The possibility glimmered of a breakaway Anglo-Scandinavian polity in this old Viking heartland.[8] To dispel it, the Normans retaliated against the resident population once the Danes had withdrawn to the Humber for the winter. Devastation of the countryside was a standard

component of medieval warfare, but William's scorched-earth programme appears to have been unusually extensive. According to
the *Anglo-Saxon Chronicle*, the king 'went northward with all of
his army which he could gather, and wholly ravaged and laid waste
the shire'. Symeon alleges that William left 'no village inhabited
between York and Durham'. Another Anglo-Norman chronicler,
Orderic Vitalis, describes how 'in his anger he commanded that
all crops and herds, chattels and food of every kind should be
brought together and burned to ashes with consuming fire, so that
the whole region north of [the] Humber might be stripped of all
means of sustenance.'[9] Seventeen years after the harrying, half of
North Riding vills and a third of vills in the East and West Ridings
were recorded as wholly or partly waste in the Domesday Book.
Yorkshire as a whole had the highest proportion of waste of any
surveyed county. Much land may have gone out of cultivation due
either to the physical devastation inflicted by the king's forces or to
subsequent estate reorganisation by his tenants-in-chief, abandoning marginal settlements to concentrate the region's diminished
resources on the most viable lowland sites.[10] An unparalleled upset
had been met with an infamous and indelible reprisal. William's
son and heir, Rufus, was able to impose shire government on Northumberland and drag Cumbria into the orbit of the English state,
establishing a garrison and peasant colony at Carlisle. For the first
time, the whole of England sat under one political roof.

Initially this was a flimsy arrangement, vulnerable to the tremors
of dynastic strife. Infighting between the Conqueror's grandchil-
dren during the Anarchy of 1135–54 saw the Border region ceded
to the Scottish king David I, consolidating his own realm on
Norman lines. David proceeded to hold court and mint coins at
Carlisle. A dip in Scottish power after his death, however, tilted
the balance of forces back the way of the English monarchy. A
Yorkshire chronicler relates how Henry II, with righteous self-
interest, warned 'that the king of England should not be cheated
of so great a part of his kingdom, and that he could not passively
endure such an amputation'. The same source adds that the Scots
'wisely decided that the king of England had the advantage in this
matter, on the merits of the case and in the strength of his forces'.[11]
An agreement struck at Chester in 1157 returned the frontier to

the Solway and Tweed. In a later treaty made at York, the Scots quitclaimed Northumberland, Cumberland and Westmorland to leave only Berwick and a sliver of 'debatable lands' in contention.

Viking conquest, regional secession, Scottish annexation – every alternative destiny for the former land of Bede and Alcuin had been closed off. Superior force of arms and feudal settlement had bonded England together at a remarkably early historical juncture compared with other European states, its feudal hierarchy topped by Norman and other French potentates forming part of a cohesive cross-Channel ruling bloc. In France, by contrast, the Capetian dynasty needed several centuries to bolt additional principalities onto its realm, one after the other, while unification of Italy and Germany would have to await the stimulus of modern-era nationalist impulses. But just as the Risorgimento, far from uniting the Italian peninsula on an equal footing, subordinated one half of the country to the other, so northern England would languish on the margins of a kingdom which cared little for it. Geoffrey Barrow, a historian of medieval Scotland, writes that

> Although the kings from William Rufus to Edward I took very seriously their grip upon Cumbria and Northumbria, they could not spend much time visiting these regions which were remote from the castles, hunting lodges, monasteries and rich trading towns of southern England, Normandy, Maine, the lower Loire valley, Poitou and Gascony whence their power derived and where, one feels, their hearts really lay.[12]

The character of the territory recovered by Henry II remains to be sketched in. Even by medieval standards it was overwhelmingly rural and underdeveloped, too remote to benefit from either the patronage of the royal court or the commercial stimulant of London, which dominated trade with Continental ports a short hop across the Narrow Sea. Urban life was especially slow out of the blocks west of the Pennines, very much off the beaten track and confined to small-time Irish Sea traffic. Ports on the east coast were better situated to access the prime commercial routes pointing to London and Europe, but they never captured more than a

fifth of the available trade. York, Hull and Newcastle, together
with Penrith, a market centre in Cumbria's Eden valley, were the
only northern representatives among the fifty richest boroughs of
pre-Black Death England. York never recovered its Anglo-Saxon
prominence but in a regional context it remained altogether
exceptional. Nerve centre of the northern church, an inland port
prosperous in the wool trade and a county capital surrounded by
good farming country, it vied with Bristol, Lincoln and Norwich
for the title of England's foremost provincial city, yet even York
had only one-seventh of London's taxable wealth in the lay subsidies of 1327 and 1332.[13]

What about the countryside? Whereas the richer soils and drier
climate of southern counties facilitate a judicious mixture of arable
and livestock farming, Defoe found north Lancashire 'all barren
and wild, of no use or advantage either to man or beast'. Westmorland was ghastlier still, 'the wildest, most barren and frightful of
any that I have passed over in England, or even in Wales itself'.[14]
The standard depiction of English feudalism is taken from the
champion country of central and southern England, where in a
landscape of common-field agriculture and clustered settlements
there was virtually a manor for every village. Here, the strength of
feudal lordship told in the preponderance of customary over free
rents and tenures. Further north, in lowland areas of Yorkshire,
Durham and Northumberland, nucleated villages and customary
tenures were also the norm, although taxable wealth was lower.
Customary tenures were even more prevalent across the Border
counties, where Henry I had established substantial lordships. In
boggy and isolated Lancashire, on the other hand, free rents were
of higher value than customary ones.[15]

The distinction ought to matter, since by the end of the thirteenth century customary tenants had been declared legally
unfree. But delayed subdivision of feudal holdings and the dispersed settlement patterns associated with pastoral farming
meant that seigniorial supervision was more thinly stretched in
the North, certainly in upland areas. Combined with the lighter
labour requirements of animal husbandry and an abundance of
reclaimable land into which peasants might flee, this made for
less onerous feudal exactions, and no automatic connection ever

obtained between customary tenure, servile status and compulsory labour services.[16] E. A. Kosminsky cautioned in a classic work that 'the division of peasants into "villein" and "free", characteristic of southern manors, can only with difficulty be applied under northern conditions.'[17]

Some parts of the North did more closely mirror the intense feudalism of the Midlands and the South. The Boldon Book, a Domesday-like survey conducted on the Bishopric of Durham's estates in the late twelfth century, provides evidence of well-functioning demesnes and villeinage with heavy labour services. But as a rule, whereas profit-minded estate holders in the South East might ramp up demesne production to serve the large London market, labour services were less important to the northern feudal economy than money rents and they decayed earlier, in many cases well before the arrival of the Black Death in 1348–9 when severe labour shortages caused landlords everywhere to pull out of demesne cultivation and become rentiers instead.[18]

The burdens of serfdom, then, were generally lighter in the North, but rural benightedness – the absence of towns and literacy – was correspondingly deeper. Musgrove, citing county-by-county statistical studies by Conan Doyle and Havelock Ellis, argues persuasively that the North was historically marked by a much lower quotient of intellectuals – thinkers, writers, artists – than the South. Jewell supplies supporting evidence, pointing out the monopoly of higher education (Oxford, Cambridge, the Inns of Court) held by the South down to the 1820s, leaving the North in a very different situation than Scotland. As Musgrove puts it, 'highly productive contexts for the intellectual life do not include militarised frontiers or heavily industrialised towns. It was the misfortune of northern England after the age of Bede that its greatness was based on both.'[19]

Accounting for no more than one-eighth of medieval England's population and wealth, the land above the Mersey, Trent and Humber presented too narrow a platform for its magnates to sustain a leading role in the elite revolts which plagued the country's weaker kings.[20] Northumberland and Yorkshire landowners of middling wealth were first to stir against King John, refusing to sponsor or enlist in his attempt to claw back French territories lost to the Capetian monarchy, so that 'Northerners' became a tag for the 1215 Revolt as a whole, but estate holders from eastern and southern counties ultimately had the run of the Magna Carta committee.[21]

It required a large inflow of resources from the centre, continued for many years, to put the northern aristocracy on a stronger footing. Conquest of the principality of Wales in 1284 left Cumberland and Northumberland standing on England's only land frontier with an independent state. The attack on Scottish independence, beginning with capture of Berwick and victory at Dunbar in 1296, opened up opportunities for rising northern dynasties to accumulate estates and offices at the Crown's pleasure.[22] Even after Edward III pivoted English aggrandisement from Scotland to France in 1337, Anglo-Scottish conflict would rumble on for centuries. Wardens of the march were subsidised by the royal court to hold the North against the Scots using private armies recruited from Durham, Yorkshire and the Border counties. Henry Percy, a Yorkshire magnate who had fought at Berwick and Dunbar, acquired the castle and barony of Alnwick from Antony Bek, Bishop of Durham, in 1310. The Nevilles, descended from Anglo-Danish thegns in County Durham, also won royal favour through military service on the frontier. In the century leading up to Bosworth, the Percys held the wardenship of the east march for eighty years and there were Neville equivalents in the west for close on sixty.[23] Extra spending power, broad jurisdiction and the prestige of high office provided them with extraordinary numbers of retainers.

The splintering of the Plantagenet dynasty into the cadet branches of Lancaster and York, after defeat in the Hundred Years War turned a rapacious English baronage in on itself, saw unprecedented intrusions into national politics by these bastard-feudal affinities. Richard Neville, Warwick the Kingmaker, controlled the marcher wardenships and other key posts in the border counties, and ruled over north Yorkshire from Middleham Castle in Richmondshire, where he briefly imprisoned Edward IV. But the support networks of such towering figures far outran any one region. Warwick also held a string of strategic commands on either side of the Channel. He was keeper of the seas, captain of the Calais garrison, warden of the Cinque Ports, constable of Dover. Moving against Henry VI in 1460, he exploited his mercantile connections to stir a popular revolt in Kent and London against the Lancastrian regime.

The dynastic struggles of 1455–85 were never, therefore, the cross-Pennine joust that their historiographical framing as a 'War of the Roses' implies. But after Warwick was cut down at the Battle of Barnet in 1471, his estates and offices fell to Edward IV's youngest brother, Richard, Duke of Gloucester, who built up the country's largest aristocratic affinity on the basis of sequestered Neville assets. Abiding on his estates in preference to spending time at court, Gloucester forged few bonds among the southern gentry – sheriffs, Justices of the Peace, servants of the royal house-hold. Outraged by his *coup d'état* in 1483, their support leaked across the Channel to the Tudor court-in-waiting. In response, Richard shoehorned a few dozen members of his ducal affinity into forfeited estates, local-government offices and military posts in southern counties, a controversial – and tellingly brief – inversion of England's normal direction of gravity.[24]

Gloucester's demise was sealed by an unexpected brittleness of his northern power base. Thomas Stanley, an officeholder in the Cheshire and Lancaster palatinates involved in multiple demar-cation disputes with the prince over the years, would intervene decisively at Bosworth on the side of his stepson, Henry Tudor, receiving the earldom of Derby in thanks. He is even said to have placed the royal coronet on Henry's head when the battle was won. What the Ricardian interlude shows is that under pre-modern conditions, not even a member of the royal line could scrabble together quite enough strength in the North to reign in defiance of Establishment opinion. The *sine qua non* of governing England was to have its southern heartland on side.

Stanley Bindoff of University College London once wrote that 'Tudor rule meant the rule of the South over the North'.[25] It also spelled the rule of London over the rest of the country. A rarity among European capitals for being both a seat of government and a major international port, London swelled to a population

of 185,000 in the course of the sixteenth century – a threefold
increase – as its merchants gained a stranglehold over the cloth
trade with the Continental entrepôt of Antwerp, while an upturn
in culture and the arts under court sponsorship culminated in the
Elizabethan theatre.[26] All but two of the twenty most prosperous
Tudor towns were located in a belt of southern England running
from Totnes in Devon to Canterbury in Kent, or else in an East
Anglian extension between Colchester and Lynn. In the reign of
Henry VIII, England north of the Trent accounted for only 8 per
cent of taxable lay wealth, sharply down from its medieval peak,
whereas the seven counties surrounding London paid 21 per
cent.[27] 'The entire economy of England was ruled from London.
Political centralisation, the power of the English Crown, the highly
concentrated nature of trade, all combined to make the capital
great,' remarked Fernand Braudel.[28] It was 'so superior to other
English towns', a Swiss travel writer opined in 1599,

> that London is not said to be in England, but rather England to
> be in London, for England's most resplendent objects may be
> seen in and around London; so that he who sightsees London
> and the royal courts in its immediate vicinity may assert, without
> impertinence that he is properly acquainted with England.'[29]

Distant from this ferment, northern England adopted a conservative posture in the seminal contests of the early modern era,
unsuccessfully championing a succession of backward-looking
causes: traditional religion, baronial privilege, Crown against
Parliament. When the Henrician Reformation moved up a gear
in 1536 through the Ten Articles of Faith, dissolution of the
smaller monasteries and legislation to extinguish the authority
of the Bishop of Rome, it set off the biggest revolt of the Tudor
age – one significant not just for its size but also for its regional
profile. Until this point, popular rebellion had been largely confined to commoners in easy riding distance of London and the
royal court at Westminster. The 1381 Peasants' Revolt centred
on populous south-eastern counties hardest hit by Richard II's
poll tax and itching to be free of labour laws imposed to prop
up seigniorial power after the Black Death. The proto-Protestant

Lollard uprising of 1414 barely made any impression north of the Trent: because literacy was less widespread in the region, there were fewer entry points for unorthodox religious ideas. The 1450 Jack Cade rebellion, at the fag-end of the Lancastrian dynasty, sprang out of a self-assertive county community of minor free-holders in Kent as news of defeat in Normandy reverberated along the London-to-Dover highway.[30] Popular unrest didn't become entirely absent from the Tudor South, as the religiously variegated commotion during Edward VI's minority would attest: the Catholic-enthused Prayer Book rebellion in the South West coinciding with Protestant-inclined unrest closer to the capital. Nevertheless, the worst upheaval was pushed out to peripheral areas, where unprecedented royal interference in parish religion ran up against the combined force of religious conservatism and regional particularism.

The Pilgrimage of Grace began on 2 October 1536 among the artisans of Louth, a Lincolnshire market town sandwiched between the wolds and the fens, as rumours swirled of an impending seizure of church goods. York opened its gates to a rebel force commanded by Robert Aske, a lawyer from Selby, on the 16th. Aske framed the uprising as a pilgrimage for the defence of the church and the upending of heretical privy counsellors.[31] Richmondshire agitators who spread the rebellion into Cumberland and Westmorland placed greater emphasis on agrarian grievances, despatching polemics in the name of Captain Poverty.

With the exception of Lancashire, where the Stanleys managed to quell the disturbances, control over nearly all of the country above the Ribble and Don slipped to nine rebel hosts, 50,000 strong in total.[32] The king guilefully said he found their grievances 'general, dark and obscure', so they gathered at Pontefract early in December to approve a petition. Aske sifted through the submissions to compile two dozen articles for debate by the lords and gentlemen present, who bowdlerised the demands of the upland peasantry for a cap on entry fines and statutory intervention to prevent enclosure of the waste.[33] Massively outnumbered by the rebels, the king's representative, Thomas Howard, Duke of Norfolk – a Tudor loyalist despite personal sympathies for the old religion – went beyond his brief to grant a general pardon and a sitting of Parliament at York to roll back the Reformation. On this basis Aske persuaded the commons to disperse.

An authority on the court and character of Henry VIII suggests that had the Pilgrimage 'been more aggressive and not trusted the king so readily', it could have unseated him.[34] But outside Cumbria, where antagonistic landlord–tenant relations were particularly strained, there were too many layers of deference – of the rebel hosts toward their landowner leaders, and of the Pilgrims as a body toward the Crown – for a regionally circumscribed movement aiming at religious restoration and tenurial fairness to propel itself forward into regime change. Aske spent Christmas at court only to find himself on the scaffold the following July. The promised Parliament at York never materialised.

The response of the Tudor state to these turbulent months was to strengthen its apparatus and set about eradicating regional autonomies in earnest. Thomas Cranmer, the first Protestant Archbishop of Canterbury and a Cambridge man by education, justified the crackdown by damning northerners as 'a certain sort of barbarous and savage people, who were ignorant of and turned away from farming and the good arts of peace, and who were so far utterly unacquainted with knowledge of sacred matters, that they could not bear to hear anything of culture and more gentle civilisation.'[35] A permanent Council in the North was instituted as a regional enforcement vehicle for the Privy Council, and a store of royal patronage – augmented by expropriated monastic land – dispensed to build up lesser landowners as a counterweight to the old magnate dynasties. 'For surely we will not be bound of a necessity to be served with lords. But we will be served with such men what degree soever as we shall appoint to the same', instructed the king.[36] Promotion of minor figures to Border offices, and cuts to the grants they received, did nothing to enhance security along the perimeter – foreign mercenaries had to be brought in – but served the more pressing need of safeguarding the monarchy from aristocratic resurgence on the periphery.

The Catholic heads of the great northern dynasties, Thomas Percy, seventh Earl of Northumberland, and Charles Neville, sixth Earl of Westmorland, made one final, doomed attempt, early in the reign of Elizabeth, to defend their religion and social primacy.

Smarting from loss of position to Elizabeth's clientele gentry, goaded into action by hot-headed members of their entourage, on 14 November 1569 they entered Durham Cathedral, overturned the communion table and celebrated a Catholic Mass. Shortly afterwards they issued a proclamation complaining of how 'diverse new set up nobles about the Queen's majesty, have and do daily, not only go about to overthrow and put down the ancient nobility of this realm, but also have ... set up and maintained a newfound religion and heresy, contrary to God's word'.[37]

Elizabeth's pick for Bishop of Durham, James Pilkington, had sermonised against veneration of aristocratic lineages.[38] A fierce Puritan, the new broom gathered around him fellow evangelicals such as William Whittingham, appointed dean of Durham Cathedral. Both men had spent part of the Marian interlude in exile in Calvin's Geneva. Pilkington went down so badly with his congregation that he confessed to William Cecil, leading statesman of the Elizabethan court, 'I am grown into such displeasure with them, part for religion and part for ministering the oath of the queen's superiority, that I know not whether they like me worse, or I them'.[39]

When the uprising broke out, Pilkington fled to London disguised as a beggar while Durham thronged with parishioners eager once again to practise Catholic rites. Despite this enthusiasm, however, only a few thousand turned out to contest the Anglican settlement in arms: yeomen farmers for the most part, some aggrieved by Pilkington and Whittingham's grasping estate management, along with poorer sorts pressed into service by threat of spoil or the promise of cash reward. Few had tenurial connections to either peer. Although reputed to love their lord better than their queen, Percy tenants in Northumberland stayed at home. After the Pilgrimage of Grace the Crown had leased out Percy manors to clients of the rival Forster clique, accelerating the decay of the family's seigniorial jurisdiction.[40] The rebels decided against hazarding an attack on York. Instead a small detachment seized control of the port of Hartlepool, vainly hoping for a landing by Spanish troops under the Duke of Alba, while the main force laid siege to Barnard Castle on the Tees. On 16 December, as royal troops advanced north to Darlington, the earls lost their nerve, fleeing from the jaws of defeat across the Scottish border.

Lawrence Stone characterised the Northern Rebellion as 'the last episode in five hundred years of protest by the Highland Zone against the interference of London'.[41] To ensure there would be no recurrence, Council of the North president Thomas Radcliffe, Earl of Sussex, summarily executed 600 rank-and-file rebels under martial law – a body count several times higher than Norfolk had inflicted after the Pilgrimage and comparable to English atrocities in Ireland, where Sussex had served as lord lieutenant. Common law trials of estate-holding rebels provided another windfall of forfeited property to the Crown. Northumberland was sold out by the Scots and beheaded at York, while Westmorland stewed in exile in the Spanish Netherlands on a pension from Philip II, his estates in Durham confiscated by the Crown and later sold to royal courtiers and coal-owning parvenus from Newcastle. Pilkington returned to his diocese triumphant. 'I am, by the blessing of God, restored to my flock', he congratulated himself in a letter to Swiss reformer Henry Bullinger.[42]

The demise of the northern earls was followed, at the end of the Elizabethan period, by a Union of the Crowns, which diminished the strategic significance of the Anglo-Scottish frontier – now 'the very heart of the country', observed James I, who did away with wardenships and marcher law.[43] The North was reduced to a periphery like any other, and like the others offered James's successor more support during the Civil War than he ever received from the capital, damned by Charles I's Secretary at War, Sir Edward Walker, as 'the head and fountain of this detested rebellion'.[44]

Musgrove dates the emergence of the Royalist North to the fourteenth century, when England's kings had exhorted the region to take up arms against the Scots as well as the French, and northern clerks, prelates, knights and merchants such as the de la Poles had assumed prominent positions in the departments of state. The Wars of the Roses of the fifteenth century then strengthened the sentimental ties linking the Crown to castle towns such as Pontefract, which would be the very last Royalist holdout against Parliament. Without the modernising impetus that Puritan ideology transmitted to London and East Anglia, northern England remained in thrall to past glories, a region marked out by its 'back-wardness and deep-seated traditionalism'.[45]

Left idling as advanced capitalist agriculture took off in East Anglia and much of the South East, the northern countryside was certainly backward. As far south as Lancashire and Yorkshire, 'tenant right' customary tenures persisted that had historically afforded yeoman farmers security of landholding in return for military service on the Border. A post-1603 landlord campaign spearheaded by James I to replace them with commercial lease-hold arrangements had become bogged down in legal wrangles. In Cumberland, to cite an extreme case, most farmers still held their land by customary tenure at the close of the eighteenth century.[46] The continuing weight of agrarian custom may do more to explain the conservativism of the rural North, and the absence of a par-liamentary party within it, than the ancient battles invoked by Musgrove.

If the tenant-right controversy tempered the popular reception of the king's cause in the region, Catholicism afforded a counter-balance.[47] The old religion survived in gentry households and out-of-the-way upland areas. In Lancashire, unusually, it retained a mass following, particularly in the western fringe of the county which traded with Catholic Ireland.[48] For its adherents, if neu-trality wasn't a viable option, the choice between Charles's High Church Anglicanism and Westminster's intolerant evangelism – the latter, in effect, a super-sized version of the old Pilkington regime in Durham – wasn't difficult, and the Crown offered a better muster point than a pair of already diminished noble lin-eages had in 1569.

Charles handed command of the far north to William Cav-endish, Earl of Newcastle, a London patron of the arts whose West Riding family had risen up the social ladder through service under Henry VIII, profiting from the dissolution of the monaster-ies. In circumstances that are obscure, Newcastle quickly raised a 'papist' northern army of some 8,000 men after being instructed to enlist loyal subjects without examining their consciences. Two-thirds of gentry families in Lancashire who engaged for the king were Catholic, as were one-third in Yorkshire.[49] 'Royalism in the North of England cannot be reduced wholly to religion or economics', insists Musgrove. But it is altogether inexplicable without them.[50]

In London, by contrast, evangelical merchants operating outside the framework of royal trading companies helped to swing opinion behind Parliament. The affinity of Puritanism with commerce, and the chafing of small clothiers at Crown restrictions on manufacture and trade, also brought growing textile handicraft towns in the North onto Parliament's side. The country linen weavers around Manchester rebuffed James Stanley, the king's commander in Lancashire and Cheshire, when he laid siege to the town in September 1642, their resolve stiffened by a Puritan preacher. Stanley was also thwarted in Bolton, 'the Geneva of Lancashire', which Prince Rupert would ultimately storm en route to Marston Moor. In keenly contested Yorkshire, Bradford and Halifax gave essential manpower and supplies to parliamentary forces under the Fairfaxes, who were short of backing from their own gentry class. The denizens of the cloth-working parishes were 'the only well-affected people of the country', Ferdinando Fairfax advised Westminster.[51]

Musgrove highlights the fact that the North provided relatively few men of national standing between Parliament's execution of Thomas Wentworth, first Earl of Strafford, in the run-up to the Civil War and the return of high Cavaliers with a Wentworth connection after the Restoration. He makes an exception for Thomas Fairfax, son of Ferdinando, commander-in-chief of the parliamentary army. According to Charles I's Secretary of State, he was 'the man most beloved and relied upon by the rebels in the North'. Fairfax sat out the Cromwellian interlude in the bucolic surroundings of his Nun Appleton home, a former nunnery seven miles south of York. Andrew Marvell, tutor to Fairfax's daughter, wrote a poem celebrating its 'fragrant gardens, shady woods / Deep meadows, and transparent floods.'[52] To take Fairfax's place in the new republic, the crowded ranks of Yorkshire's gentry class offered up John Lambert, a minor gentleman landowner from Calton in the Yorkshire Dales. Lambert, ignored by Musgrove, authored the 1653 Instrument of Government, the original template for Cromwell's protectorate and England's first written constitution. It defied Leveller demands for universal manhood suffrage but struck a modern note by redistricting English and Welsh constituencies, the towns of Leeds and Manchester among the beneficiaries. The scheme lapsed under the replacement constitution of 1657, the Humble Petition and Advice, the adoption of which caused Lambert to part company with Cromwell and retire from public life. Another 175 years would elapse before key northern cities regained parliamentary representation.

When the republic imploded after Cromwell's death in 1658, Fairfax joined the bulk of England's landed classes in opting to stabilise the social order by reinstating the Stuart monarchy. He raised the Yorkshire gentry to prevent Lambert, 'inveterate against the king', from impeding the progress of George Monck's army from Scotland to London, from which the Restoration would issue. Monck crossed the border into England the day after York capitulated to Fairfax's troops.[53] But although Yorkshire's outsize county community was an appreciable factor in the national political balance, only London carried decisive weight. By far the most important reserve of popular and financial support for the Roundhead cause, effectively bankrolling the New Model Army, the capital controlled four-fifths of England's foreign trade and was a magnet for people as well as commodities, on its way to supplanting Paris as Europe's largest city. John Lilburne and Gerrard Winstanley, leaders of the Leveller and Digger movements respectively, both migrated from northern England to the City as apprentices in the textile trade.[54] It was the moderate majority opinion in the City that gave the necessary ballast to Monck's decision, in February 1660, to settle matters by throwing open Parliament to Royalist opinion. Fairfax joined the delegation sent to invite Charles II back from The Hague, supplying the king with the horse he rode at his coronation. For all the talk of clemency that surrounded the Restoration, Lambert was kept under lock and key until his death in 1684.

The Restoration settlement, even when modified in Parliament's favour by the Glorious Revolution, created the paradox of a monarchical *ancien régime* coexistent with a modern capitalist society in the South East. When large-scale industry made its advance in the nineteenth century, a wider contrast would open up between northern economic modernity and southern political archaism. Until then, however, pressure for parliamentary reform proved to be containable. Christopher Wyvill, a wealthy North Riding gentleman landowner and an absentee Essex clergyman, raised the question of reform in 1779 as the American War went from bad to worse, but had to take no for an answer. Unlike the Anti-Corn Law League of the Lancashire mill owners, fifty years into the future, Wyvill's Yorkshire Association wasn't based on the emerging factory towns but instead addressed itself to 'gentleman of weight and character' in England's largest county community, drawing the bulk of its support from the lesser gentry and clergy – including the deans of York and Ripon, much to the embarrassment of their archbishop. Through this extra-parliamentary vehicle, a sizeable landed interest threatened with higher taxes sought to impose economy measures on the royal court and on the Tory administration of Lord North.⁵⁵

The Yorkshire Association was the first provincial outfit to wrest the leadership of extra-parliamentary agitation from London, vying for control of the reform agenda with metropolitan radicals active in the Quintuple Alliance of London, Middlesex, South-wark, Surrey and Westminster who urged annual parliaments and universal manhood suffrage. Wyvill wanted more modest changes – triennial parliaments, a purge of Crown placemen from the Commons, additional MPs for the counties and large towns – to clean up politics and reduce royal influence. Much of his campaign work was innovatory, but hitched to an ideology no less traditional than the reverend's social base: 'the restoration of national morals' and 'the preservation of our Constitution on its genuine principles'. He abhorred the root-and-branch democratic ideals associated with Thomas Paine's Rights of Man and wished to keep the vote restricted to men of property.⁵⁶

Wyvill's energetic, if fruitless, campaigning moved the Whig reformer Charles James Fox to remark that 'Yorkshire and Middlesex between them make all England'. A couple of generations later the statement couldn't stand without alteration. 'You may add Lancashire,' advised mill owner Richard Cobden in 1846.⁵⁷ The failure of the Yorkshire Association proved that the aristocrats and merchants who ruled from London's palaces and counting houses weren't going to be dislodged by the provincial squirearchy or by curates of advanced opinions. If anyone was going to storm Britain's constitutional citadel, it would be a task for the industrial classes who were about to take centre stage.

3

Industrialisation and Revolt

When Rochdale mill owner John Bright was elected to Westminster by Manchester's bourgeoisie in 1847, a local newssheet hailed a 'new alliance of industrial independence with political power'.[1] The merchants and manufacturers of Cottonopolis had successfully pressed Sir Robert Peel's Westminster government to abandon tariff protection on imported grain, to the great political cost of the Tory prime minister and the discomfort of the southern landed interest. 'It is to this and a neighbouring county that the great element of power in this country is henceforth to be found,' celebrated Bright in his valedictory address to the Anti-Corn Law League. 'Lancashire, the cotton district and the West Riding of Yorkshire, must govern England.'[2] Simultaneously, factory hands and ancillary workers massed under the Chartist banner mounted a political jailbreak attempt. As Marx observed, the proletarian demand for universal suffrage, in English conditions, amounted to 'a war slogan'.[3]

The Industrial Revolution converted Lancashire 'from an obscure, ill-cultivated swamp', in Engels's words, to the hub of a mechanised factory system that would be emulated the world over. Liverpool and Manchester grew 'as if by a magic touch' into the largest provincial cities in Europe, between them coordinating the cotton trade which kick-started the age of industry.[4]

An order sent from Liverpool in the morning, is discussed by the merchants in the Manchester Exchange at noon, and in the evening is distributed among the manufacturers in the environs.

> In less than eight days, the cotton spun at Manchester, Bolton, Oldham or Ashton, is woven in the sheds of Bolton, Stalybridge or Stockport; dyed and printed at Blackburn, Chorley or Preston and finished, measured and packed at Manchester.

So reported a Parisian journalist in 1844, as Engels penned *The Condition of the Working Class in England* based on surveys of his adopted Manchester home.[5] Manchester had a more sophisticated business structure than the outlying mill towns, cotton production accounting for less than a fifth of employment in a townscape thronging with general labourers, servants, craftsmen and dressmakers, as well as a bourgeois layer of merchants, shopkeepers and professionals. In Liverpool, working-class men relied on casual dockside or warehouse employment; women on domestic service and the clothing trade.

The manufacturing revolution spread across the Pennines as Yorkshire woollens followed Lancashire cotton down the path of machinofacture. Small-scale clothiers attacking the cheaper end of the market had already started to get the better of counterparts in the West Country and East Anglia. Worsteds, made from long wool, take their name from a Norfolk village but it was Bradford which earned the moniker Worstedopolis. Neighbouring Leeds organised much of the rest of the woollen business but also diversified into ready-made clothing, tanning, engineering and printing. The low-woollen trade, reworking leftover rags, focussed on Batley, Dewsbury and Ossett. Huddersfield was known for its quality worsted coatings, Guiseley and Yeadon for tweeds, Saddleworth for flannels, Halifax and Liversedge for carpets and rugs. Sheffield's cutlery and tool-making trades made it the largest West Riding town outside the textile zone. In the North East, coalmining created a rash of pit-head villages and the beginnings of larger colliery settlements like Ashington. Prototype railways shuttled Durham coal and Manchester textiles to the sea.

Viewed close up, the Industrial Revolution looks like a dull sort of bourgeois self-help success story. The first factory masters came from local manufacturing, mercantile or gentry families, tapping local wealth to cover modest start-up costs. Lancashire wasn't the only scene of early experimentation in factory production but it possessed a well-established textile handicraft industry, run on a capitalist basis. Colonisation of the Pennine moors followed by subdivision of landholdings in an open market had yielded a mass of smallholders and cottagers unable to live off the land. Commercial middlemen put out materials to these dependent homeworkers, each equipped with a spinning wheel or handloom.

Towards the end of the eighteenth century, the spinning part of the cotton-making process was transformed by a series of technological breakthroughs called forth by local 'needs. James Hargreaves's jennies, Richard Arkwright's water frame and Samuel Crompton's mule concentrated production in large workshops and early factories. Crompton and Hargreaves were both weavers, from the vicinities of Bolton and Blackburn respectively, while Arkwright started out as a Preston barber. The water-powered spinning mill trialled by Arkwright at Cromford, Derbyshire, in 1771 was imitated in several northern and Midland counties before Boulton and Watt's steam-power technology – an offspring of Scottish expertise in scientific instrumentation and capital supplied from the Birmingham metal trades – brought a general relocation to Manchester and other non-incorporated towns, unfettered by guilds, close to the Lancashire coalfield and its canals. By 1800 there were over fifty steam engines in use in Manchester and Leeds.[6] Related engineering, chemical and finishing trades grew up alongside the factories and storage units.

To staff these new enterprises, industrialists recruited the local surplus of a growing rural population and also cast their net over pauper children from the London slums and southern parishes, taking the pressure off the poor rate to the benefit of well-to-do ratepayers. The abuse-ridden apprentice system gifted early industrialists about a dozen years' unpaid labour from each infant conscript, typically bound over at the age of ten. The Bury mills of Sir Robert Peel, father of the Tory prime minister, ran almost entirely on unfree child labour. Peel sponsored a modest statutory scheme to regulate factory 'apprenticeships', but it was hardly enforced. Many other mill workers migrated to Lancashire from British-ruled Ireland, propelled by famine, state coercion, an iniquitous land system and a decline in handicraft employment after the imposition of a common market with England. 'The moment I have a turn-out and am fast for hands', explained Newton Heath silk manufacturer James Taylor, 'I send to Ireland for ten, fifteen or twenty families, as the case may be. I usually send to Connaught and I get the children, chiefly girls, of (I suppose) farmers and cottiers. The whole family comes, father, mother and children. I provide them with no money.'[7]

Windfalls of cheap fuel and raw material added to manufacturers' good fortune, as industrialisation changed the balance of regional comparative advantage. Fast-flowing Pennine streams provided plentiful water power; unrewarding agricultural land disgorged abundant coal deposits and other minerals. 'Such has been the bounty of nature to this otherwise frightful country', wrote Defoe of proto-industrial Halifax in 1725,

> that two things essential to the [clothing] business, as well as to the ease of the people are found here, and that in a situation which I never saw the like of in any part of England; and, I believe, the like is not to be seen so contrived in any part of the world; I mean coals and running water upon the tops of the highest hills: This seems to have been directed by the wise hand of Providence for the very purpose which is now served by it, namely, the manufactures, which otherwise could not be carried on; neither indeed could one fifth part of the inhabitants be supported without them, for the land could not maintain them.[8]

Gloucestershire clothiers paid two or three times more for coal than competitors in Leeds, on account of their distance from the major sources of supply.[9]

Defoe's 'wise hand of Providence' omitted to supply a local source of raw cotton, however – the plant won't grow in such a climate – so the vanguard industry of the Industrial Revolution was reliant on overseas markets not only to sell its wares, but for the key ingredient needed to produce them in the first place. It's necessary, therefore, to zoom out from Lancashire to consider the general situation of England's foreign trade, which had slipped its traditional north European moorings to go intercontinental by the time the manufacturing revolution got under way. The Navigation Acts, first laid down by Parliament after victory in the Civil

War, combined with a series of wars against Dutch mastery of the global carrying trade, cleared the seas for British merchants, prising open the sort of long-distance trading opportunities identified by Braudel as 'the only doorway to a superior profit level'.[10] These incremental steps to imperial hegemony weren't geared to serving the tiny cotton interest. The City of London also reaped the benefits, funnelling the world's goods and funds through its wharves and counting houses, indifferent to a provincial manufacturing complex which developed in parallel to it. Nevertheless, the UK's head-start mercantilism constituted a massive helping of state aid for both Lancashire and London.

With all this geopolitical wind behind them, Liverpool merchants could sail to the West African coast to exchange Indian calicoes and Lancashire textiles for slaves, whom they shipped to the Americas, where planters responded to soaring demand by massively increasing cotton cultivation on estates expropriated from the indigenous population and worked by forced labour. The cotton was shipped to Lancashire to be woven, spun, dyed and finished, and then despatched to the Indian subcontinent – formerly the world's leading producer of cotton textiles, but reduced under strengthening British hegemony to production of primary commodities and Lancashire's largest overseas market.

Liverpool accounted for one-half to three-quarters of British slave-ships sailings in the late eighteenth century and forced over a million Africans across the Atlantic during its involvement in the trade.[11] Even after abolition in 1807, Merseyside merchants were free to own slaves and plantations and to deal in slave-produced cotton and other commodities. William Gladstone's father, John, directly owned over a thousand slaves in the West Indies.[12] In his maiden parliamentary speech in 1833, Gladstone Junior defended his family's estate management and urged British lawmakers to proceed cautiously when considering a scheme for phased emancipation. Some slaves were 'idle', he warned. 'I would not free the slave without assurance of his disposition to industry: I would not redeem him from the hands even of an oppressor and an enemy, to place him in a state where he would himself be his own worst enemy'. At the age of twenty-three, the future Liberal prime minister was already a talented moralist.[13]

It isn't to be wondered at that a Westminster legislature crammed full of landowners converted to capitalist business practices in the countryside should have smiled on the advance of machinofacture in the North, nor that MPs proved indifferent to the distress of handicraft workers displaced by mechanisation. As Hobsbawm wrote, 'On issues of agrarian, commercial or financial policy Lancashire might be in conflict with London, but not on the fundamental supremacy of the profit-making employer.'[14] Many of the great landowners stood to gain from urban growth and exploitation of mineral rights. Rents from the factory towns swelled the incomes of aristocrats like the Howards, Dukes of Norfolk, who remodelled Arundel Castle in Sussex using receipts from steelworks in Sheffield. Hugh Percy, third Duke of Northumberland, a descendant of the old Percys in the maternal line, sat back as his family's income from colliery rentals rose tenfold between 1790 and 1831.[15]

Such were the origins, in brief, of the manufacturing revolution. What were its effects? To paraphrase Marx, the steam mill created the North of the industrial capitalist and the wage-earning factory worker. Industrialisation didn't make a clean sweep of existing social relations in the North: machine production and cottage industry coexisted in the textile district; many Chartists were outworkers rather than factory hands; the Liverpool docks were no more mechanised than those which lined the Thames; large swathes of the border counties remained overwhelmingly agricultural.[16] But there was no doubting the direction of travel.

The appearance of new social forces in the region threatened to catch the majority of officeholders at the apex of Britain's governing structure wrong-footed. 'The Home Counties, the South East and the West country filled their horizons', writes Michael Bentley of Tory Cabinet ministers in 1815; 'and this at a moment when the axis of working-class unrest and political radicalism had swung sharply north and west'.[17] Industrial society was disfigured, according to Edward Thompson, by the 'intensification of two intolerable forms of relationship: those of economic exploitation and of political oppression'.[18] In a business matrix dominated by small private firms, few of which had business partners or bank accounts in London, economic exploitation was pushed along by resident mill owners rather than distant shareholders. Left to their own devices, however, the 'factory despots', as Marx called them, wouldn't have held out long against the handloom weavers' fury, nor the disgruntlement of their own misused mill workers.[19] The classic industrial novels are correct, up to a point, to emphasise the isolation of the factory capitalist – adrift on a proletarian sea, at any moment likely to be 'borne down by numbers' and by 'the awful power' of trade unions. Never, it seems, was there such a need for damsels to rescue manufacturers in distress.[20]

Where the bourgeois romances went wrong was to suppose that industrial peace was attainable through capitalist philanthropy. At the close of Gaskell's *Mary Barton* (1848), John Carson becomes the very model of a mill owner, binding management and workers together 'by the ties of respect and affection, not by mere money bargains alone'. Disraeli posited in his condition-of-England melodrama *Sybil, or The Two Nations* (1845) that 'proximity to the employer brings cleanliness and order, because it brings observation and encouragement.'[21] What actually kept a lid on the North in these tumultuous decades were the forces of law and order coordinated by the Crown in Parliament, as the tumbrils of Paris encouraged the Westminster old guard and the new captains of industry to huddle together for mutual protection.

During the Anti-Jacobin Wars of 1792–1815, the British state spearheaded the counterrevolutionary effort abroad while cracking down on domestic unrest through emergency laws, troop deployments and barrack building. Prime Minister William Pitt warned in 1793 that 'a spirit had appeared in some of the manufacturing towns which made it necessary that troops should be kept near them.'[22] English Jacobinism was strongest in old craft communities such as Norwich and Sheffield, but the mill towns were also stirring. Pitt sounded the tocsin that illegal and conspiratorial combinations of workers 'existed to a very great degree in the northern parts of the kingdom' and passed the Combination Acts to strengthen the armoury of anti-trade-union legislation. He was goaded into action by William Wilberforce, a venerated anti-slavery campaigner and Christian philanthropist but also the son of a wealthy Hull merchant who sided with the bastions of authority against working-class organisation, 'a general disease in our society'.[23]

State repression drove industrial grievances into subterranean alliance with political radicalism, hence, in Thompson's words, 'north of the Trent we find the illegal tradition'.[24] The Luddite movement began at the Trent more or less exactly: in the village of Arnold near Nottingham, on 11 March 1811, during a war-related economic slump. Skilled workers in the framework-knitting trade, still a handicraft industry at this point, targeted wide stocking frames producing inferior goods. Missives signed by the mythical ringleader, General Ned Ludd, were sometimes addressed from Sherwood Forest, that traditional haunt of English outlawry. The insurgency was transmitted by emissaries and by example north-wards into Lancashire and Yorkshire, taken up by handworkers battling against the diffusion of factory machinery. They came up against Establishment barricades erected through the Crown's pre-rogative powers and Westminster legislation, and manned locally by sheriffs, Justices of the Peace, mayors, bailiffs, constables and other civil officers – reinforced by the military as needed.[25] With opponents ranged against them high and low, Luddites in the West Riding recognised that the founding of a just republic would require the downfall not just of 'the Hanover tyrants' but of 'all our Tyrants from the greatest to the smallest'.[26]

In April, a Luddite band led by George Mellor, a cropper from Longroyd Bridge near Huddersfield, staged an assault on the Liversedge mill of William Cartwright, targeting what fellow machine wreckers in Leeds called 'those detestable Shearing Frames'. Two attackers were fatally wounded in a shoot-out with soldiers and loyalist workmen. The incident is replayed in Charlotte Brontë's *Shirley* (1849), which makes a hero of the mill tenant while dismissing the principal Luddites as 'chiefly "down-draughts," bankrupts, men always in debt and often in drink – men who had nothing to lose, and much – in the way of character, cash, and cleanliness – to gain'. Cartwright reportedly denied medical aid to the dying men, whereas his fictional coun-terpart sends for help at full gallop.[27] Two weeks after the raid at Liversedge, Mellor assassinated mill owner William Horsfall, who had expressed a wish to 'ride up to the saddle-girths in Luddite blood'.[28] On the other side of the Pennines, meanwhile, a crowd of several thousand attempted to force entry into the Middleton mill of Daniel Burton, an early adopter of the power loom. The rioters pelted the building with stones. Four or five were shot dead by musket fire from Burton's men; more were killed by a troop of Scots Greys when hostilities resumed the next day. The coroners returned a verdict of 'justifiable homicide'. The Luddites rued that 'if Burton's infamous action was "justifiable", the laws of Tyrants are reason's dictates'.[29]

The government of Lord Liverpool fielded 12,000 troops to lock down Luddite areas that summer.[30] Home Secretary Henry Addington, first Viscount Sidmouth, the son of a London physician, obtained additional powers to seize weapons, disperse meetings and apprehend Luddite delegates. Ten rioters were hanged at Chester and Lancaster, and Sidmouth stressed the 'urgent expediency of accelerating' the mass trial of other suspects held at York. The prosecuting counsel in York duly wrapped up his work within days, impressing the Home Secretary by his zeal. Mellor and sixteen others were hanged. 'I confidently anticipate the happiest effects in various parts of the kingdom,' celebrated Sidmouth. A royal proclamation urged manufacturers 'not to be deterred from continuing the use and employment' of their machines. They could be confident in their 'recourse to the salutary measures which the wisdom of Parliament has provided for the protection of persons and property'.[31]

Home Office draconianism, an improvement in trade and a good harvest drew the strength out of this main outburst of Luddism, but the domestic emergency would resurface shortly after British victory at Waterloo. In March 1817 Liverpool and Sidmouth threw another military cordon around the textile districts to prevent a workers' march on London from Manchester. Three hundred handloom weavers set off for the capital on the 10th equipped with blankets and a petition for the Prince Regent. Their opening rally at St Peter's Field was broken up by the King's Dragoon Guards and many of the Blanketeers were arrested at Lancashire Hill near Stockport, where a local labourer was shot dead by a dragoon. Harried by soldiers, only a handful made it as far as Derby. A plot to free those detained was penetrated by government spies.

Official harassment of the Blanketeers was a prelude to the Peterloo massacre two years later, dramatised for the screen by director Mike Leigh to mark the bicentenary. 'If the Magistrates shall see an opportunity of acting with Vigour,' Sidmouth's permanent under-secretary had counselled,

> they will recollect that there is no situation in which their Energy can be so easily backed by Military aid as at Manchester, where the Troops are at hand, and may be kept on the alert, if the Civil Power should appear likely to stand in need of their assistance.

On 16 August 1819, a troop of the Manchester and Salford Yeomanry Cavalry charged into a peaceable crowd of 60,000 gathered on St Peter's Field to hear Wiltshire radical Henry 'Orator' Hunt call for parliamentary reform. The yeomanry were mill-owner and shopkeeper volunteers captained by Hugh Hornby Birley, proprietor of a city-centre cotton factory on the banks of the Medlock. They were ordered into action by a special committee of magistrates chaired by William Hulton of Hulton Hall near Bolton, a coal-owning Pittite who venerated 'Our Glorious Constitution'.[32] Hulton then sent in the regular 15th King's Hussars – veterans of Waterloo, as were some of their victims. At least 654 people were injured by state forces, eighteen of them fatally. Sabre blows were the commonest cause of injury; there were also wounds from truncheons, bayonets and gunshots. 'The proceedings at Manchester on Monday will, I trust, prove a salutary lesson to modern reformers,' Sidmouth confided to his daughter. He relayed the thanks of the Lord Regent to Hulton and the yeomanry 'for their prompt, decisive and efficient measures for the preservation of the public peace', and had Whig grandee Earl Fitzwilliam dismissed as Lord Lieutenant of the West Riding for his part in a meeting of Yorkshire freeholders which demanded an inquiry into the Manchester outrage.[33] Under Hunt's direction, the working-class response to Peterloo was no more pushing than that of the Yorkshire gentry. Hunt shifted his oratory from the streets to the courts, where all impetus was lost.[34]

Musgrove makes an extravagant attempt to demonstrate the unity of industrial society in the North against the common foe of the landowning class, depicting workers and employers dancing in the streets together at Repeal of the Corn Laws, with only archaic petty capitalist malcontents – not workers – causing trouble at Peterloo and elsewhere. 'Peterloo was a protest by manufacturers against the old political order which excluded them,' he contends, pointing to the involvement of bourgeois radicals like John Knight and Joseph Johnson, small-scale cotton and brush manufacturers respectively. Yet half of the dead and wounded in St Peter's Fields for whom an occupation is known were weavers; others were spinners, labourers, hatters, shoemakers, dyers, tailors. A large number resided in factory-worker districts such as Ancoats and New Mills. In other words, the crowd comprised domestic workers, artisans, factory hands and the labouring poor, not industrial capitalists, who were to be found on the other side of the confrontation, in the ranks of the yeomanry and special constabulary, alongside the shopkeepers, publicans and professional men.[35]

The activists who battled through these difficult times left their imprint on working-class theory and organisation. William Benbow, a Manchester shoemaker who had helped to organise the Blanketeers, went on to propound the idea – hesitantly taken up by Chartism – of combining a general strike with a congress of the working classes mandated to devise a plan, before the month-long stoppage was over, for getting idle land, property and capital into circulation, 'whereby, if it is possible, the privation, wretchedness and slavery, of the great mass of us, may be diminished, if not completely annihilated.' Benbow may have had the isolation of the Blanketeers in his mind when he stressed the need for this Grand National Holiday to involve 'every city, town, village and parish throughout the United Kingdom', so that 'the festival be not partial but universal'.[36] The first attempts by Manchester factory spinners to build a general trade union and to agitate for effective legislation to curb excessive working hours – particularly those of children, with hoped-for knock-on effects on adult shifts – also date to this period.

The Manchester spinners had cause to confront the rapacity of the factory system. While the textile masters made small fortunes, their mill hands faced long hours, harsh discipline and dangers to

life and limb. Richard Oastler's characterization of a set of Bradford industrialists as 'Messrs. Get-all, Keep-all, Grasp-all' had
broader applicability.[37] 'Talk of vassals! Talk of villains! Talk of
serfs!', exploded Surrey popular journalist William Cobbett on
one of his rural rides,

> Are there any of these, or did feudal times ever see any of them,
> so debased, so absolutely slaves, as the poor creatures who, in
> the 'enlightened' North, are compelled to work fourteen hours
> in a day, in a heat of eighty-four degrees; and who are liable to
> punishment for looking out a window of the factory![38]

But there were also plenty of apologists for the factory system.
Writing from Manchester's York Hotel, a favourite haunt of
the mill owners, the economist Nassau Senior, promoter of the
amended Poor Law, assured the Board of Trade that 'the exceed-
ing easiness of cotton-factory labour renders long hours of
work practicable'. Keeping an eye on the machines and piecing
broken thread was really no more onerous than shopkeeping.[39]
Leeds liberal Edward Baines Junior, who ran the Whiggish *Leeds
Mercury* with his father, was equally forgiving to the factory
masters in his celebratory *History of the Cotton Manufacture in
Great Britain* (1835):

> The only thing which makes factory labour trying even to
> delicate children is, that they are confined for long hours and
> deprived of fresh air: this makes them pale, and reduces their
> vigour, but it rarely brings on disease. The minute fibres of
> cotton which float in the rooms, and are called *fly*, are admitted,
> even by medical men, not to be injurious to young persons.[40]

In fact, Gaskell's depiction in *North and South* of a nineteen-
year-old cardroom worker dying from cotton dust in her lungs
was warranted. Statutory compensation for byssinosis, a disa-
bling and life-limiting respiratory disease, would not be awarded
until the Second World War, a century after Baines – a man of the
same stamp as his father, dubbed 'the great liar of the North' by
Cobbett – was pushing these sham certainties.[41]

The focus of the factory-reform effort shifted to the West Riding at the start of the 1830s as the worsted industry converted to the industrial system. The campaigner Richard Oastler disturbed the moral calm of the Yorkshire bourgeoisie in a series of letters to the *Leeds Mercury* deplored by the Baineses. With proto-Dickensian outrage, he adopted the vernacular of abolitionism to call middle-class worthies to account for neglecting the 'magazines of British Infantile Slavery – *the Worsted Mills in the town and neighbourhood of Bradford*'. His targets included the supporters of Yorkshire MP Henry Brougham, a prominent figure in the Anti-Slavery Society:

> Thousands of our fellow-creatures and fellow-subjects, both male and female, the miserable inhabitants of a *Yorkshire town* (Yorkshire now represented in Parliament by the giant of anti-slavery principles), are this very moment existing in a state of Slavery *more horrid* than are the victims of that hellish system – 'Colonial Slavery'.[42]

Oastler had started off as a Methodist preacher and Leeds cloth merchant, but switched tracks when he became a land steward for an absentee gentry family outside Huddersfield. The Dissenting tradition of the textile trade was jettisoned in favour of Anglican rural paternalism. The result was a rabble-rousing Church-and-King Tory engaged in a long rhetorical war with the advocates of laissez-faire. Contact with Huddersfield radicals channelled this high-profile fulminator into the operatives' world of the short-time committee and mass meeting. Oastler constituted a rare outcrop of upper-class humanitarianism, becoming to the factory-reform movement what Fergus O'Connor was to Chartism: a gentlemanly rallying point for working-class protest.[43]

The master worsted spinners of Halifax spoke for manufacturers as a body when, in response to Oastler, they deplored 'the pernicious tendency and effects of all *legislative enactments*, whether protective or restrictive, which propose to regulate the details of trade and manufactures'.[44] It needed two further impulses, beyond steady trade-union pressure, to achieve a legal ten-hours' restriction. One was inadvertently supplied by the free-trade radicals of

Manchester's Anti-Corn Law League, incurring the wrath of the country gentry, who took their revenge by meddling in factory matters on behalf of the mill hands. 'Had not these passions interposed', admitted Lord Ashley, 'there would have been no unusual humanity.'[45] The other spur came from the popular radicalism of renegade Lancashire cotton master John Fielden, who unlike Oastler kept his relevance to working-class politics by following the mass move into Chartism. It was Fielden who roused the North in support of the Ten Hours Bill and piloted it through Westminster in 1847. By this point, mill owners had been flourishing essentially unregulated for half a century. They responded to the political setback with measures to reverse and circumvent the restrictions, to resist any further 'meddling legislation' and to squeeze more work out of their employees within a somewhat shorter day.[46]

The Yorkshire factory campaign, combined with a fresh effort at general trade-unionism emanating from Manchester, compounded Establishment alarm during the Reform crisis of 1829–32, when Grey's patrician Whigs conceded a Reform Bill to break an unprecedented bout of civil disorder afflicting both London and the provinces, town and country, in the shadow of the July revolution in Paris. Tricolour flags had greeted the Duke of Wellington, head of the preceding Tory administration, at the opening of the Liverpool–Manchester railway in September 1830. 'The spirit of the district was detestable', complained one of his ministers.[47] At the end of that year, Henry Hunt's by-election victory over Edward Smith Stanley, the future fourteenth Earl of Derby, at Preston – a rare potwalloper constituency with almost universal manhood suffrage – gave further evidence of popular restiveness.

It's striking that all three major instalments of franchise reform in the nineteenth century were passed under the aegis of prime ministers with family backgrounds in the hinterlands of the Industrial Revolution. Grey grew up at Howick Hall on the edge of coal-mining Northumberland; Stanley, who would oversee the Second Reform Act of 1867, had his family seat at Knowsley, eight miles north-east of Liverpool, where Gladstone – sponsor of the Third Reform Act of 1884 – was born on a fine Georgian street.

They weren't, of course, industrialists themselves. Grey's politics were those of the Whig notables gathered at Devonshire House on Piccadilly, while Gladstone's merchant-prince father had eased his son into the Establishment by enrolment in Eton and Oxford, followed by marriage into the minor aristocracy. Nevertheless, the northern origins of this trio of public-school men left them well placed to appreciate the need to make room for industrial society on terms as favourable as possible to the institutions of the old regime. As Grey's biographer puts it, 'Only by making these institutions acceptable in a new age and to new and influential classes could they survive into the era of Britain's transformation into a great commercial and industrial country.'[48]

The unreformed political system had worked well enough in a pre-industrial context, notwithstanding Christopher Wyvill's tirades against its venality. Old Corruption may have been domiciled in London, mainly representing southern territorial and commercial interests – more than half of English borough MPs had their seats in counties on the coastline below the Severn and the Wash – but landowners and urban mercantile oligarchies in the North were thoroughly implicated in its processes.[49] Each northern county sent two members to Parliament, with the exception of oversize Yorkshire which returned four. There were also an appreciable number of parliamentary boroughs in the region. The Westmorland pocket borough of Appleby, where the vote was vested in tenants of the aristocratic Lowther and Tufton families, helped three prime ministers – Grey, Pitt the Younger and Robert Banks Jenkinson – to climb the parliamentary ladder. George Canning, meanwhile, the liberal Tory who was twice Foreign Secretary and briefly prime minister, had his parliamentary base for ten years in Liverpool. He was a stranger to Merseyside, arriving there in 1812 at a low point in his career by the invitation of John Gladstone and other West Indies traders, who afterwards lobbied him assiduously.[50]

Where Old Corruption left itself open even to bourgeois criticism was in not providing growing urban centres in the North and the Midlands with a direct line to Westminster. There were no borough constituencies in south-east Lancashire: the chief spokesman for the cotton lobby, George Philips, had to make use of a series of rotten boroughs outside the county. Pontefract was the only enfranchised borough anywhere near the Yorkshire cloth towns.[51] The 1832 Reform Act would fill in these empty spaces. It was an undeserved victory for the millocrats, gained by virtue of pressure from more effective campaigns mounted in other parts of the country. In the opinion of John Lambton, Baron Durham – a major North East coal owner and son-in-law to Grey – 'the country owed Reform to Birmingham'.[52] In a world of petty workshops, artisans and small masters, Birmingham banker Thomas Attwood was able to arbitrate between the masses and the Whig ministry, rallying local opinion behind the tepid reform proposals of Grey and Lord John Russell. Attwood's vehicle was a Political Union of the Lower and Middle Classes inspired by the Irish example of Daniel O'Connell's Catholic Association. Birmingham in turn provided the organisational model for other municipalities. One of its more influential counterparts was Newcastle's Northern Political Union (NPU) led by Attwood's younger brother, a Gateshead glass manufacturer. While Birmingham had the best lines of communication to Whitehall, the NPU was also in friendly correspondence with Grey, who professed to welcome the 'reaffirmation of my countrymen' but kept them at arm's length.[53]

Class antagonism was too sharp in the main textile centres for middle-class reformers to pose, like Attwood, as natural civic leaders, and this reduced their leverage on events. 'There is an unhealthy disparity of condition in the factory towns, with its millowner employing his thousand hands, which will always militate against a hearty and fearless cooperation on ordinary political questions,' commented Lancashire calico printer Richard Cobden, whose opposition to factory legislation didn't endear him to the working man or woman. 'In Birmingham where a manufacturer employs his three or four hands only, and sometimes but an apprentice or two, there is much more cordial and united feeling among the two classes'.[54] Archibald Prentice of the *Manchester Times* headed a small group of pro-Reform Bill radicals in Manchester backed by the shopocracy, while a working-class splinter group damned the Whig proposals for their paltriness. In Leeds, caught in the cross-current of Oastler's factory-reform campaign, a middle-class grouping around newspaperman Edward Baines

Senior – a resolute opponent of universal suffrage – was just as unpalatable to the labouring population.

But Birmingham must have the vote, so Leeds and Manchester could hardly be left out. The Whigs cauterised the general unrest by admitting the middle classes into the Constitution. For Russell, seats for the manufacturing towns and a uniform property-based franchise broadening the borough electorate in England from 170,000 to 270,000 would reclaim 'a mass of industrious, intelligent, prosperous men' produced by manufacturing growth

> from the political desert to which they have been confined; to recall them from wild prospects and hostile schemes, in order to bind them to our institutions; to make them a part of the great family of the Constitution, partaking in all its privileges and defending it in all its dangers.[55]

One peril to be avoided was that of swamping large-town constituencies with a class of persons 'hostile to property'. Russell corresponded with Edward Baines Senior to ascertain the likely effect of a £10 household qualification on the Leeds electorate. Baines assured the Whigs 'that the £10 qualification did not admit to the exercise of the elective franchise a single person who might not safely and wisely be enfranchised'; his canvassers were in fact 'surprised to find how few comparatively would be allowed to vote'. Writing from the *Leeds Mercury* office, Baines continued, 'It appeared that in the parts occupied chiefly by the working classes, not one householder in fifty would have a vote. In the streets principally occupied by shops, almost every householder had a vote.' Factory workers were left out, shopkeepers ushered in. Russell relayed the information almost verbatim to the House. He marvelled that anyone could confuse the recommended alterations with universal suffrage.[56]

Grey and Russell ensured that their landed kin survived the Reform Act, obliging the manufacturing centres to share the spoils of redistribution not only with a handful of southern towns – Brighton, Stroud, etc. – but also with the counties. Of the forty counties in England, only six or seven of them are usually claimed for the North. Under the new arrangements, Lancashire (population 1,400,000) returned twenty-six county or borough members; Devon (population 500,000) returned twenty-two, only four fewer than before. The Devonian borough of Totnes still sent two MPs to Parliament; so did Liverpool, a city fifty times its size. Russell was within his rights to protest that 'the last charge which ought to be made against ministers was, that they had neglected the interests of the Southern or Western counties, or that they had overlooked the agricultural districts.'[57] But at least the textile masters now had unmediated access to Westminster, and over the next three decades they would account for a third of all Lancashire's MPs. A broader base of support among the propertied classes emboldened the reformed House of Commons to maintain a firm line against working-class interests, notably in the Poor Law Amendment Act 1834 which condemned penniless operatives to the workhouse. James O'Brien, a Manchester Chartist delegate, commented that reform had simply 'united all property against all poverty'.[58]

The disappointment of 1832, sharpened by economic distress in the late thirties and forties, yielded Chartism, a precocious working-class campaign for the partial democratisation of the British state. Meanwhile the millocrats used their entrée into the political system to press for liberalisation of the country's commercial relations. The inaugural conferences of the Chartists and the Anti-Corn Law League coincided in Westminster Palace Yard at the opening of a new parliamentary session in February 1839. The Anti-Corn Law League achieved its objective within a decade. Chartism failed utterly in the period of its existence but laid down a marker for the future. Once the threat of mass insurrection finally spread from the provinces to London in 1848, a section of the Whigs became convinced that further reform could not be delayed indefinitely.[59]

Metropolitan artisans and a revived Birmingham Political Union (BPU) made the early running in the Chartist endeavour. London cabinetmaker William Lovett drafted the movement's founding document, which demanded the vote for every male inhabitant of Britain and Ireland. To complement the Charter, BPU secretary Robert Douglas, editor of the liberal-radical *Birmingham*

Journal, added a national petition. But the movement they engendered drew mass strength from the depressed outworkers and industrial operatives of the North, whose energies had already been stirred by the factory-reform campaign and the hated New Poor Law. Joseph Rayner Stephens, a Methodist preacher from Ashton, contended that Parliament had rendered itself 'constitutionally defunct' by this obnoxious piece of legislation.[60] Simple mill towns like Halifax and Stockport were easiest to mobilise for Chartism, but command functions belonged to the big cities. In Engels's opinion, Manchester was 'the central point of Chartism'.[61] A meeting of Chartist delegates at the Griffin Inn on Great Ancoats Street, chaired by power-loom weaver James Leach, launched the National Charter Association (NCA), a prototype workers' party based on individual subscriptions. Together with a radical print culture in Leeds, where Irish landowner Feargus O'Connor – 'the apostle of the North' – established the *Northern Star* newspaper, the NCA lent coherence to the Chartist effort through the hungry forties.[62]

One of the finest public speakers of early Chartism, Stephens told a monster rally of 300,000 undernourished people at Kersal Moor outside Manchester – under banners that had seen service at Peterloo – that the fight for the vote was a 'knife-and-fork question'.[63] From political power would follow material relief. Whigs and Tories in Parliament, jealously guarding their privileges, understood this logic, seeing in Chartism not just a public-order problem but also a threat to property. In the implacable Wellington's rendering, 'Plunder is the object. Plunder is likewise the means'. The senior military commander in the North, Charles Napier, wrote from Manchester, 'There may be, and there may not be a general insurrection; but the people menace the use of the pike and fire in all directions, which is perfectly practicable.' Napier, who would later apply his generalship to furthering the cause of British imperialism in India, annexing the Sindh region, outlined plans to intercept a Chartist march on London in the hill country of Derbyshire – 'full of strong positions where, with artillery, large bodies might be arrested'. A cousin of Charles James Fox, he had some sympathy for the Chartist rank and file, 'rather to be pitied than blamed'. But it only went so far. 'If they fail an oligarchy becomes triumphant,' he despaired. However, 'if they succeed we shall have carnage.'[64] Stephens's arrest was effected by a Bow Street Runner sent north for the purpose.

Notwithstanding his crowd-drawing popularity, Stephens's attitude towards Chartism was ambivalent. He advised Ashton supporters who wanted him as their delegate to the convention that 'he was for physical force and the promoters of this question were for moral force; they were for petitioning, and in that he could not join them. The day had gone by when people ought to petition; it was already proved that their prayers were not listened to.'[65] On 12 July 1839 a poorly attended House of Commons rebuffed the first national Chartist petition. By this point, mass arrests orchestrated by the Whigs had thinned the ranks of the Chartist Convention, which drew back from plans for a general strike, though there were a number of localised shutdowns, notably in the cotton district around Manchester.[66]

Carlyle dubbed the second Chartist upsurge of 1842 'the Manchester insurrection'.[67] A hot summer of stoppages and civil disturbances, amidst the worst economic slump of the century, began on the north Staffordshire coalfield before spreading into the textile belt, as the idea of a general strike for the Charter was taken up by activists. In the first week of August, power-loom weaver Richard Pilling moved a resolution at Dukinfield, just east of Manchester, that 'the people should turn out, and stop out, till they got a fair day's wage for a fair day's work, and until the Charter became the law of the land'. A conference of trades delegates at the Carpenters' Hall in Manchester made this the official position. Conservative Home Secretary Sir James Graham, a Cumberland baronet, instructed that gatherings of striking workers be suppressed, moved troops into mill towns and the Potteries, and ordered the incarceration of members of the Manchester trades conference, believing that 'a blow struck at the heart of this Confederacy goes to the heart of the evil'. Two strikers were shot and killed by the military at Preston. At least two more men and a soldier died in clashes in Halifax on the 16th. 'You must whop these fellows without loss of time; if once they get ahead we shall find them troublesome,' Graham warned the colonel of the Yorkshire Hussars. Hundreds of men were sentenced to transportation by special commissions at Chester, Liverpool and Stafford. Hunger and state repression brought a return to work in Manchester by the end of September.[68]

The Plug Plot was not a fully national affair. Lord Liverpool had fretted to Chateaubriand, the royalist French ambassador, 'A sudden insurrection in London and all is lost'.[69] But the capital's vast size and occupational diversity made it a tough nut for the Chartists to crack. 'London is always the last to stir,' complained the *Northern Star*; 'or when it takes the initiative, such is its overwhelming bulk, and the consequent segregation of its parts, that no powerful and well-compacted concentration of popular energy is produced.'[70] The peak organisations of Chartism, the NCA and the *Northern Star*, both came to be run from the capital in the years after 1842, but it took until 1848 for metropolitan Chartism to pick up speed, fired by Continental and Irish revolutionaries, and even then, all forward momentum was immediately lost in the Kennington Common fiasco, when O'Connor and other Chartist leaders organised a rally on the wrong side of the Thames and decided against defying a police ban on a procession to Parliament. 'The Chartists and Confederates made the challenge, and chose the field and trial of strength,' exulted *The Times*. 'They chose to disturb the metropolis for the chance of something coming of it. They fished for a revolution and have caught a snub.'[71] The subsequent arrest of several hundred Chartists and Irish Confederates in London and the North finished off the movement. The mayor of Manchester, Elkanah Armitage, a Salford bedding manufacturer, rallied Liberal Dissenting magistrates to the Establishment's defence and received a knighthood from Russell's Whigs. 'He was anti-aristocratic in the way these northern businessmen were, but with no anxieties or hesitations when the social order was threatened by democracy,' writes John Saville in his study of the British experience of 1848. Chartist activists turned in defeat to cooperativism and town-hall politics.[72] For the time being, national politics was out of reach.

This was not the case for Lancashire's factory capitalists, who, having been brought within the Pale of the Constitution in 1832, proceeded to press for the dismantling of the commercial protection enjoyed since the end of the Napoleonic Wars by the country's rentier landowners. For the protagonists of the Anti-Corn Law League, the economic rationale for unilateral tariff reduction – cheaper bread, hence potentially cheaper labour; expanded world trade, to the benefit of world-beating British manufactures – was intertwined with political considerations of the greatest moment. Richard Cobden's antipathy towards the landed aristocracy has been traced back to a yeoman family background in Sussex. But though he kept his country accent and returned in later life to what he called 'the pastoral charms of the South of England', Cobden was probably more guided by his Manchester experience than by his rustic upbringing.[73] According to Victorian biographer John Morley, his politics were those of an unusually clear-sighted cotton exporter for whom the factory was 'the foundation of the new order of things, which demanded a new kind of statesman-ship and new ideas upon national policy'. Aristocratic politics and commercial restriction, as conjoined in the Corn Laws, were 'fatally incompatible with an industrial system'. Cobden himself argued that since the nation's prosperity no longer depended on its land, the political monopoly of the great landowners was an anachronism. It was a case of 'adapting the government to the changing and improving the condition of its people'. Marx was moved to describe the league as 'the party of the self-conscious bourgeoisie'.[74]

Though it attempted to shed its sectional image, including by making a pretence of relocating its head office from Manchester's Market Street to London's Fleet Street, the Anti-Corn Law League remained based squarely on the cotton interest – a sizeable one, given how large cotton goods loomed in the national ledger, each year accounting for between 40 and 50 per cent of UK exports by value.[75] To translate this commercial predominance into politi-cal leverage, Cobden threw himself into campaign mode, carrying on where Wyvill's Yorkshire Association had left off. There was pamphleteering, petitioning and public speaking galore, plus manipulation of electoral registers in the hope of packing the Commons with free-trade MPs. Contra John Bright, the league never became an all-embracing 'movement of the commercial and industrious classes against the lords and great proprietors of the soil'.[76] Factory operatives were hostile toward exploitative employers who opposed Chartism and factory reform. The same parliamentary session that brought forth Corn Law repeal saw Bright doggedly resist the Ten Hours Bill. Cobden was desperate to make free trade more than 'a mere mill-owners' question' but couldn't even achieve a consensus among the country's bourgeoisie. In Manchester business circles there was friction between free-trade ultras and other bourgeois liberal voices, not least the *Guardian*, over the pace of reform and the stridency of the league's agitation. The City of London was more deeply divided, colonial shipping interests among those supporting the status quo. 'There is little hope of doing anything here – the change of feeling is something like descending into an ice-box compared with Manchester,' the league's president, J. B. Smith, reported to Cobden on his first sally to the capital in 1839.[77]

But in spite of this coolness, the Leaguers won through. Prime Minister Robert Peel, the Harrow- and Oxford-educated son of a Bury calico printer taken to country living, passed the buck to Cobden for a repeal measure which split the Tories and broke his government. The member for Stockport, he told the House, 'ought to be chiefly associated' with it. Possibly he gave Cobden more credit than was his due. The immediate problem faced by Peel was pacification of Ireland after the crop failure, not placation of Lancashire business interests. The definitive history of the league concludes that it 'had the part of a chorus which did not play a decisive part in the action; the decisive steps were taken in Parliament and the influence of the league was confined to whipping up enthusiasm out-of-doors in support of a measure which was not its own work'.[78] The Manchester school wasn't the only transmitter of free-trade economics: the *Economist* magazine, founded in London with the Anti-Corn Law League's assistance in 1843, made a more lasting impression on the subject, while Board of Trade ministers with mercantile connections – William Huskisson, succeeding Canning as MP for Liverpool; Charles Poulett Thomson, the Benthamite son of a London merchant adopted by the Manchester bourgeoisie, who elected him as one of their first MPs; William Gladstone, moving with Peel toward free trade – had already set about rationalising import duties and regulations.[79]

Nevertheless, Cobden's well-funded campaign in and out of Parliament made its presence felt in the corridors of power. Disraeli berated Peel for recapitulating Anti-Corn Law League propaganda and for scaring his colleagues with the spectre of 'a third party' based on the league 'being called into the management of public affairs'. Peel maintained in his resignation speech that abandonment of protection was wholly necessary to 'terminate a conflict which, according to our belief, would soon place in hostile collision great and powerful classes in this country'. Better in his eyes to complete a managed transition to a new commercial regime, one that proved beneficial to City merchants and financiers as the volume of international transactions increased. Southern English agriculture would have the run of the domestic market until the 1870s and, in any case, the incomes of large landowners were propped up by urban ground rents and financial investments.[80]

The scale of Cobden's triumph in 1846, accredited by the king's first minister as the prime mover of a shift in national policy on a touchstone domestic issue, is best measured against his subsequent disappointments. Cobden immediately wrote to Peel urging him to go to the country and to rule thereafter through free-traders of all parties, with the mill owners for support. 'Do you shrink from the post of governing through the *bona fide* representatives of the middle class?' he asked. 'You must know them better than to suppose that they are given to extreme or violent measures. They are not democratic.' Peel politely declined the suggestion, replying that the country needed a period of calm, and instead Russell took power at the head of a Whig administration.[81]

Cobden then tried his hand at promoting two other causes, anti-imperialism and fiscal retrenchment, holding each as dearly as the other. He became involved in the London Peace Society and attended a number of international conferences, urging cuts to defence spending and non-intervention abroad.[82] Little came of these endeavours, however. 'I thought free trade was the beginning of a new era,' Cobden lamented, 'but it is evident we repealed the Corn Laws by accident, without knowing what we were about.' Thwarted by the popularity of Palmerston's gunboat diplomacy, by 1852 he was complaining to Bright about all the 'blank cartridges' they were firing from Manchester. Then came the Crimean

War, opposed by both men, and a flag-waving general election in which Cobden went down to defeat in Huddersfield and Bright in Cottonopolis itself, where the *Guardian* rebuked him for lacking patriotism. 'We are dead as a Manchester party,' mourned Cobden, his one later achievement an Anglo-French free-trade treaty negotiated as Gladstone's envoy in 1859–60. Bright, meanwhile, decamped to Birmingham for the second half of a long parliamentary career.[83]

'Our mercantile and manufacturing classes as represented in the chambers of commerce are after all the only power in the State possessed of wealth and political influence sufficient to counteract in some degree the feudal governing class of this country', Cobden insisted to a Bolton mill owner in 1862.[84] But to Cobden's despair, his fellow industrialists proved to be too unpopular in their localities, too distracted by the demands of business in a competitive small-firm environment, and too overawed by wealthier aristocrats and financiers in the South to mount a sustained bid for seniority within the ruling bloc. Still less able were the outworkers and factory hands of the North to combine with London's artisans and labouring poor in a bid to end the combined tyranny of landowner and cotton lord.

The problem for Cobden was that once granted the vote and free trade, the average factory capitalist rested content as a northern civic adjunct to Britain's liberal-imperial governing elite. What was true of the cotton lords also held for Yorkshire's wool magnates, 'loath to involve themselves in national issues'.[85] All the mudslinging between uncouth industrialists and aristocrats waxing rich off unearned increments shouldn't disguise the confluence of interests between men of property. Dependence on colonial markets and concern about the creeping advance of organised labour gave the mill owners solid common ground with fellow businessmen and public-school imperial functionaries. Not even in their Anti-Corn Law phase had they attempted to sweep away the established order *in toto*; still less would they do so afterwards. One of their spokesmen, *Economist* leader writer W. R. Greg, told Gladstone in 1852, 'We still consider ourselves earnest reformers, but thorough anti-democrats.'[86]

Deference to the traditional governing classes had a material basis in the vaster fortunes enjoyed by the great landowners, preponding in the ranks of the very rich until the 1880s. The City of London was the other major source of top wealth.[87] The millocrats were caught in a force field of superior affluence and cultural hauteur. 'I find that nothing seems to be considered so decided a stigma as to brand a man as a mill-owner', said Cobden of the House of Commons, which was not above disparaging Peel for his family's industrial antecedents. Unlike leading City figures, manufacturers lacked the social lubricant of a public school and Oxbridge education. Clunky fellows, they were grateful to be allowed onto the lower echelons of the honours system. Musgrove observes that the new industrial bourgeoisie of mill owners and manufacturers in the North was provincial and philistine in ways that bankers and merchants, clustered in the South, with much more leisure time on their hands and situated at international crossing points, were not, still less a landowning class that did not even have to exert itself in any counting house, and always produced much the greatest number of intellectuals. Cobden was the exception who despaired at the rule, lamenting how fellow members of his class were 'glorying in being the toadies of a clod-pole [i.e. blockhead] aristocracy'.[88]

The pre-industrial mould of British politics remained unbroken, with fateful consequences for the North once its commercial fortunes began to slide. Gaskell perhaps anticipated this outcome in her curious ending to *North and South*, in which Margaret Hale becomes the landlord of factory master John Thornton after he is almost bankrupted by a strike, having inherited his mill and much real estate besides from an Oxford don who 'has lived an easy life in his college all his days'. Even in the land of long chimneys, Gaskell seems to say, business survival will depend on the attitude taken by the traditional landowning and monied interests of the South.[89]

4

The Tide Turns

In the second half of the nineteenth century, industrialism broadened out from the mill towns to become the dominant pattern of northern working-class life 'and not merely a regional anomaly of Lancashire'.[1] The capital-goods phase of the manufacturing revolution, stimulated by railway construction funded by profits from textiles and coal, saw heavy-industrial complexes of shipbuilding, iron and steel, engineering and sundry supply trades form around the coal ports. *The Times* likened the 'astonishing' enlargement of Barrow-in-Furness to the sudden emergence of Chicago in the American Midwest.[2] Middlesbrough on the eastern seaboard, turning out iron rails and ship plates, developed at similarly breakneck speed. The region's shipyards were sustained by the expansion of the merchant marine and by the naval race between the Great Powers which outstripped the capacity of royal dockyards in the South. Warship-maker Armstrong-Whitworth had two-fifths of Tyneside metalworkers on its books by 1914.[3]

Meanwhile the heavy-chemicals industry exploited Lancashire coal and Cheshire salt to produce soda for Merseyside soap and glass works, and for the textile and paper mills of Manchester. The Leblanc process of alkali production blanketed the chemical towns in pollution. 'St Helens is eminently what Cobbett meant by a *Hell-hole* ... and what Lord Derby and Mr Bright would call a centre of manufacturing industry', observed the poet and critic Matthew Arnold.[4]

The output of such hellholes increased the North's share of UK gross domestic product from 22 to 27 per cent between 1861 and

1911 at the expense of the rural periphery: Ireland, south-west England and East Anglia.[5] Yet the novelty of its industrial society was wearing off. Clydeside launched more ships than the Tyne or Wear, although not more than these two taken together. The South Wales coalfield increased its output until it almost matched the Great Northern. Overseas, the factory system advanced beyond early encampments in New England and the Low Countries, the export by Platt Brothers, an Oldham textile-engineering firm, of huge amounts of spinning machines to Germany, Russia and Japan storing up problems for domestic cotton production.[6]

It would require the addition of the West Midlands, holding on to 7 per cent of GDP as machinofacture began to make headway in the metal trades, to bring the economic output of the North up to parity with high-financing, empire-ruling London and its hinterland. A separate growth pole organised around international commercial and financial transactions and a burgeoning consumer economy, the South East increased its share of national output from 28 to 33 per cent.[7] Disconnected from the bulk of domestic industry, free of government restrictions on capital export, the City poured money overseas into railways and foreign-government bonds. Only 7 per cent of national income was reserved for investment in the home economy, compared to 12 per cent in rapidly modernising Germany and America.[8]

Even the industrial bourgeoisie could be *tête montée*, as Richard Cobden put it, about investing in far-off ventures. He got his fingers burnt speculating on the Illinois Central Railroad. 'Everything has gone as unluckily as possible with me', he complained.[9] The price deflation of the closing decades of the century was particularly strong and sustained in the cotton industry, warding off fresh outlays. Liverpool and Manchester wealth holders were second only to Londoners in their readiness to put money into foreign undertakings outside the empire.[10] Capital was not offered by the City, nor was it sought by complacent manufacturers, to keep updating the North's industrial technology and organisation, or to move the region beyond textiles and heavy industry into newer growth sectors.[11] For the North it was a case of so far and no further: from now on, it would have to sink or swim with its nineteenth-century coal mines, textile mills, steelworks and shipyards. In the years after the First World War these basic industries would account for between one-third and one-half of insured workers in the region.[12]

One of the few notable late developments in the North, the Ship Canal, opened up Manchester to large seagoing vessels in 1893. It was comparable in length (thirty-six miles) to the Panama Canal and reduced cargo-transportation costs by breaking Liverpool's stranglehold on North West shipping. Completed only after a municipal bail-out, the waterway represented a determined bid by the original industrial city to hold its position. 'People have talked of the decline of Lancashire. But Manchester declines to decline', editorialised the *St James's Gazette*.[13] Nevertheless, it is suggestive that such a word was being bandied about.

Alongside the docks appeared a planned industrial estate, a new innovation created by a shady Nottingham company promoter on parkland put up for sale by a local baronet. 'Trafford Park is a modern miracle', wrote Salford novelist Walter Greenwood:

> Where the drives once wound their serpentine paths through the woods, the fungus of modern industry, huge engineering shops, flour mills, timber yards, oil refineries, automobile works, repositories for bonded merchandise, choke and foul the prospect ...
> A Five Year Plan thirty years ahead of the Russian. Yesterday the country seat of an aristocrat, today the rowdy seat of commerce. Revolution! and not a drop of blood spilt or a shot fired![14]

The park provided a landing strip for incoming American multinationals in the leading-edge sectors of electrical engineering and car manufacture. Westinghouse constructed Europe's largest factory complex there, modelled on a Pittsburgh original. Ford Motors of Detroit arrived in 1911. A British spokesman for Westinghouse congratulated his employer on finding such an ideal location, 'in the thick of the vast industrial life of the North, with the Manchester Ship Canal and the Bridgewater Canal hard by, and several lines of important railway in close attendance.' Westinghouse's arrival, he claimed, heralded an 'era of rehabilitation and return to that great place in the world's history of effort and achievement, which we were in danger of losing for ever.'[15]

☙

Although Manchester and Birmingham remained prominent in public affairs, far more so than in any subsequent period, London was the 'pet and fancy' of the age.[16] Amidst the financial prosperity of high imperialism, it would be impossible to uphold Gaskell's judgement of southern England as a stagnant region. Spoiled in its exceptional wealth and its control of the country's governing institutions and of increasingly unified corporate and banking sectors, the capital set the tone for national life to a greater extent than had been possible in the days of Chartism and the Anti-Corn Law League. By the end of the Victorian era, Greater London was home to 6.6 million people, virtually equalling the combined total for the south-east Lancashire, west Yorkshire, West Midland, Merseyside and Tyneside conurbations. It had a larger and richer middle class than all the big provincial towns put together. 'Forsytes were numbered by the thousand!' exclaimed Galsworthy. The City of London, around which the wider metropolis sprawled, was assessed for four times as much income tax as Manchester.[17]

Further out, the surburbanised Home Counties filled up with City commuters and rentiers living off private investment pots – in J. A. Hobson's delicate phrase, 'incomes dissociated from any present exertion of their recipients'. Colonial retirees were also ten a penny in this part of the world. 'The South of England is full of men of local influence in politics and society whose character has been formed in our despotic Empire, and whose incomes are chiefly derived from the maintenance and furtherance of this despotic rule', Hobson observed in 1902, during the long period of Conservative rule under Salisbury and Balfour. 'Not a few enter our local councils, or take posts in our constabulary or our prisons: everywhere they stand for coercion and for resistance to reform.'[18] All these well-off elements fuelled the high end of a consumer economy characterised by small trades and services. Robert Tressell's novel *The Ragged Trousered Philanthropists* (1914) gives an idea of the exploitative, casualised employment practices underpinning the belle époque.

Lancashire's millocrats were losing not just political impetus but also national economic heft and notoriety. 'All roads led to Manchester in the 1840s', wrote Asa Briggs. It proved merely a temporary diversion. Cotton's share of UK exports dropped below 40 per cent at the end of the decade for the first time in thirty-three years.[19] Immense hardship came to the mill towns when a downturn in the business cycle coincided with the Union's blockade of Confederate ports in America, interrupting the supply of slave-produced raw cotton. The dislocation was amplified by speculation on the Liverpool Exchange and the re-export of raw cotton at scarcity prices. However, a more diverse export portfolio and the decoupled prosperity of London meant that the Cotton Famine barely exerted any drag on the wider economy. 'Outside Lancashire it would not be known that anything had occurred to injure the national trade', marvelled *The Times*.

> An industry which we conceived to be essential to our commercial greatness has been utterly prostrated, without affecting that greatness in any perceptible degree. We are as busy, as rich and as fortunate in our trade as if the American war had never broken out, and our trade with the States had never been disturbed. Cotton was no King, notwithstanding the prerogatives which had been loudly claimed for it.

Fleet Street's paper of record announced that England could 'dispense with the special industry of Lancashire'.[20] Cobden, the onetime leader of Lancashire business opinion, died in his Pall Mall lodgings a few days before General Lee's surrender concluded the Civil War in America. There could be no question of the younger generation of mill owners setting the political tempo. Crowed the *Spectator*,

> We may be allowed to doubt the truth of the saying ... so flattering to Lancashire self-esteem – that what Lancashire thinks today England will think tomorrow. The influence acquired by the County Palatine during the Anti-Corn Law agitation has passed away; and since the rejection of Cobden, Bright, and Milner-Gibson, followed by that of Gladstone, it has ceased to lead, or greatly to modify, political opinion. Its Members [of Parliament] are mostly mediocrities.[21]

Chartism's collapse had sucked the life out of working-class politics: monster demonstrations and insurrectionist plotting giving way to economistic trade unionism, temperance and cooperativism, which under Rochdale principles relinquished Owenite anti-capitalism for dividend-paying, politically neutral shopkeeping. Nevertheless the quietude of Lancashire during the Cotton Famine came as a relief. Edward Stanley, fourteenth Earl of Derby, praised the 'noble manner, a manner beyond all praise, in which this destitution has been borne by the population of this great county'. In the years after the cotton dearth, rising real wages and statutory concessions including legalisation of trade unions ensured that mill workers' patience wasn't stretched beyond all limits.[22]

A respectable culture was one of the North's chief contributions to the renewed debate about votes for labouring men.[23] 'The town of Rochdale', declared Gladstone, 'has probably done more than any other town in making good to practical minds a case for some enfranchisement of the working classes'. If mass disturbances in London made the introduction of male household suffrage expedient, the 'extraordinary intelligence and self-governing power' of the Pioneers made it seem sound.[24] There was also the queasy spectacle of Samuel Smiles delivering evening classes in self-help to autodidacts in Leeds. Mill owner John Bright, who kept up his Rochdale residence despite now sitting for Birmingham in the Commons, assured MPs that the men of his home town were but 'a fair sample of the general run of the industrious, intelligent and independent population' either side of the Pennines.[25]

Something of a Smilesean himself, Bright was far from being in perfect sympathy with the wage-earning classes. 'The bulk of them could live moderately well on half their present incomes,' he confided to Cobden when the Cotton Famine struck, 'and they and their employers might well learn something useful by a little suffering.'[26] But if the rough, demoralised poor – the 'residuum', he called them – were still entirely beyond the pale, petty retailers and factory workers might become allies of the bourgeois radicals. Cobden had once dabbled in the franchise question vainly hoping to supply the Anti-Corn Law League with 'something in our rear to frighten the Aristocracy'. Bright proceeded in the same spirit. Dished by middle-class Manchester voters in 1857, he reached down the social ladder to enlist support for a continued attack on unearned privilege at its top.[27]

Bright latched onto the working-class Reform League, run by men of the London Trades Council and the First International. The league had three times as many members as Manchester's bourgeois Reform Union. 'The movement in the provinces is this time wholly dependent on that of London', commented Marx.[28] Galvanised by the Hyde Park riots of July 1866, Bright embarked on a speaking tour of the manufacturing towns to champion their claims to fuller representation. He told a packed meeting at Leeds town hall, on a platform shared with Reform League president Edmond Beales, that a gigantic agitation was needed to break the political duopoly of landowners and 'moneybags' boroughmongers and to restore a free Constitution. He said, 'We believe that there is a spirit created in Birmingham, in south Lancashire, in the West Riding of Yorkshire, in the Newcastle and Durham districts, and in Glasgow and the west of Scotland – that there is a power rising which fairly combined can do all this.'[29]

Bright's collaboration with Beales was eased by the latter's shift away from the Chartist demand for manhood suffrage through a qualifying emphasis on 'registered and residential' working men. This spelled the exclusion of itinerant workers and the vagabond and doss-house poor, and aligned the Reform League with the ratepayer franchise aimed at by Bright and the Reform Union. The desire to keep the vote away from poor men, and from women of all social grades, was fully shared by the protagonists inside Westminster. Derby had endorsed the concessions of 1832 even while coordinating political repression on the other side of the Irish Sea as Chief Secretary for Ireland during the tithe war. He resigned his Cabinet post over Corn Law repeal, aggrieved that Peel had surrendered the landed interest 'to the hostility of urban envy'. There were reasons to envy the Stanleys: the Industrial Revolution quadrupled their estate income in a few decades thanks to bulging ground rents from Bury and Liverpool. Granted a shot at government office in June 1866, Derby seized the mantle of reform to make the Tories the arbiter of events for a change. The queen, he advised Disraeli, wanted the question 'settled by *us*'.[30]

Living on Disraeli's wits in the Commons, Derby's minority administration accepted the key amendment opening up the borough franchise less than two weeks after the Reform League had forced the resignation of the Home Secretary by pulling off a mass demonstration in Hyde Park in defiance of a government ban. Lord Liverpool's warning echoed through the West End: a sudden insurrection in London and all is lost. The second front opened up in the provinces by Bright and the Reform Union added strength in depth to this agitation. A speaker from Bradford told the 150,000 protestors gathered in the park that a crowd twice might descend on the capital from the North to see that reform was enacted. Gladstone warned MPs that if the great political problem of the franchise were not settled, it 'may become to us a source of public danger'. Disraeli in reply strenuously denied even the existence of a popular clamour but in private said he wanted to destroy it. Speaking at a Manchester banquet, Derby argued that 'safe and sound' ratepayer suffrage would 'leave no ground for future agitation'. In this matter, he counselled, 'boldness was safety.'[31] Not everyone was convinced. Lord Cranborne, the future Marquess of Salisbury, berated his colleagues for their surrender to 'the mobs who beat down the palings of Hyde Park, or went out marching with bands and banners in the towns of the North.'[32]

The immediate upshot of the Second Reform Act was an 1868 general election in which a predominantly working-class borough electorate, in the world's most proletarianised society, dutifully voted in Liberal and Tory candidates from the business and professional classes. Manchester Chartist and Reform Leaguer Ernest Jones proclaimed that 'rich and poor, employer and employed, moderate Liberal and advanced, now stand united upon the same platform for one common object, the prosperity of each through the good of all.' The West Riding wool boroughs were solidly Liberal, as was Sheffield, although the Steel City afterwards grew mistrustful of Liberal parsimony on military procurement.[33] Leeds returned two Liberals, Edward Baines Junior and former Chartist Robert Meek Carter, alongside a barrister representing the minority Conservative vote. The North East, another

Nonconformist stronghold, offered almost total support for the party of Gladstone. Newcastle and Gateshead stuck by incumbent Liberal coal owners, the former also re-electing a Liberal barrister. South Shields returned a senior partner of the Jarrow Chemical Company; newly enfranchised Middlesbrough plumped for steel magnate Henry Bolckow, also a Liberal; Whitby voted in one of Gladstone's sons. In Cumbria, a Liberal calico printer held Carlisle alongside a radical baronet, while a carpet manufacturer maintained the party's grip on Kendal. Even after the introduction of a secret ballot a few years later, the *Spectator* could sigh with relief that 'property is still a political power'.[34]

Thomas Burt, the Northumberland miners' leader, won the coal borough of Morpeth under Liberal colours in 1874 to become one of Britain's first working-class MPs alongside Lanarkshire miner Alexander Macdonald. Burt hated strikes ('an ugly weapon'), resisted the introduction of a national minimum wage for coal, and thwarted the national miners' Eight Hour Campaign. Coal hewers in Northumberland were on seven-hour shifts and not greatly troubled that the boys who assisted them as putters and transit workers toiled for ten hours straight. When the Miners' Federation affiliated to Labour in 1908, Burt and two other Lib-Lab stalwarts on the Great Northern refused to budge. 'He helped to make the working class respectable in both collective bargaining and politics', says Burt's biographer. By the time he retired from the Commons in 1918, Burt was Father of the House.[35]

For Gladstone to emerge as the standard-bearer for popular liberalism in the regions, organised around the themes of liberty, retrenchment and reform,[36] was quite a turnaround for a defender of New World slavery, a special constable against the Chartists and a young Tory reactionary who, while a student at Oxford, had organised a petition against Whig reform during the crisis of 1829–32, fearing a breakdown of the social order, which had earned him a dinner with the college dean. During the American Civil War he recognised the Confederacy's claim to independent nationhood. 'He was born of a great slave-holding family,' commented Bright to Cobden, 'and I suppose the taint is ineradicable.' His commitment to retrenchment was unimpeachable. Disapproving of welfarism, he resisted state intervention during the Cotton

Famine ('a public grant in my opinion is not to be thought of').[37]
What were his credentials when it came to liberty and reform? He
proved reluctant to embrace a popular constituency despite affecting to be 'Oxford on the surface, Liverpool below', and only went
in for south Lancashire when his alma mater was lost in 1865.
Beginning to thrill at his ability to excite large crowds, he declared
himself willing to bring working men into the Constitution except
for an unspecified number 'presumably incapacitated by some
consideration of personal unfitness or of political danger'.[38] But
the legacy of his multiple stints at the Exchequer – strict Treasury oversight of public expenditure, balanced budgets, small-state
parsimony – ensured that even once possessed of the vote, the
working class would struggle to gain access to state coffers.

Embarrassingly for the People's William, the Liberals were out-
polled in his Lancashire backyard where the strong liberalism of
the mid-century industrial bourgeoisie meant that Toryism took
on a more populist complexion. Ethnic tensions also made for
Conservative strength. In 1868 Disraeli raised the banner of 'No
Popery' to capitalise on evangelical unease at Gladstone's attempt
to disestablish the Irish Church, amidst Fenian jailbreaks and
anti-Irish riots whipped up by William Murphy, a Protestant ultra
from County Limerick. Conservative candidates around Manchester supplemented xenophobia with Tory Democracy, reconciling
themselves to trade unionism and statutory regulation of factory
conditions.[39] The Conservatives retained Blackburn, Preston
and their two Liverpool seats; took full control of Bolton; and
recorded their first ever gains in Ashton, Manchester and Salford.
'Once again the proletariat has disgraced itself terribly', Engels
wrote to Marx.

> Manchester and Salford return three Tories to two Liberals ...
> Bolton, Preston, Blackburn, etc., practically nothing but Tories
> ... Everywhere the proletariat is the tag, rag and bobtail of the
> official parties, and if any party has gained strength from the
> new voters, it is the Tories.[40]

The Liberals also lost all eight county seats in Lancashire, including
Gladstone's. The party leader was obliged to flee to Greenwich.[41]

The 1868 poll was the high-water mark of political anti-Catholicism except in stubbornly sectarian Merseyside, where the Conservatives harvested virulent religious bigotry to prolong their electoral hegemony into the 1950s.[42] Irish Catholics accounted for about a third of Liverpool's population at the turn of the century, forming an electoral majority in the Scotland division where they returned Home Ruler T. P. O'Connor. Prejudice against them had originally been 'catalysed' by the admixture of Protestant Ulster immigrants. The Operative Protestant Association of pastor Hugh McNeile, the Ian Paisley of early Victorian Merseyside, was embedded within the local Tory apparatus. Disraeli awarded McNeile the deanery of Ripon as part of his electoral manoeuvring. Local party bosses sat sometimes uneasily atop a populist Protestant bloc comprising Orange lodges, other preacher–agitators in the McNeile mould, and the country's largest Working Men's Conservative Association – a Protestant-only body presided over by the sixteenth and seventeenth Earls of Derby, son and grandson of the prime minister. In essence, sectarianism was to Merseyside what Radicalism was to the West Midlands: the glue for a cross-class alliance behind one of the governing parties. When the Conservatives took eight of nine Liverpool seats in 1885, Tory chairman Arthur Forwood called it his 'answer to Birmingham', where the Liberals had just swept the board.[43]

Forwood was the first shipping magnate to become an Admiralty minister but remained 'a misfit at Westminster, steeped in municipal business so long that he once addressed the Speaker as "Mr Mayor"'.[44] Industrialists also made little headway in a Parliament which preserved its aristocratic flavour. On the rare occasions when Conservative shipbuilders John Laird (Birkenhead) and Ralph Ward Jackson (Hartlepool) ventured an opinion in the House they stuck to a maritime theme. Wirral soap maker William Lever, a lifelong admirer of Gladstone, entered Parliament for the Liberals at the fifth attempt in 1906 only to find the going so hard that he retired three years later.[45] It fell to local-government supremo Joseph Chamberlain, following in the footsteps of Thomas Attwood, to translate municipal authority into national political leverage. His well-drilled Birmingham Liberal caucus was the biggest provincial influence in the modernising party system.

When Chamberlain led the Midlands into Unionism over Irish Home Rule in 1886, the National Liberal Federation (NLF) had to evacuate its Birmingham base. Sir James Kitson, owner of a Leeds locomotive works, squandered the opportunity to lay claim to the NLF for west Yorkshire. Kitson addressed delegates squeezed into Leeds's Albert Hall,

> Now, he (the President) was not prepared to deny that Leeds was a great centre of commercial activity – (cheers) – and a great centre of political intelligence – (hear, hear, and laughter) – and he assured them that it required a considerable amount of self-denial ... on the part of himself and those with whom he acted to decline the blandishments of those who would have fixed the headquarters of the Federation in Leeds, but they felt that the time had now arrived – the importance of this association was such, that it could not be a merely local association – (hear, hear).

The federation needed to be 'conducted for national ends', Kitson concluded, therefore 'the proper course was to remove the head-quarters of this association to London.'[46]

This fine example of regional abdication reflected a broader trend. The more that companies scaled up their operations, the stronger the pull became to transact their affairs close to Westminster and the City. By 1904, only thirty-two of the country's 250 largest businesses were registered in the North West or North East, while Yorkshire lost the head office of Vickers to London as the arms giant cosied up to its Whitehall client.[47] The firm's ties to Sheffield had been loosened by its acquisition of a naval yard at Barrow, a motor company in Birmingham, and weapons factories in south-east London turning out Maxim guns for the British in Africa, not to mention joint ventures in Spain, Italy, Austria–Hungary, Turkey and Russia.[48]

Among organisations of labour rather than capital, the draw of London was sometimes less insistent, but still a factor. The bosses of the amalgamated unions turned the London Trades Council into what the Fabians Sidney and Beatrice Webb described as 'an informal cabinet of the trade-union world', the Junta. 'From

1851 to 1863', they write, 'all the effective forces in the trade-union movement were centred in London.' There followed a shift in organisational impetus back to the regions as unionisation took permanent hold among the miners and cotton workers.[49] Neither offered a clear national-political lead, however: 'their work was confined to certain districts, and their interest in politics was an essentially local one,' observes Harry Hanham in his study of Victorian electoral politics.[50] Manchester hosted the founding conference of the Trade Union Congress in 1868, the Conservative-supporting secretaries of its local trades council begging to suggest the propriety of holding the event in Cotton-opolis since it was 'the main centre of industry in the provinces'. However, the London societies remained aloof until the publication by the first Gladstone administration of a trade-union bill in 1871 which fell short of general expectations. A broader-based symposium held in Marylebone authorised the creation of a parliamentary committee 'to watch over the political interests of its constituents', operating from Buckingham Street off the Strand under George Potter of the London Working Men's Association.[51]

If matters had ended there – an industrial bourgeoisie humbled by the Cotton Famine, a factory proletariat marking its ballots for Liberals and Conservatives as 'lib-lab' collaboration held back the formation of independent party of labour, London edging ahead of the regions economically and drawing in more and more of their peak organisations – it would have been quite a comedown from the time when (to borrow a phrase from the English Civil War) the Chartists and Anti-Corn Law League had attempted to call the conclusions of England to the Bar of Lancashire.[52]

But history's tectonic plates, local and global, don't stop moving, and by 1914 the Northern Question was setting off new tremors. Lancashire reverberated with bimetallist arguments against the gold standard, because exporters were hit by sterling's appreciation against the rupee and other non-gold currencies, while its cotton lobby fought a running battle against import duties imposed by the colonial administration in Calcutta for revenue-raising purposes.[53] On the tariff-reform controversy which split Edwardian Westminster – provoked by the erosion of Britain's position in world markets – the chambers of commerce in Bradford and Sheffield, facing rising import penetration in worsteds and steel respectively, joined sides with West Midland's metal-bashing and engineering trades (the main constituency for Chamberlainite imperial preference and commercial retaliation), while free trade retained adherents not just in the City of London but in staple industries like cotton yet to be squeezed by foreign competition.

Conservative MPs were defenestrated by Lancashire cotton workers in the 1906 general election for questioning the Cobdenite shibboleth of tariff-free commerce, by now popularly associated with the area's commercial well-being. Party leader Arthur Balfour had first gone in for Manchester East in 1885 on his uncle's recommendation, for the same reason that had attracted Canning to Liverpool: the prestige of representing a wealthy commercial city. Balfour never expected to 'waste too much brain' on his working-class constituents, believing it was 'enough to strain one's vocal chords without straining one's intellect at all'. He roused himself when disaster loomed. To a boisterous audience inside Ardwick public hall, he said, 'I do not absolutely cut myself adrift from what is known with some injustice to Mr Cobden as the Cobdenite programme.' Met with a mixture of cheers and groans, he lapsed into an ill-judged harangue against the Manchester school:

> What are you in Lancashire dependent on largely? (Cries of 'Cotton.') And how are you going to keep your markets open for cotton? (A voice – 'And free imports.') How are you going to keep your markets open for cotton? Are you going to war? (Cries of 'No,' and a voice – 'We have been to war.') That is quite right. I accept the answer. You are not going to war; then the only other instrument you have is the instrument I have suggested, the instrument of retaliation. (Cries of 'No.') You have no means of bringing diplomatic pressure to bear upon any other nation except the means I suggest.[54]

In a posthumous victory for the Anti-Corn Law League, Balfour lost to a Liberal lawyer by 2,000 votes. He relocated to the City of London – 'the most desirable seat of all, from my point of view'.[55]

At the next general election in January 1910, Manchester East was captured by Jack Sutton of the Independent Labour Party, a check-weigher and branch secretary at the local Bradford colliery. 'I have been sent here from a very important constituency,' Sutton told the Commons. 'I say an important constituency, because it was represented by the leader of the Opposition for over twenty years; but the democracy of this country is taking a different view from what it did during those twenty years.'[56]

With no intimation of misgiving or dismay, Frank Musgrove describes the Labour Party as 'the North of England's great twentieth-century triumph'.[57] Although never exclusively of the North, Labour rested heavily on the region's mass trade unionism and Dissent-imbued ethical-socialist political culture. Bradford hosted the first general conference of the Independent Labour Party, the most important socialist group among Labour's founder organisations, after an industrial defeat sustained by woollen workers at the town's huge Manningham Mills.[58] 'The [Social Democratic Federation] on the one hand and the Fabians on the other have not been able, with their sectarian attitudes, to absorb the rush towards Socialism in the provinces, so the formation of a third party was quite a good thing', commented Engels. 'But the rush now has become so great, especially in the industrial areas of the North, that the new party came out already at this first congress stronger than the SDF or the Fabians, if not stronger than both put together.' He added that 'the mass of the membership is certainly very good, as the centre of gravity lies in the provinces and not in London, the home of cliques.' Within two years, the ILP had a network of 305 branches. Well over half (175) were in Yorkshire or Lancashire. Bradford alone had as many as London (29).[59]

The cotton unions, forming one of the country's biggest blocs of organised labour, overcame their aversion to the Labour Representation Committee in 1903 after a court injunction ('Taff Vale Number Two') was issued against picketing weavers in Blackburn.[60] Their enlistment boosted the party's performance at the ballot box, but increased the conservative element within its ranks. The Manchester spinners had led efforts at alliance building between the organised trades in the early days of the factory system. They grew introverted as their industry aged, resisting attempts to organise their assistant piecers, whom they employed on a low fixed wage, into an independent union. The official history of the spinners' amalgamation comments, 'Industrial self-confidence, the ability to help oneself within the confines of a trade, was a most effective antidote to socialism and no trade union had greater justification for this feeling than the spinners.'[61] James Mawdsley, its general secretary until his death in 1902, had urged his members to channel their energies into 'the domain of legitimate social reform and the conditions in which we live and work, without troubling our minds with the unworkable theories of Mr Hyndman or of the communistic ideas which occasionally dribble over from the Continent'.[62] Lancashire accounted for two-fifths of Labour members returned in the 1906 general election, their progress eased by a pact with the Liberals. Among the new intake was A. H. Gill of the Bolton spinners, a Gladstonian critic of high public spending. 'Reference is made to Socialism and our party is spoken of as though this was a Socialist party', said Gill to his fellow MPs. 'This party is not a Socialist party. It is a Labour party. There are Socialists in it and there are those who are not Socialists.'[63]

Far more significant, in the immediate term, than a minor reformist Labour presence in Parliament was the growing strength of trade-union chapels in northern England. The Webbs counted 1.2 million trade-union members in England as of 1892, noting 'how thickly the trade unionists are aggregated in the thriving industrial districts of the North'. Lancashire contributed more than a quarter of the total; the West Riding, Durham and Northumberland another quarter. On the other hand, unionisation was negligible in the rural South and underwhelming in the capital, which mustered less than 200,000 members out of its assorted trades. Notwithstanding the great East End dock strike of 1889, most industrial action occurred in coalfields, shipyards, textile mills and engineering works well away from London, where union density measured as a proportion of the general population was only a third (3.5 per cent) of the figure for the North East (11.2 per cent).[64]

Sheer numbers ensured that the North remained front and centre on the industrial-relations map. The surge in trade-union organisation – from half a million members in the 1870s to four million by 1914 – obliged Whitehall to treat directly with the biggest unions to prevent national disputes boiling over. In the summer of 1911 the first countrywide walkout by railway workers began with an unofficial stoppage at Liverpool, coinciding with a general transport strike in the city. Prime Minister Asquith and Home Secretary Churchill despatched 2,000 soldiers, a battleship and a cruiser to Merseyside.[65] The *Manchester Guardian* compared Liverpool to 'a city of which a besieging army has just taken possession'. On 13 August, police reinforced from Birmingham and Leeds baton-charged a mass meeting on St George's Plateau in the city centre. 'The officers could be seen using their truncheons like flails', the *Guardian* reported. A policeman was killed in the ensuing street violence. Two days later, hussars shot dead a docker and a carter.[66] Warning of complete economic paralysis, Churchill urged additional troop movements. Chancellor Lloyd George browbeat the rail companies into talks by raising a war scare over Franco-German tensions in Morocco.[67] The following spring, Foreign Secretary Sir Edward Grey, a Liberal imperialist descended from the Greys of Howick and Fallodon in Northumberland, likened a national coal strike to a state of civil war. Asquith conceded the principle of a statutory minimum wage for coal, implemented in as loose a form as he could get away with.[68]

As Asquith's Liberal ministry grappled with industrial unrest of unprecedented proportions – and the threat of armed revolt by Unionist diehards in Protestant-majority Ulster, opposed to Irish Home Rule – it also had to contend with the militancy of Mancunian suffragettes who shattered the calm of London's more salubrious neighbourhoods, bringing the multi-form domestic crisis of 1910–14 to the doorsteps of the governing class.

The question of women's suffrage had been shelved by previous generations of male reformers. 'Among the suggestions we received for improving this Charter', explained the London Working Men's Association in 1838,

is one for embracing women among the possession of the franchise. Against this reasonable proposition we have no just argument to adduce, but only to express our fears of entertaining

it, lest the false estimate man entertains of this half of the human
family may cause his ignorance and prejudice to be enlisted to
retard the progress of his own freedom. And, therefore, we deem
it far better to lay down just principles, and look forward to the
rational improvement of society, than to entertain propositions
which may retard the measure we wish to promote.[69]

The campaigners who pushed for the Second Reform Act of 1867
were also united in their indifference to the enfranchisement of
women. When Rev. Samuel Alfred Steinthal of the trailblazing
Manchester Committee for Women's Suffrage tried to interest a
conference of the Reform League's northern department in the
question, national president Edmond Beales 'doubted whether the
amendment could be put, inasmuch as it was not in accordance
with the platform of the Reform League'. The amendment *was* put
nevertheless at Steinthal's insistence, only to be voted down by a
large majority.[70]

To end this impasse, two suffragist groups immersed in the
socialist and trade-union cultures of *fin de siècle* Manchester
broke away from the drawing room respectability of Millicent
Fawcett's National Union into contrasting strategies of grass-roots
activism and guerrilla militancy. Esther Roper, an Owens College
graduate born to badly off African missionaries, plunged into the
mill towns intent, she said, on 'making women's suffrage a trade-
union question'. This ran contrary to generations of bourgeois
campaigning focussed on the claims of 'women of business' and
'ladies of property'.[71] Roper had some success in wearing down
opposition within male-dominated Labour and trade-union hierarchies, but her petitioning and lobbying of the governing Liberals
met with endless prevarication.

The Pankhursts' Women's Social and Political Union (WSPU),
comprising a small number of middle-class Manchester ILP-ers,
quickly tired of foot-slogging around Lancashire. 'What is the
good of a constitutional policy to those who have no constitutional weapon?' demanded Christabel, whose first experiment in
militancy came at a Manchester Free Trade Hall meeting graced
by Churchill and Sir Edward Grey on 13 October 1905.[72] Thrown
out for heckling, she ensured a seven-day stretch in Strangeways

by spitting at a policeman. She and Emmeline ditched the project of building a working-class base in favour of elite-cadre militancy concentrated on the capital, where Sylvia Pankhurst set about marshalling East End labourers, tacking left politically as her mother and older sister veered right.[73]

Grey and Asquith's decision to take Britain into the First World War eased their domestic headaches for a spell. The July Crisis exposed political cross-currents within the women's suffrage and labour movements. Most of the WSPU joined forces with erstwhile critics in support of trench warfare, as did the bulk of the Labour Party, whereas Esther Roper and Sylvia Pankhurst entered the peace camp along with ILP-ers such as Ethel and Philip Snowden. The peace party was very much in the minority. Lancashire and Yorkshire with their vast stores of industrial manpower provided nearly a quarter of the infantry battalions for the first three of Kitchener's New Armies. James Sexton of the National Union of Dock Labourers defied a Fenian family background to set up dockers' battalions on Merseyside as work gangs under the command of the seventeenth Earl of Derby. In Lloyd George's estimation, Derby was 'the most efficient recruiting sergeant in England'. Asquith made him director-general of recruiting in October 1915 to squeeze every last drop out of voluntary enrolment before resorting to conscription. The North West grandee raised several battalions of the King's (Liverpool) regiment, popularising the creation of 'battalions of pals' beginning with the clerks of Liverpool's commercial houses. Derby's good friend, General Haig, sent his Merseyside recruits into the slaughterhouse stalemates of the Somme, Arras and Passchendaele.[74]

By 1914 the forward ranks of the industrial working class had caught up on the factory masters of 1832: they had gained entry to what Gramsci termed 'the complex of state life', reciprocating with a social-patriotic commitment to a national ruling order that pre-dated either social class.[75] Among the many repercussions of the First World War would be a loosening of Lancashire's grip on British India, the biggest outlet for its cotton goods. A Burnley manufacturer had warned a royal commission, 'On India we rely, and if we lose India, Lancashire is practically ruined.'[76] Outpaced by late-start competitors in Europe, America and the Far East, dependent on imperial privileges approaching expiry, the world's first industrial region was about to experience the ground giving way beneath it. Once that happened, how much purchase would its footholds within the British state afford?

5

Dereliction

Considering what was to come, northern manufacturing exited the First World War in remarkably giddy mood. The release of four years' worth of pent-up demand carried the basic trades aloft in a fleeting trade boom. 'All over Lancashire there could be heard whispers of fortunes that left the riches of pre-war days far behind', recounted Benjamin Bowker in his 1928 jeremiad *Lancashire under the Hammer*. Half the cotton-spinning industry was 'cast on to the gambling tables' as local syndicates traded furiously in mill company shares at inflated prices.[1] The irrational exuberance extended to shipbuilding, where virtually overnight a London shipbroker backed by merchant banks Sperlings and Kleinworts threw together a huge dockyard combine around the Northumberland Shipbuilding Company of Howdon on the Tyne.[2]

The economic upswing was cut short by the retrenchment of Lloyd George's Conservative-dominated coalition, beating a path back to balanced budgets and the gold standard. As shipyard output on Tyneside fell to its lowest figure for three decades, the over-leveraged Northumberland Shipbuilding Company buckled and broke. Howdon was sold to National Shipbuilders Security Ltd, an industry body supported by the Bank of England to eliminate struggling dockyards. The same vulturish organisation dismantled Palmers of ill-fated Jarrow.

Baldwin and Churchill carried through the return to gold at the pre-war parity of $4.86 to the pound in 1925. Their failed attempt to reboot the belle époque, sponsored by the City, aggravated the North's hangover from its bout of bubblenomics. Exporters already struggling with heavy financial liabilities and shrinking markets also had to grapple with an overvalued exchange rate and tight credit conditions. 'This gold standard is a fetish,' said mill director Cecil Hilton, a Tory MP for Bolton.

> It does not create a yard of cloth, it does not work a single loom or a single spindle. It stops them; it is not in the interests of Lancashire. It is done in the interests of what we call finance and economics. The mistake of it and of the government is that the gold standard should not rule England, should not rule Lancashire and should not rule employment.[3]

Overcommitted to depressed basic industries, the North's share of British GDP dropped from 30 to 25 per cent between 1921 and 1931.[4] The manufacturing sector was growing briskly, but in the South rather than the North as the construction of a national electricity grid and improvements to road transport reduced the appeal of coalfield locations. The *Economist* underlined 'the remoteness of the areas of heavy unemployment and the bleakness of life in them; the bad housing; the absence of amenities and social life; the tradition (generally unfounded) of labour unrest; the superior social attractions of the Home Counties for the directorial and managerial grades'.[5] Firms in growth sectors such as auto and electronics homed in on the Greater London market and the West Midland supply chain, setting up shop in suburban and green-belt areas which had taken the lion's share of wartime light-assembly factories readily adaptable to mass production of consumer durables.[6] Ford abandoned Trafford Park for Dagenham in Essex. Other carmakers were based in Birmingham, Coventry, Luton and Oxford. In *English Journey* (1934), Bradford-born J. B. Priestley cast a rueful eye on the stridently modern factories lining the western approaches to London. 'They are tangible evidence, most cunningly arranged to take the eye, to prove that the new industries have moved south.'[7] Further buoyed by trade in services and by real-estate development, the South East, including London, increased its share of national output from 35 to 39 per cent. The West Midlands drew level with Yorkshire and Humberside at 8 per cent.

&

While the affluent Home Counties 'danced all night', the towns and cities of Outer Britain suffered industrial desuetude and political defeat.[8] Trade union membership rose from 4.1 million to 6.5 million during the war and went on to peak at 8.3 million in 1920. This doubling of the number of organised workers was accompanied by a parliamentary breakthrough for the party named in their honour. In 1924 Labour under Ramsay MacDonald staked its claim to be a party of government. The North supplied most of the administration's Big Five: Chancellor Philip Snowden, the son of Yorkshire weavers; Newcastle ironmoulder Arthur Henderson, appointed to the Home Office; Lord Privy Seal J. R. Clynes, once an Oldham cotton piecer.

Despite these advances, the two wings of the labour movement took turns to court disaster through the timidity of their leaders. Snowden's career offers an example of that sad process by which an anti-Establishment figure may come, with equal fervour, to hero-worship the rich and powerful. After a strict Methodist upbringing in the Pennines, Philip had trained revivalist fire on the immorality of allowing the owners of land and machinery to monopolise access to the necessities of life. In an industrial society, he argued, there ought to be enough for all, and enough for each. He prophesised an imminent purge of social ills as the spirit of Christ took possession of men's minds. 'The horrible social conditions existing today will give way before this divine impulse, and the poverty of the many and the luxury of the few will join hands in a union of contented happiness for all.'[9]

Philip and his wife Ethel made a lot of money out of journalism and speaking engagements. By the time he made the Treasury, they had moved to a big house in Tilford, Surrey, and got mixed up with high society. Millennial utopianism evaporated to leave behind a stony residue of self-help and fiscal prudence. Estranged from the unions, ignorant of Marxism, awestruck by Bank of England governor Montagu Norman, Philip emerged at the despatch box nothing more than a purse-proud Gladstonian. He said,

> It is no part of my job as Chancellor of the Exchequer to put before the House of Commons proposals for the expenditure of public money. The function of the Chancellor of the Exchequer,

as I understand it, is to resist all demands for expenditure made by his colleagues, and, when he can no longer resist, to limit the concession to the barest point of acceptance.[10]

As for the others, Henderson was primed to wield the Emergency Powers Act against former trade-union colleagues. Clynes maintained that ministers 'played properly the part of a national government and not of a class government'.[11] Post-war radicalism emanated not from the ageing manufacturing zones of northern England but from the Celtic fringe, where a mass industrial character developed relatively late in the day and threadbare social amenities did little to cushion working-class discontent. In a period of flux, overcrowded Glasgow, with its high housing costs, was liable to flare up. Clydeside MPs exerted the only left-wing pressure on MacDonald within the Parliamentary Labour Party. John Wheatley, a veteran of the 1915 rent strike, pushed through a Housing Act which constituted the first Labour government's only legislative achievement.

Although shop-floor militancy wasn't absent from northern England, Lloyd George had turned to the cotton unions of Lancashire confident that they would set 'an example of moderation'.[12] He knew better than to expect the same from South Wales, its coalfield now the largest in Britain, accounting for a fifth (19 per cent) of the country's 1.1 million miners.[13] Militant in war and peace, the Welsh miners panicked Whitehall into assuming emergency control of the industry in 1917. The peak organisations on either side of the negotiating table were led by men from the Valleys: Sir Evan Williams, president of the employers' association, and A. J. Cook, left-wing general secretary of the Miners' Federation of Great Britain (MFGB).

In broad regional terms, however, coal was chiefly a North of England affair. Its six coal-working districts – from largest to smallest Yorkshire, Durham, Lancashire–Cheshire, Derbyshire, Northumberland and Cumberland – accounted for half (51 per cent) of the national workforce. What they added to the industrial-relations dynamic was immovable bulk, as personified by MFGB president Herbert Smith, a miner from Castleford in the West Riding. Smith prided himself on an imperturbable manner and what his biographer calls a 'capacity for the bare negative'. In negotiations with the government, the Yorkshireman cleaned his dentures before telling the prime minister, 'Nowt doing'.[14]

The Lloyd George Cabinet considered state control of the coal industry perverse once the slaughter in Europe was over. It disregarded the majority opinion of the Fabian-ish Sankey commission in favour of full nationalisation. When Sankey suggested that Yorkshire might be taken into public ownership as an experiment, ministers unquestioningly accepted the colliery owners' argument that the miners would skew the result by working hard in Yorkshire and slacking off elsewhere. Conservative hardliner Frederick Smith, first Earl of Birkenhead – a barrister's son from Merseyside who achieved social success at Oxford after ditching his northern accent – pithily remarked, 'It would be possible to say without exaggeration of the miners' leaders that they were the stupidest men in England if we had not had frequent occasion to meet the owners.' Yet he refused to consider taking the industry out of the latter's hands. Talk of nationalisation was 'antagonising the whole of the commercial world', he complained.[15]

To return coal to private management was tantamount to inviting the colliery owners to transfer the cost of an overvalued pound onto their staff through wage cuts. The miners were 'the victims of an economic juggernaut', argued Keynes in *The Economic Consequences of Mr Churchill* (1925).

> They represent in the flesh the 'fundamental adjustments' engineered by the Treasury and the Bank of England to satisfy the impatience of the City fathers to bridge the 'moderate gap' between $4.40 and $4.86. *They* (and others to follow) are the 'moderate sacrifice' still necessary to ensure the stability of the gold standard.[16]

In County Durham nearly one-third (29 per cent) of men and boys over twelve were miners.[17] Not for the last time, Whitehall was prepared to squeeze the living standards of working-class communities in peripheral regions to help London keep up with New York in international finance.

In autumn 1925, Prime Minister Baldwin appointed another

commission chaired by Sir Herbert Samuel, a former Cleveland MP, to gain ideological cover for decontrol and to buy time for officials to finalise their strike-breaking preparations. Business interests were represented by Kenneth Lee of cotton firm Tootal Broadhurst Lee, who, like many a Lancashire industrialist, 'had a certain reputation in Manchester commercial circles but no national profile'.[18] The LSE's Sir William Beveridge and City banker Sir Herbert Lawrence completed the Liberal-leaning quartet. They duly backed the demand of colliery owners for wage reductions ('the necessary downward revision of district minima').[19] The Conservatives terminated state support for the industry on 30 April 1926 and colliery owners in Durham and other districts proceeded to lock the miners out.

It was untenable for the TUC to abandon the country's largest union at the crunch point of post-Armistice industrial relations, despite previous tergiversations, without firing off some rounds of ammunition first. But a general strike to force a government intervention in the coal stand-off stuck in the craws of Ernest Bevin of the Transport Workers' and like-minded union leaders. 'There can rarely have been in the history of labour a more revolutionary decision taken with so little hope and so little fervour', commented the *Manchester Guardian* after a special conference of TUC affiliates held in London on May Day.[20]

Acting TUC general secretary Walter Citrine, a Liverpudlian electrician, reflected the conservativism of fellow office holders in the movement. 'By temperament and habit of life Citrine is an intellectual of the scientific type,' recorded Beatrice Webb. 'He is sedentary, takes too little exercise for his health, he is assiduous, always improving himself by reading and writing and working at his job unremittingly.'[21] Despite finding himself at the head of the biggest industrial conformation in British history, Citrine feared communists and Labour radicals more than he did Conservatives or the employer class. In his memoirs he wrote, 'Much of my energy had been consumed in combatting subversive doctrines and policies designed to create confusion and to sow distrust in the minds of the rank-and-file members. I had to be constantly on the alert against such machinations'. He published a handbook on the *ABC of Chairmanship* with helpful pointers on how to restore order at mass meetings using police powers under public-order legislation.[22]

The TUC general council's safety-first leadership ensured that the nine-day general strike from 3 to 12 May was confined to selected industries. Citrine preferred not to think of it as a general strike at all. But the strike call was impeccably observed in the big cities. On arriving in Manchester to edit a northern edition of the *British Worker*, ILP journalist Fenner Brockway remarked that 'realisation of the success of the strike is much completer than in London. At Westminster one was conscious of the power of the government. Here the men are absolutely on top'.[23]

At TUC headquarters in Eccleston Square, Pimlico, union bosses couldn't mentally sustain a politicised confrontation which government propaganda presented as unconstitutional. The *Morning Post* accused them of having 'exchanged an industrial dispute for a political *coup d'état*'.[24] (Its proprietor was a baron of the old school: Alan Percy, eighth Duke of Northumberland, a leading coal owner with fascist tendencies.) Shaken by this ideological barrage, Citrine forecast disaster and acted according to the premonition. 'We can hold out for three or four weeks at the longest,' he wrote in his diary. 'I do not think it possible to continue longer than that.' Although the strike was holding firm, Citrine fretted that 'a gradual decline in [the unions'] economic power must ensue. Then we shall have dribblings back to work here and there, and possibly large desertions.'[25]

The *Guardian* reported on 13 May how 'Manchester received the news that the General Strike had been called off, somewhat incredulously, about the time that it finished its lunch.' The North Western District Strike Committee telegrammed Eccleston Square to protest at the climbdown. Employers were refusing to reinstate workers except on the basis of reduced wages and inferior terms and conditions. The government responded with a statement offering moral support to the bosses. Some displacements were inevitable, it advised.[26]

The general council's loss of nerve 'was the culmination of days and days of faint heartedness', observed A. J. Cook, a shrewder judge of the situation than Birkenhead allowed. 'They had been prepared to force *us* to retreat in order that *they* might carry

out the retreat they longed for. When the truculence of the Tory
cabinet thrust them willy nilly into the General Strike they had
not ceased in their endeavour to "smooth it over".' Citrine went
on to accept a knighthood from MacDonald and Baldwin's pro-
austerity National Government. After the war Attlee made him
Baron Citrine of Wembley and enlisted him in government service
as chairman of the British Electricity Authority, apparently the
happiest period of his working life.[27]

Abandoned by other unions, Cook and Smith persevered until
the miners' solidarity fractured in inland districts sheltered from
the crisis in the export trade, where projected pay cuts were less
severe. Four-fifths of Midland coal workers had returned to work
by mid-November compared to only one-tenth in the North East
and an even smaller proportion in South Wales.[28] Nottinghamshire proved the weakest link, its 'butty' subcontractors splintering
off from the Miners' Federation into company unionism.

Organised labour didn't have the forward momentum after this
debacle to influence national policy until the Second World War.
Things worked out differently in America, where mass strikes
in 1933–4 gave popular impetus to Roosevelt's New Deal programme.[29] In the immediate aftermath, British Conservatives put
aside the hoary notion of each man's home being his safest refuge,
and attempted to drive the defeated miners into flight. Charged
by the Labour opposition with neglecting distress on the coalfields, Baldwin adopted measures to accelerate the outmigration of
surplus labour to southern growth points like Slough and Watford,
where rising wage costs needed to be dampened down. The government would subsidise relocation costs and juvenile wages.[30]

Board of Trade president Sir Philip Cunliffe-Lister insisted,
however, that transference was 'primarily not a matter of new
expenditure, but rather of driving force'. Presumably he had in
mind the rationing of poor relief in mining districts: compulsory
belt tightening to weaken people's resolve to sit out the trade
depression. Whitehall advisers recommended, 'As an essential condition of the will to move, nothing should be done which might
tend to anchor men to their home district by holding out an illu-
sory prospect of employment. We therefore reject as unsound
policy relief works in depressed areas.'[31] An annual average of

28,000 individuals migrated to employment through labour exchanges over the next decade, although around a third afterwards returned home. Several times more upped sticks without official aid.[32] The exodus was modest in relation to the scale of the jobs crisis. Those who stayed put, in defiance of official pressure, resigned themselves in Orwell's words to 'living a reduced version of their former lives'.[33] When MacDonald took over from Baldwin in 1929 he intervened in the coal industry not to nationalise it, but to protect colliery owners from competition through a price-fixing scheme.

After the great strike came the Great Depression, its worst and more enduring effects felt in industrial monotowns well away from the stockbroker belt, in what was otherwise a good decade for consumers and wage-earners. Unemployment recorded by the 1931 census, before the slump had bottomed out, ranged among women from 42 per cent in Blackburn to 3 per cent in Luton, and among men from 37 per cent in Sunderland to 4 per cent in the north London suburbs of Southgate and Finchley. What need for a New Deal when large parts of the South could get through the slump unscathed?[34]

The collapse of export demand and business confidence compounded an already rotten situation for the smokestack industries. Once their post-Armistice euphoria wore off, it struck home to cotton producers that their grip on South Asia had been loosened by wartime disruption and conflicting imperial considerations. Lloyd George granted tariff autonomy to Delhi to subdue the nationalists, balance the budget and service the external debt. The colonial administration welcomed Japan, a sometime ally of the British and a rising regional power, into the Indian market. By the late thirties, British exports to the subcontinent were down to a tenth of their pre-war peak and Japan had established itself as the world's leading vendor of cotton goods.[35] Diversification into man-made fibres offered Lancashire an escape route from appalling trading conditions in coarse cottons. But although most rayon factories were to be found in the textile belt, the development of 'artificial silk' was spearheaded by Courtaulds, an Essex silk and mourning-crape company with historic links to Spitalfields in east

London.[36] Courtaulds would eventually expand to a point where it could swallow the stricken cotton industry whole.

Oriented toward a sturdy domestic market, the woollen industry lost fewer jobs than cotton. Nevertheless, J. B. Priestley noted how merchants in Bradford had to 'snatch at every crumb of business'.[37] Further north, heavy-industrial centres on the Cumbrian seaboard were fast becoming ghost towns. 'The condition of Maryport is desperate,' reported University of Manchester economists. 'Since the partial closing down of the Risehow colliery in 1928, about half the insured population has been unemployed, and there appears little hope of revival. The ironworks at Maryport has been permanently closed down; and another colliery and brickworks has worked very spasmodically since 1926.'[38]

The party of organised labour occupied national office for the second time when Wall Street crashed. The North returned 108 Labour MPs in the May 1929 general election, nearly twice as many as at the previous poll. Scotland and Wales added another 61. Taken together, these regions and nations provided a clear majority (59 per cent) of the party's total number of seats.[39] It was a vote of confidence in Labour that its leaders scarcely warranted. MacDonald had just taken a safe County Durham seat. 'They offer me a constituency which I need not visit more than once a year and where, at a general election, three or four speeches at the outside would be all they would ask of me.'[40] The closest bonds the prime minister forged in Seaham Harbour were with its wealthy aristocratic colliery owners rather than its miners. 'Oh Seaham, Seaham! How I am letting you down,' he wrote to Lady Londonderry.[41]

An opportunistic Lloyd George went into the election campaign armed with a plan he said would conquer unemployment. Labour in power didn't so much as take the field against it. All that could be done was to weather the economic blizzard, said MacDonald, and await a revival in trade. Snowden supported the Bank of England's decision to raise interest rates to 6.5 per cent in September 1929, their highest level since the 1919–21 slump, to stem the flow of gold into a bullish Wall Street ahead of Black Tuesday. He continued to defend the gold standard after the financial meltdown despite continuing protests from industry groups. 'It would be fatal if Lancashire were led to suppose that a change in monetary policy offered them a cure for their troubles,' he said.[42] The chancellor wouldn't deviate from free trade even as chambers of commerce in Bradford, Leeds and Manchester joined the drift of business opinion toward protectionism. ('Whether or not Cobdenism was the right policy for the years preceding the war has nothing to do with us today', shrugged Manchester's *Daily Dispatch*.[43]) He also ruled out additional borrowing to fund a large-scale public-works programme. A deficit of any size was unaffordable, he insisted, on the grounds that investors wouldn't wear it.[44] Thus Snowden sat on his hands while the jobless total doubled to more than three million. Two-thirds of the registered unemployed were in northern England, Scotland or Wales, left stranded on a diet of bread and margarine with no New Jerusalem in sight.[45]

The *Economist* noted that in selecting ministers from the Labour right, MacDonald 'spared Cheltenham and the City from alarm'.[46] He and Snowden further demonstrated their reliability by parking the problem of industrial reorganisation with the Bank of England. The times were so out of joint, and the bare possibility of Labour interference in British capitalism so objectionable, that governor Montagu Norman ordained that 'a marriage can take place between the industry of the North and the finance of the South.' Declining overseas investment opportunities, frozen over-drafts and unpayable loans had already embroiled the banking sector in the problems of the staple trades.[47] Norman launched a Bankers' Industrial Development Company to eliminate surplus capacity. Nearly a hundred debt-laden textile firms were corralled into an amalgamated Lancashire Cotton Corporation 'partly to help the cotton industry, partly to keep the question away from politics, but more especially to relieve certain of the banks from a dangerous position'.[48] This extraordinary *mésalliance* between domestic manufacturing and the City wouldn't last. Even in the thirties, industrial issues accounted for only a tenth of the value of quoted securities on London's Stock Exchange, and the Bank of England was uninterested in funding the development of growth industries in depressed areas.[49]

Faced with lengthening dole queues, City schmoozer Jimmy Thomas, Minister for Unemployment, told lunch guests of the

Manchester Chamber of Commerce, 'There is too much tendency to be spoon-fed. All that a government can do, when all is said and done, is infinitesimal compared with what businessmen can do for themselves.' MacDonald was privately of the same creed. 'I have no heart for these doles,' he confided to his diary. 'To establish people in incomes which represent no effort to get or to do work is the very antithesis of Socialism. The State as Lady Bountiful may be a fatal extension of Toryism but it is not the beginning of Social-ism.'[50] The prime minister, of course, was one of those messianic Labour figures for whom socialism was whatever he happened to be doing at the time. In spring 1930 he took Thomas off unemploy-ment and assumed responsibility for a ministerial panel supported by Sir John Anderson, the permanent under-secretary at the Home Office, nicknamed Pompous John. Anderson advised the prime minister to 'sweep away ruthlessly any lingering illusions that a substantial reduction of unemployment figures is to be sought in the artificial provision of employment'. MacDonald was in full concord. His panel went on to advise the Cabinet,

> there are natural forces at work encouraging development in the South and Midlands as against the North or Scotland or south Wales. Any attempt completely to turn the stream of industrial development back into the older industrial areas is not only doomed to failure but is probably fundamentally uneconomic.

In view of which, 'local self-help and initiative must be the key-notes of any effort to bring new industrial activities into the depressed areas.'[51] Outer Britain, even under a Labour Party it had propelled into Downing Street, was on its own.

When a European banking crisis broke out that summer, Snowden, of all people, was accused of undermining investors' confidence in sterling by failing to crack down sufficiently on a budget shortfall. A Committee on National Expenditure, chaired by George May of the Prudential and representative of pro-austerity feeling in the City, prompted a full-scale run on the pound by inflating the scale of the deficit. Jimmy Thomas had earlier commended to Manchester business leaders the 'sagacity, the single-minded effort, integrity and wisdom of the governor of the Bank of England in steering this country through a difficult period'.[52] Now Threadneedle Street held off financial assistance from foreign central banks while the Labour Cabinet sweated over deep spending cuts, including totemic reductions to the dole. MacDonald relayed a warning from the bank that it was 'essential, particularly from the point of view of the foreign interests concerned, that very substantial economies should be effected on unemployment insurance. In no other way could foreign confidence be restored'.[53] Under union pressure, a minority of ministers refused to endorse a 10 per cent cut to standard unemployment benefit. MacDonald and Snowden deserted to form a National Government, taking Thomas with them. The prime minister, according to Snowden, gleefully anticipated the kisses of every duchess in London.[54]

Renewed financial turbulence quickly made it impossible for Britain to stay on the gold standard. Nevertheless, MacDonald and Snowden persevered with their secondary purpose of balancing the books on the backs of the unemployed. Orders in Council issued under the National Economy Act of 30 September cut the dole by the desired 10 per cent – supposedly an emergency device, though not reversed until 1934. The new administration also introduced a household means test for the long-term unemployed along Poor Law lines.

Activists within the communist National Unemployed Workers' Movement (NUWM), led by indefatigable London toolmaker Walter Hannington, risked police beatings and jail terms to protest at Snowden's economy measures. Several thousand demonstrators singing the *Internationale* and the *Red Flag* marched on Salford town hall on 1 October to demand that the council – in which the Conservatives were the largest party – abandon dole cuts, loosen the means test, abolish boot-camp training centres for the unemployed, and provide free milk for the under-fives and a hundredweight of coal per week to help families through the winter. Police blocked the entrance to Bexley Square and baton-charged the crowd, dragging arrested men across the square into riot wagons. Inside the civic centre, one councillor protested, 'Men are being frog-marched about the square and thrown about. It is most un-British and I think it is a great shame.' The novelist

Walter Greenwood witnessed the police operation, which he revisited in *Love on the Dole* (1933). There were also skirmishes in Manchester after the authorities diverted a procession en route to Albert Square. 'Firemen appeared,' reported the *Guardian*, 'and a couple of hoses quartered the crowd like machine guns spraying water.'[55]

MacDonald took his Tory-heavy administration into the polls on 27 October brandishing German banknotes from the twenties to scare Seaham voters with the spectre of hyperinflation. Presenting himself as a stalwart of the labour movement, he mustered a majority of 6,000 despite a dire record in office and the hostility of miners' leaders. It helped his cause that Seaham was in better shape than the rest of the coalfield – only 12 per cent of insured workers unemployed, compared to a county average three times that figure – but the result was also symptomatic of a general Labour rout against a united Tory–Liberal opposition. Elsewhere in Durham, miners' candidates were defeated in straight fights by Conservative chartered accountants in Houghton-le-Spring and Sedgefield, and by National Liberals in Bishop Auckland and Consett.[56]

In the North West, MacDonald's lacklustre replacement as party leader, Arthur Henderson, lost Burnley to a retired Royal Navy rear admiral standing as a National candidate. Notwithstanding anti-government rancour among the unemployed, the eight constituencies with Labour incumbents in Manchester and Salford all switched to the Conservatives. Support for a demoralised Labour Party dipped by a few thousand votes in each case, while most Tory majorities were boosted by the withdrawal of Liberal competition. 'We no doubt lost large blocks of votes because our opponents had a great asset in appealing to the emotions of the people to back up a government which they had called National', said J. R. Clynes, defeated in Manchester Platting.[57] In Yorkshire, Snowden opted not to defend Colne Valley. Instead he accepted a viscountcy and stepped up to the House of Lords, an institution he had once deplored as a 'standing disgrace to the intelligence of the British people'.[58]

The National Government's landslide victory (554 of 615 seats, nearly all in Conservative hands) made certain that deficit hawks would continue to dominate the politics of the Depression. Mac-Donald farmed out the unemployment problem to a committee of junior ministers under Treasury chairmanship, with instructions to 'bear in mind that the number of persons for whom it is impossible to find permanent employment will probably remain at a very large figure, which is not likely to be reduced materially for some years to come'.[59] The following summer an NUWM member was killed by a blow from a police truncheon in Castleford. Police brutality also provoked several nights of disturbances in Birkenhead, obliging the local Public Assistance Committee to make concessions on benefit scales.[60]

Local-authority administration of unemployment relief proved too unreliable for the National Government, which first stripped the Durham and Rotherham Public Assistance Committees of their powers for noncompliance with the means test and then centralised the entire benefits system. A uniform scale formulated by an unelected national board brought widespread reductions in weekly payments. Protests organised by local labour organisations and leftist activists spread from the Rhondda and Merthyr to towns and cities in northern England and Scotland. When the furore reached the Commons, MPs from wealthy southern constituencies 'listened to the often virulent attacks on the new regulations in a puzzled silence'.[61] Minister of Labour Oliver Stanley – younger son of the seventeenth Earl of Derby – suspended the regulations and reintroduced the old allowances, pending a delay. He was forced to concede an immediate restoration in Sheffield after fierce clashes between police and demonstrators. That Stanley's U-turn ranks as 'the most severe legislative defeat of any of the interwar years' speaks volumes for the relative ease with which a Conservative Party unassailable in the Commons navigated the pitfalls of regional mass unemployment.[62] Stanley's retreat ensured that the principle of means-tested relief was not upturned, despite its enormous unpopularity in working-class communities.[63]

In 1934, unemployment among insured workers fell back to single digits in London and the South East as cheap credit and tariff protection boosted trades focussed on the home market. In the North and in Scotland, by contrast, joblessness remained stuck above 20 per cent. In Wales it was higher than 30 per cent. *The Times* ran a series of despatches from the Durham coalfield headed 'Places without a future'. Their special correspondent noted that in the comfortable South, people were 'beginning again to think in terms of prosperity'. However, 'There are districts of England, heavily populated, whose plight no amount of general trade recovery can ever cure, because their sole industry is not depressed but dead. It would be a failure of humanity to forget them, a failure of statesmanship to ignore them.'[64] Read aloud by MPs in the Commons, this outburst from the paper of record put the National Government on the spot. It looked like one of those enjoyable moments when the Establishment turns in on itself. In fact the pieces were written by Henry Brooke of the Conservative Research Department at the bidding of Neville Chamberlain, Snowden's replacement at the Exchequer, who was on friendly terms with *Times* editor Geoffrey Dawson. Chamberlain was convinced that the government had to have something positive to say about the depressed areas and he needed to overcome Cabinet resistance. 'It was not a question of spending a great deal of money,' he said, 'but of showing that the matter had not been pigeon-holed, and that the government was doing its best to help matters.'[65]

A poor tactician at home and abroad, Chamberlain stoked expectations he proved reluctant to meet. Four ministers were sent out to conduct investigations. He warned them not to expect significant help from the Treasury, believing the situation of the depressed areas to be hopeless.[66] Hornsey MP Euan Wallace, a parliamentary private secretary at the Admiralty, went off-piste when, in his study of Tyneside and Durham, he took up the arguments of Tory backbench radicals by mooting 'some form of national planning of industry' – not just to break the vicious circle of industrial depression and unemployment in the North East, but to check the unwanted further expansion of Greater London. An interdepartmental committee under chief industrial adviser Sir Horace Wilson poured several gallons of cold water on the suggestion:

> under existing powers industry cannot be compelled to go to a locality which the manufacturer does not consider the best for his purpose, and in the opinion of the Board of Trade the more

far-reaching suggestion for what may be called the 'locational control of industry' would require much work and much research before the controlling body possessed the necessary knowledge for giving directions as to how industry should develop; nor would the opinion when formed be likely to command universal consent. Under such a system some industrial development would be prevented unless a guarantee were given to a prospective manufacturer to compensate him for going to what he might regard as an unsuitable locality. It seems probable, too, that the assumption of powers to settle the location of factories (except perhaps on defence grounds) would involve the state in embarrassing questions of management.[67]

A separate proposal to appoint a technocrat to coordinate local urban-regeneration schemes was more palatable. Chamberlain brought forward a Depressed Areas Bill for the purpose. The House of Lords put a euphemistic gloss on the wording, transforming 'depressed' areas into 'special' ones. The areas so designated were west Cumberland; Tyneside and most of County Durham; the central belt in Scotland; and west Monmouthshire and the greater part of Glamorgan. Chamberlain cautioned MPs, 'It would be very unfair to expect these commissioners to perform miracles. We do not anticipate spectacular results.' Nor were any forthcoming. Financial incentives to attract manufacturers into these areas were precluded. Harold Macmillan, progressive Conservative MP for Stockton, damned the legislation as defeatist.[68]

It didn't take long for special-areas commissioner Malcolm Stewart, a brick and cement businessman doing well out of the South East housebuilding boom, to deduce that 'there is little prospect of the special areas being assisted by the spontaneous action of industrialists now located outside the areas.'[69] He ruffled the City by drawing attention to difficulties encountered by entrepreneurs in raising capital for new undertakings. 'Criticisms of the financial machinery available for financing the development of business, and particularly small businesses, in the special areas can no longer be ignored,' warned Norman's assistant at Threadneedle Street. Stewart called for the creation of a special fund – 'pretty horrible, tho [*sic*] it may be unavoidable', regretted a Treasury official – as well as state-funded trading estates. This was a good deal too interventionist for Chamberlain, who was privately of the opinion that his appointment had been a mistake.[70] Whitehall still wanted to leave it to labour migration to ease Outer Britain's jobs crisis. In words freighted with suspicion of the unemployed, Horace Wilson insisted, 'the people *who wish to work* must go where the work is.'[71]

Nevertheless, with another general election looming, the National Government promised to establish industrial estates where firms could rent ready-made factories. It wasn't enough to save MacDonald, trounced at the polls on 14 November 1935 as the Durham coalfield swung back to Labour. 'To thousands of Seaham voters the government's chief monuments were the means test and the indignities associated with it,' writes David Marquand. 'Seaham's patriotism in sending him to Westminster had been rewarded by four years of stagnation and neglect.'[72] But the government held on to a string of borough constituencies on the North East coast, including Gateshead, which was rewarded with the country's first state-funded industrial estate, Team Valley.

Autumn 1936 brought another minor breach in the wall of Whitehall obstructionism. On 5 October 200 unemployed men from Jarrow set out for London under Special Branch surveillance with a petition calling on the government to 'actively assist resuscitation of industry'. Jarrow is situated on the south bank of the Tyne, a few miles downriver of Gateshead. The town was reduced to dereliction by the business failure of the Palmers Shipbuilding and Iron Company, a mid-nineteenth-century innovator in the design of steam colliers for the coastal coal trade. Its steelworks closed in 1930. Minister of Labour Henry Betterton asked the National Government's employment committee to waive procurement rules and award a naval contract to Jarrow. The Admiralty was against it and so, it turned out, were Betterton's colleagues.[73] Within months, Palmers had fallen into receivership. The receiver sold the Jarrow works to National Shipbuilders' Security, a Bank of England-backed rationalisation vehicle which disposed of sites under restrictive covenants to prevent them re-entering the shipbuilding trade. The machine shops and blast furnace were bulldozed. J. B. Priestley was reminded of scenes he had witnessed in wartime France. 'The whole town looked as if it had entered a perpetual penniless bleak Sabbath. The men wore the drawn masks of prisoners of war.'[74] Over 7,000 people were on the dole, four-fifths of the insured population. 'There was no work,' recalled Ellen Wilkinson. 'No one had a job, except a few railwaymen, officials, the workers in the cooperative stores, and the few clerks and craftsmen who went out of the town to their jobs each day.'[75]

Wilkinson had dislodged the Conservatives to take Jarrow at the 1935 general election. A working-class, university-educated Mancunian, she had started out on the hard left and was one of the first to join the Communist Party of Great Britain. Returning from a trip to Moscow in 1921, she observed,

> Russians are rather weary of explaining to naive new-comers that communism in Russia has only begun as yet, and it cannot succeed until the communists in other countries have done their part. It is no more possible to have a communist Russia in a capitalist world than to have a communist Manchester in a capitalist Britain.[76]

She quit the CPGB when it was proscribed by Labour in order to stand for the latter in Middlesbrough. When the National Government parties closed ranks against her in 1931, Middlesbrough was lost and Wilkinson switched her attention to the Tyne. She arrived in Jarrow in time to see a private-sector initiative for a major new steelworks blocked by Teesside firms within the Iron and Steel Federation, despite rising demand for basic steel, much of which was being met by imports. The federation was a state-sanctioned cartel, yet Baldwin and Board of Trade president Walter Runciman – a shipowner's son from South Shields – denied any responsibility for the steel imbroglio. Runciman advised a delegation from Jarrow that the town would have to 'work out its own salvation'.[77]

Such was the background to the Jarrow Crusade, which got under way just as Labour delegates were assembling in Edinburgh for their annual conference. Wilkinson detoured to Scotland to berate her chosen party and the TUC for cold-shouldering the Jarrow men: 'What has the National Council [of Labour] done? It has disapproved of it. What has gone out from our General Council? Letters saying, in the politest language, "Do not help these men".' For Labour and the Conservatives alike, hunger marches smacked of communist agitation. The NUWM had been organising them ever since the post-Armistice slump. In the era of the Popular Front, however, Wilkinson demanded that delegates set aside factional prejudices. If they couldn't do this, she wondered aloud, what was the point of a Labour Party? A biographer laconically comments that 'her speech was not welcomed.'[78] The same could be said of the Jarrow marchers in Whitehall. The Cabinet issued a statement in advance of their arrival:

> Ministers have under consideration the fact that a number of 'marches' on London are in progress or in contemplation. In the opinion of HM Government such marches can do no good to the causes for which they are represented to be undertaken, are liable to cause unnecessary hardship for those taking part in them, and are altogether undesirable.[79]

Herbert Henson, the reactionary Bishop of Durham, put it more strongly in a letter to *The Times*, accusing the Jarrow Crusade of 'substituting for the provisions of the Constitution the method of organised mob pressure'.[80]

In truth Wilkinson had moved sufficiently rightwards not to entertain thoughts of upturning the Constitution or anything else. The Jarrow Crusade was a labourist creation, devoid of wider political ambition. Wilkinson described it as 'quiet and constitutional' in tacit contrast to the NUWM. She bundled the marchers onto a pleasure cruise down the Thames before introducing the town's petition in Parliament, where it was picked over for discrepancies, logged and forgotten.

The Jarrow demonstration at least pushed the problem of the depressed areas once more to the forefront of the public mind. It held its place there thanks to the largest ever NUWM march, about 1,500-strong – including a small contingent from forlorn Maryport – which began to make landfall in London the day after the Tyneside men had departed the capital by train from King's Cross. NUWM protestors tramped up and down Whitehall until they were granted the ministerial audience that Wilkinson's group had been denied. 'The Jarrow marchers', commented the *Guardian*, 'will probably draw in their dismay the dangerous moral that they did not make themselves sufficient of a nuisance'.[81]

In the context of an industrial boom in the South, stagnation in the North couldn't be dismissed as merely a cyclical downturn. It looked bad for a government with any kind of One Nation pretensions not to evince concern about the plight of regions which weren't being lifted by the rising economic tide. Baldwin's public-relations headache was compounded by a stray comment from Edward VIII during a visit to impoverished South Wales ('something must be done to find them work') and by the resignation of special-areas commissioner Malcolm Stewart, citing a need for a rest after a period of strain and anxiety. The *Spectator* roundly condemned the Baldwin government for hanging the commissioner out to dry. 'He is without direct contact with ministers, without adequate funds, without adequate powers, his freedom of action is hopelessly restricted, his proposals are ignored, he is hampered by departmental delay and red tape.'[82]

Stewart's final report vented its author's frustration that after he had been in post for nearly two years, there were still 130,000 registered unemployed (25 per cent of insured workers) in the Durham and Tyneside special area. In the smaller labour market of west Cumberland another 12,000 (35 per cent) were without work. 'It has to be admitted that no appreciable reduction of the number of those unemployed has been effected,' said Stewart. He pointedly added, 'This, however, was not to be looked for seeing that the Special Areas Act makes no direct provision for this purpose.' Attempts to persuade industrialists to avail themselves of facilities in depressed areas had proved futile, he complained. In the previous year over 200 new factories had been established in Greater London, compared to just two in Durham and Tyneside. 'The macrocosm of London grows with a rapidity which is beginning to cause alarm,' the outgoing commissioner warned. 'Every new factory built creates a demand for more material, transport and services. Local prosperity abounds; nothing succeeds like success. Manufacturers instinctively follow in the footsteps of those whose success is obviously demonstrated.'

Although dismissive of full-blown state control over the location of industry, Stewart urged the introduction of direct financial subsidies – tax relief and long-term, low-interest loans – to attract manufacturers into the depressed areas, together with an embargo on factory construction in Greater London. It was foolish to concentrate so many industrial resources in the south-eastern segment of the country, acutely vulnerable to air attack from the Continent. With any luck, the special areas would claim their share of new developments diverted away from the bloated capital.[83]

Young Tory progressives threatened a backbench revolt over government inaction. As pressure from below met pressure from above, the politics of regional economic imbalance slipped momentarily out of Chamberlain's control. With no choice but to cede ground, he legislated for rent and tax rebates, as well as Treasury loans, to be made available to new industrial undertakings in high-unemployment districts. By September 1938 Stewart's successor had committed £100,000 in financial inducements. The Treasury ultimately provided £1.2 million in loan finance. The *Economist* thought the money on offer 'insufficient to attract entrepreneurs to areas which they regarded as remote and bleak.' By the outbreak of war, around 4,000 people were working at Gateshead's Team Valley – a modest total set against the exemplar industrial estates of Slough and Park Royal in west London, each employing some 30,000.[84]

Chamberlain meanwhile kicked the suggestion of an embargo on London into the long grass by means of a Royal Commission on the Distribution of the Industrial Population under former Salford MP Sir Anderson Montague Barlow, an old Cabinet friend with whom he went fishing.[85] The commission wouldn't report until 1940. It represented the last in a series of ruses to get London governments through the interwar emergency without resort to regional economic reflation. The Conservatives hadn't fought and won the General Strike merely to ride roughshod over the locational privileges of private-sector manufacturers. The politicians and bankers of the slump were aghast enough to be adrift of the gold standard and free trade, and embroiled in schemes for the rationalisation of domestic industry. They refused to countenance further misadventures in a market economy until the exigencies of total war forced their hands.

Without a socialist programme to combat the slump, Orwell argued, 'the very best the English working class can hope for is an occasional temporary decrease in unemployment when this or that industry is artificially stimulated by, for instance, rearmament.'[86] So it proved. Defence expenditure, increasingly funded by government borrowing, provided a shot in the arm for the staple trades. The full mobilisation of national resources in the course of the Second World War would reduce the concentration of national economic activity on the South East and achieve the revitalisation of Outer Britain that peacetime politics at Westminster had singularly failed to deliver. The number of registered unemployed in the North tumbled from 830,000 to 60,000 between January 1939 and January 1942.[87] One of the many issues debated in Whitehall, even as the bombs fell, was whether this accidental solution to the regional problem would long outlast the war.

6

Forged in Yorkshire

L ifted out of the long slump by the war effort, the next step
for the smokestack regions after 1945 was to overhaul their
manufacturing base before the resumption of commercial competition from continental Europe and Japan. Burnt by the Depression,
however, it was obvious that the staple sectors, if left to their own
devices, would opt rather to coast along in a temporary buyers'
market. Still less likely was it that, with government and corporate
research and development activity heavily concentrated in south-
east England, Outer Britain would blaze a trail of innovation in
new product lines.

The question, therefore, was whether there would be any *diri-
gisme* from either Whitehall or the City. Fatally, neither of these
institutions required a modernised industrial base in order to
recover a position in the world. Instead the imperial mentality sati-
rised by Belloc – 'Whatever happens we have got / The Maxim gun,
and they have not' – persisted. A nuclear-weapons programme,
Attlee's forgotten legacy, would reassert this military vanity under
changed conditions. The pound sterling offered another 'ticket
to the world's top table'.[1] David Kynaston, historian of the City
and the Bank of England, notes a 'sharp and lamentable' contrast between the UK and German post-war banking systems
when presented with the latter's record of nurturing small and
medium-sized domestic firms, a task that the Square Mile has
always abjured in pursuit of business abroad, its path to overseas
markets cleared by earlier rounds of British imperial expansion.[2]
Viewed from Downing Street or Bank Junction, therefore, the

Northern Question still seemed like small beer compared with the overriding imperatives of keeping the pound strong and British imperialism intact. If the deflationary supports needed for these strategies clashed with the investment requirements of domestic industry, it would be so much the worse for the latter.

Hedged in by these traditional preoccupations, post-war governmental action under the rubric of 'regional policy' came to involve merely a modest stimulus to private-sector investment and job creation, aimed at indemnifying the ruling parties against accusations of neglect, should slump conditions return to the industrial towns of northern England, Scotland and Wales. Its parameters were laid out by Labour and the Conservatives during their wartime coalition. In January 1940, the majority report of Sir Montague Barlow's Royal Commission on the Distribution of the Industrial Population recommended the creation of a board equipped with veto power over new industrial undertakings in London and the Home Counties. The minority report called for a dedicated Whitehall department to control industrial location throughout the country, not just in the congested South East. There was general agreement that something had to be done to promote 'a reasonable balance of industrial development' and 'appropriate diversification of industry in each division or region'.[3]

Chamberlain's ouster in May 1940 ushered into the corridors of power Labour politicians who had been arguing ineffectually along these lines from the opposition benches. Their spokesman was Hugh Dalton, a stentorian, supremely self-confident old Etonian raised in the shadow of Windsor castle. Dalton had had enough of depressed areas, so much so that he preferred to live in Wiltshire rather than anywhere near his Bishop Auckland constituency. Inspired by a Fabian Society trip to the Soviet Union in the depths of the Depression, he made it an object of Labour policy that the state 'should aim at the transfer of work into these areas, rather than the transfer of workers away from them'.[4] The war took him first to the Ministry of Economic Warfare and then to the Board of Trade, where he upped the ante on industrial dispersal through selective allocation of building licenses and construction of standardised factories and industrial estates. 'It is a very simple problem,' he wrote. 'These areas had too few factories in them and too little variety of industry. The remedy is to put more factories in them with a greater variety of industries. If this is persistently followed for several years, the problem will be solved.' His assistant, Douglas Jay, a former City journalist, worked out the details without getting round to reading the Barlow reports.[5]

Supported by Bevin, Dalton hardwired these wartime improvisations into Whitehall's preparations for the coming peace. 'It will be an object of government policy to secure a balanced industrial development in areas which have in the past been unduly dependent on industries specially vulnerable to unemployment', pledged the keynote 1944 White Paper on employment. To this end, a Distribution of Industry Act mandated the Board of Trade to build factories in enlarged versions of the old special areas, renamed 'development areas'.[6] The Treasury could issue grants and loans to manufacturers setting up in these zones. No provision was made for either rent subsidies or tax breaks, and a clause to regulate industrial activity in the South East was dropped on Dalton's say-so to appease the Conservatives. Nevertheless, as the *Economist* observed, 'the Board of Trade will be able to exercise a powerful direct influence over industrial location so long as building materials and labour are in short supply through the issue of building licenses, without which no firm can build.' It was a matter of 'how much hay can be made in the existing development areas while the sun of wartime controls shines'.[7]

Attlee, condemned by one of his successors as 'tone deaf as far as all economical questions were concerned', evinced no interest in using such controls as a springboard toward planned industrial modernisation.[8] Beneficiary of a landslide victory at the polls, the first majority Labour administration, taking office on 26 July 1945, would expand the welfare state as an essential component of the peace dividend and take into public ownership a rundown coal industry upon which Churchill had already imposed dual control. It also placed the Bank of England under formal Treasury supervision, without, however, meddling in its inner workings. The Old Lady remained 'in essence Montagu Norman's bank'. Kynaston's verdict on the new administration: 'The City was safe in their hands.'[9]

Loath to upset the Establishment applecart by going further

than circumstances dictated, the Labour Cabinet prevaricated over whether also to add steelmaking to the state sector and categorically ruled out nationalisation of cotton, despite the failure of mill owners to invest in new machinery. Unlike in 1924, none of the Big Five – Attlee, Bevin, Cripps, Dalton, Morrison – were born north of a line running between Buckinghamshire and Glamorgan. It was left to junior ministers like Ellis Smith, who resigned from the Board of Trade in January 1946, to protest at the government's timidity. 'My whole make-up, technical training and industrial experience meant that I should lean towards the planned road,' explained Smith, a former Metropolitan Vickers patternmaker at Manchester's Trafford Park. 'I have documentary evidence of my ideas and many notes of thanks, but no action was taken.'[10]

Instead of channelling private investment to the North, Labour allowed private capital to leak overseas into the colonies and dominions. There were no restrictions on investment within the sterling area, so British wealth holders could relieve the tedium of austerity by placing bets abroad. Gold mines in South Africa were a particular favourite. 'Neither Dalton nor his colleagues seriously questioned the national desirability of a strong sterling area,' writes Kynaston, 'an assumption that inevitably demanded that sterling be a powerful (or anyway, as powerful as possible) world currency, whatever the domestic deflationary consequences'. Capital export in 1947 totalled £640 million, equivalent to 8 per cent of national income.[11] In February that year, the Cabinet raised concern about what it deemed 'excessive' industrial diversification in Lancashire, where light-engineering firms had sprung up in decommissioned munitions works and were competing for fuel and manpower with the cotton industry, whose exports were needed to close the trade deficit. Dalton assured his colleagues that except on Merseyside and in St Helens, 'no positive action had been taken on behalf of the government to promote industrial development in the rest of this area.'[12] Broadening the economic base of the original industrial region would have to wait. Labour's priority was 'to cut a dash in the world considerably above our means' – Keynes's words – while cash-rich Britons chased windfall profits in the Transvaal.[13]

Government expenditure on military encampments stretching from Germany and Austria to Egypt and Iraq, Malaya and Hong

Kong, added to the strain on the balance of payments. A more substantial downsizing of imperial ambitions was called for. But although less bellicose than Bevin at the Foreign Office, Attlee wasn't going to force the issue. 'He was an old India hand; he retained his veneration for the Crown and the imperial connection, for all his socialism.'[14] To keep up Britain's deployments, Keynes negotiated a $3.75 billion loan from the Americans. In return, Attlee undertook to restore the convertibility of pounds into dollars by July 1947.[15] With greenbacks in high demand, Britain's reserves began to give out. Dalton and Stafford Cripps frantically reintroduced exchange controls, cut domestic expenditure and mounted a dollar-earning export drive. 'New industrial building had had to be restricted to those projects which would make a substantial contribution to the solution of our overseas-payments problem,' recalled a young Harold Wilson, who took over at the Board of Trade that September. 'This had meant that even in the development areas, projects which were capable of providing much-needed employment could often not be sanctioned.'[16] In private, Wilson went so far as to allege that the reduction in regional-policy spending to less than £7 million per annum

> condemns the development areas to the grim prospect of mounting unemployment and offers no hope whatever to those areas. In these circumstances, full employment, the Ark of the Covenant in the government's economic policy, is in danger of being a mockery. There are already a number of areas where one cannot quote the phrase in a political speech.[17]

Under the 1947 Town and Country Planning Act, new industrial undertakings of over 5,000 square feet required Board of Trade certification that they were consistent with the proper distribution of industry. In practice, this left plenty of room for manoeuvre. One of Wilson's ministerial colleagues, Blackburn MP John Edwards, confessed that 'distribution of industry principles were being overridden in case after case because of production considerations.' A government White Paper made a point of noting that 'there is of course no positive power to direct an industrialist to build a factory in any particular locality.' Increasingly there was a sense that anywhere would do. Over the course of the Attlee years, the factory floor space awarded to the development areas fell from one-half to one-fifth of the national total.[18] The Cabinet minutes for 15 June 1950 record that 'recovery in the development areas was in fact beginning to lag, mainly because of increasing difficulty in persuading firms to establish new enterprises there.'[19]

Even when the going was good, the most that Labour accomplished was the provision of sorely needed overspill production facilities in designated areas for big manufacturers such as Dunlop and Siemens. Ministers were well aware that 'many firms in these areas were only subsidiaries and would be the first to feel the effect of any depression of trade.'[20] A survey by economists at Durham University found that in the North East, 'a number of branches were being exploited by their main factories, used to cope with demands beyond the capacity of the central factory and made to cut their output if any cutting had to be done.'[21]

It isn't the case that Attlee lacked the resources to keep up investment in the industrial regions. The sums involved were trifling compared to the ramping up of projected military expenditure to £4.7 billion over three years in support of the US's escalation of the Cold War in Korea. In addition, the Labour leadership was prepared to plough limitless amounts of money into its clandestine nuclear-weapons programme. 'We have got to have this thing over here whatever it costs. We've got to have the bloody Union Jack flying on top of it,' said Foreign Secretary Bevin, the Bristol trade unionist turned Cold War warrior, about the atom bomb.[22]

The plutonium for Britain's first nuclear weapons came from Sellafield, a Second World War TNT works hidden behind the Lake District mountains on the Cumbrian coast. Courtaulds had wanted the site for a rayon factory; instead Attlee repurposed it for nuclear-age warfare, changing its name to Windscale to avoid confusion with the Springfields uranium-processing facility outside Preston. Construction of two atomic piles to irradiate uranium fuel elements supplied by Springfields began in 1947. Five years later, Churchill's Conservatives detonated the first British nuclear device off the north-west coast of Australia, then ordered Windscale into overdrive in pursuit of a more destructive hydrogen bomb to keep up with the Cold War superpowers. The Atomic Energy Authority 'always put as the paramount issue the necessity of meeting the defence programme', confessed a senior official. 'Shortages of men or materials or knowledge were not allowed to jeopardise this. The times given were such that risks had to be accepted.'[23] On 10 October 1957, technicians at Windscale discovered that fuel cartridges in Pile No. 1 were on fire. The blaze continued through the night and into the following morning, until emergency teams became desperate enough to hazard a catastrophic explosion by dousing the chimney with water. Radioactive debris from the fire may have caused up to 100 fatalities through lung and thyroid cancer.[24] In a remarkable coincidence, the Soviets suffered a reactor disaster of their own, at Kyshtym in the southern Urals, only a fortnight prior to the Cumbrian emergency. Outdistanced by the Americans, Macmillan and Khrushchev were both furiously stockpiling weapons-grade plutonium; mishaps followed as a matter of course.

Anti-nuclear protest in Britain can be traced back to a speech by Bob Edwards of the Independent Labour Party in St Helens in 1943. The location is not as arbitrary as it may seem. St Helens was a centre of chemical manufacture; Edwards a senior figure in the Chemical Workers Union. He appears to have picked up stray hints about the Manhattan Project from contacts in the US chemical industry. His response was to sound a warning that the secretive race to weaponise atomic power risked 'devastating frightfulness and destruction'.[25] Windscale vindicated his concerns closer to home than he might have anticipated. But so deftly was the incident underplayed by the authorities – 'at no time was there any risk of explosion,' *The Times* misinformed its readers – that J. B. Priestley's influential *New Statesman* article calling on the British people to make a declaration to the world that they rejected the evil of nuclear warfare didn't even mention it.[26] Thus although the Campaign for Nuclear Disarmament launched within months of the Windscale fire, the impulse for the largest protest movement of the post-war period came rather from British test explosions in the Pacific. At home, public unease focussed on those installations most immediately associated with the new doomsday devices: the Aldermaston bomb factory in Berkshire and Holy Loch near Glasgow, where Macmillan bowed to pressure from

Eisenhower to allow the US to dock its nuclear-armed Polaris submarines.

Even CND barely made an impression on the torpid years of Conservative rule between 1951 and 1964. A long world-economic boom buoyed up the former depressed areas, near-full employment allowing the Churchill government to continue a winding down of regional policy that had started under Attlee after the 1947 sterling crisis. Disregarding warnings from his officials about the problems looming over the staple industries, Peter Thorneycroft, the doctrinaire liberal put in charge of the Board of Trade, directed that 'no new building should be sponsored in the development areas unless it satisfies the strictest tests of essentiality.'[27]

The representatives of labour were as complacent as those of capital. The number of days lost to strikes was unexceptional by international standards and there were few set-piece confrontations. Officials from the stolidly labourist North devoted their energies to bearing down on communists and the Labour left, wielding their block votes and committee powers in the Gaitskellite cause. Organised labour 'should never hold the country to ransom', insisted Tom Williamson of the Municipal Workers', the son of a St Helens glass-blower and one of nature's bureaucrats, garlanded with a life peerage by Macmillan.[28] Others deserving a mention in despatches include Sam Watson, a Durham miners' official and key Labour Party insider, who talked Nye Bevan into renouncing unilateral nuclear disarmament, and Teesside bruiser Harry Douglass, fondly remembered by his steelworkers' union for 'smiting the Bevanites hip and thigh'.[29]

If the political waters appeared to hold few surprises, beneath the surface of events, the spread of secondary education and access – of course, to a far more limited extent – to higher education saw a large number of writers, directors and artists of popular origin emerge from the North, who came to express or represent the region on a national stage: David Hockney in painting; Ted Hughes, Tony Harrison, Philip Larkin (if only by residence) in poetry; David Storey, Beryl Bainbridge, Pat Barker, Stan Barstow in fiction; Tony Richardson, Terence Davies, Mike Leigh in film; and Shelagh Delaney, Jim Allen, David Mercer and

Alan Bennett in drama; not to speak of the worldwide impact of the Fab Four.

How did this late cultural florescence relate to the onset of the North's economic decline? One account floated by Dave Russell in *Looking North* is that the idea of Englishness took on a more northern complexion from the fifties because the tightly knit working class with which the region had become indelibly associated was the only even partially viable bulwark against American cultural imperialism.[30] 'Working-class people are a good deal less affected than they might well be,' averred Richard Hoggart in *The Uses of Literacy* (1957), a study of the seepage of Americanised mass-market literature into the terraced-street communities of his native Leeds. 'The question, of course, is how long this stock of moral capital will last, and whether it is being sufficiently renewed.'[31]

For the youth, on the other hand, constrictive working-class milieus were not changing nearly quickly enough. 'I wanted an Aston-Martin, I wanted a three-guinea linen shirt, I wanted a girl with a Riviera suntan,' exclaims Joe Lampton, the anti-hero of John Braine's debut novel *Room at the Top*, published the same year as *The Uses of Literacy* and adapted for the screen by Jack Clayton in 1959. Anxious not to miss out on the advent on mass consumer prosperity, and doggedly intent on social promotion, Lampton quits his glum-looking Victorian mill town – 'the back-to-back houses, the outside privies, the smoke which caught the throat and dirtied clean linen in a couple of hours, the sense of being always involved in a charade upon *Hard Times*' – in favour of a more salubrious locale where Yorkshire businessmen trading in textiles, coal and groceries enjoy all the conveniences of the automobile age: 'the garage for each house, the taste of prosperity as smooth and nourishing as eggnog'. Lampton's itinerary mirrors Braine's own progress from Thackley, a suburb of industrial Shipley near Bradford, to the market town of Bingley, only four miles distant as the crow flies but a world away in terms of social class and standards of living.

Progress is always relative, and if the North enjoyed some updraft from the post-war boom, the South gained altitude at a faster rate. Braine was acutely conscious that by southern standards, bourgeois oases such as Bingley were no great shakes. As his protagonist acknowledges, 'anyone who lives on a private income in Bath will consider me a cross brute.'[32] The author abandoned Yorkshire for Surrey in 1966 in the course of a failed attempt to revitalise his flagging career closer to London's literati.

This was by then a well-worn route. Even the leading representatives of the northern new wave were quickly snapped up by a London record label – Penny Lane remembered from the greater comfort of Abbey Road. Emblematic of the capital's tightening grip on the national culture was the *Guardian*'s decision to bid adieu to Manchester in 1964. The newspaper had been founded by a cotton and twist dealer after the Peterloo massacre to preach reform, liberty and political economy to the large Nonconformist interest among the millocracy. In those days, as the paper's official history nostalgically observes, 'Manchester was neither an island backwater nor a cultural dependency of London.'[33] It was fast acquiring these unwanted traits. By the early 1950s, editor A. P. Wadsworth could note,

> Although the paper is directed from Manchester the most considerable part of it is already written in or supplied through London. Already the main specialist writers work from London: parliamentary, political, industrial, financial, diplomatic, air and science correspondents. There are also staff writers there on music, art, theatre, etc. A good many leaders are also written from London, especially on finance and international affairs.[34]

Wadsworth's successor, Alastair Hetherington, dropped 'Manchester' from the masthead so that the publication appeared less provincial in the national advertising market, then relocated the editorial staff to Gray's Inn Road. 'The advantages of detachment from the capital are great, and the decision to move the main editorial office has been taken reluctantly,' the paper claimed. 'It would be foolish, however, not to recognise now that the job can be done more easily and efficiently in London.' The *Spectator* suspected that it protested too much:

> Fleet Street is crowded with provincial journalists who have joined the drift to London without any discernible reluctance

at all, but evidently the *Guardian* men are of a different stamp. They dream of Salford and Moss Side. One sighs for the rigorous sense of duty which has exiled them from their beloved haunts.[35]

One aspect of the migration of artists and journalists to the capital, highlighted by Russell, is that the critical distance it afforded 'allowed for both affection and wry mockery'. For the larger part of the London establishment, already *in situ*, that distance had always been there, but without the close familiarity that effective satire requires. Russell cites Hartlepool-born cartoonist Reg Smythe's famous comic-strip northerner Andy Capp, and Keith Waterhouse's early novel-cum-play *Billy Liar* (1959), set in Leeds. Half-remembered 'Lowryscapes' of the North – one adorns the cover of this book – risked lapsing into stereotype as the class and region they targeted changed out of all recognition.[36]

Among those left behind, a sense of malaise became increasingly palpable. According to Geoffrey Moorhouse, a *Guardian* journalist from Bolton,

> no one who lived in Lancashire, in Yorkshire, and in the North East during the late fifties and early sixties could fail to be aware that these areas were gradually falling behind the national average in many ways – in tolerable housing conditions, in mortality, in investment, and, above all, in employment.[37]

For every 1 per cent rise in the UK jobless rate under the Tories, unemployment increased 1.7 per cent in the North West, which was already in the throes of deindustrialisation: regional manufacturing employment fell by 4 per cent over these years, in stark contrast to an 8 per cent rise in the national total.[38]

The difficulties facing areas still reliant on old basic industries beginning to wilt under the glare of resurgent foreign competition were compounded by the side effects of Conservative liberalisation of the UK's external financial arrangements. The Treasury and Bank of England held that the pound needed to be a major trading and reserve currency in order for the Square Mile to flourish once again as an international financial centre. But with the US dollar now the world's top currency, sterling's position wasn't easily assured. The loosening of exchange controls exposed it to hostile financial-market opinion whenever confidence waned in the government's ability to hold its fixed exchange rate against the dollar.[39] To demonstrate national solvency and lure hot money back to the City, Whitehall countered periodic runs on the pound with interest-rate rises, credit restrictions and spending cuts. Not only was regional-policy expenditure a casualty of retrenchment, but these repeated 'stops' on domestic expansion were anathema to long-term investment in the industrial regions. 'Continuity is vital', the chairman of North Eastern Trading Estates Ltd complained to MPs.[40]

In the autumn of 1957, the Macmillan government fended off severe financial-market speculation by tightening credit for private industry, reducing capital expenditure in the state-owned sector and raising interest rates from 5 to 7 per cent, their highest level for thirty-seven years. The sterling parity was saved, but business confidence in the productive sector took a bad knock. The national jobless total exceeded 500,000 and unemployment in the development areas rose further above the national average.[41]

It was in Lancashire, where the cotton industry lost market share faster than its US and European counterparts, that grievances about Whitehall neglect were most acute. For the first time since the Industrial Revolution, the UK was importing more cotton goods than it exported. Mill directors pleaded again and again for protection in the home market from low-wage South and East Asian producers, the heirs of Cobden and Bright reduced to arguing that 'free entry would never have been conceded in the first place if conditions had then been as they are today'.[42] But Board of Trade president Thorneycroft was unwilling to abandon the precepts of Cobdenism for Lancashire's sake. His response to such appeals was unequivocal: 'The government has no feather-bed to offer you and very little shelter in the harsh winds of competition which are blowing through the world today.'[43]

More than a century may have passed since cotton called the national tune, but it was impossible for London to ignore ill feeling in Lancashire indefinitely. Even Thorneycroft was aware that a trade depression in the cotton belt 'could not be devoid of all political significance'.[44] For despite their electoral orientation towards southern England, the Conservatives usually stand in need of northern votes. In the 1955 general election they secured 43 seats in the North West and a Commons majority of 59. Three years later, a by-election defeat in Rochdale gave Macmillan pause for thought. It was the first televised electoral contest in the UK – a Granada innovation. Voters dumped Conservative candidate John Parkinson at the bottom of the poll, behind the Liberals. Cotton still accounted for nearly half of total employment in the Rochdale area and the district cotton employers' association had taken Parkinson to task over his party's refusal to cap imports from Commonwealth producers. Parkinson in response accused them of driving a knife into his back.[45]

The Rochdale upset came as 'a tremendous shock', Macmillan confided to his diary. Other Tory marginals began to look vulnerable. He feared that unless the government take action, 'we shall lose a lot of Lancashire trade and 9–14 Lancashire seats!'[46] Ministers hurriedly negotiated voluntary import quotas with India, Pakistan and Hong Kong and allocated funds to Lancashire for the scrappage of surplus spindles and looms. Further lobbying also yielded a less generous subsidy for new equipment.

Trouble in the mill towns fed into a larger public-relations headache for the Conservative administration. Within weeks of the Rochdale poll, Chancellor Derick Heathcoat-Amory reported to the Cabinet, 'The Economic Policy Committee have discussed the problem of local unemployment, on which public and parliamentary attention is being increasingly focussed'. The committee's conclusion: 'we must take all the action we reasonably can to deal with this problem; and, equally important, we must be seen to be doing so'. For his own part, Macmillan was anxious 'to concentrate on the weak spots', since general measures to stimulate demand 'would inevitably result in a renewed inflation, with all that this means to our balance of payments and to sterling'.[47] After years of disuse, regional policy suddenly came back into fashion. The development areas gave way to smaller 'development districts' targeted at unemployment blackspots, and regional aid recovered from £3.6 million in 1958–9 to £11.8 million in

1960–1.[48] A tightening of location controls induced carmakers Ford, Standard-Triumph and Vauxhall to set up assembly plants on Merseyside, which had some of the worst unemployment in the country. The new Board of Trade president, Reginald Maudling, would have preferred Vauxhall to go to the North East, but felt that any further interference 'would commit us deeply to a policy of planning the "proper distribution" of the motor-car industry. This is what the Opposition would like, but I do not believe it is a sensible policy.'[49]

This flexing of state power achieved its immediate objectives, allaying public criticism and preventing a haemorrhage of Conservative support among northern voters. Macmillan won by a landslide in the 8 October 1959 general election by hoovering up seats in the booming Midlands and London. His position further upcountry was more or less unchanged. South-east Lancashire bucked the national trend to swing Labour's way, but not by enough to cause the Tories substantial damage. Only one seat in the cotton district was lost, that of Oldham East, and this was more than made up for by Conservative gains in a number of tight contests on the North East coast.

The Tories would have fared less well in the North East had Macmillan not waited until after polling day to publish a revised Plan for Coal with reduced output targets and up to 240 additional pit closures. The party had always wanted to lessen the country's reliance on coal in order to reduce the industrial power of the National Union of Miners. Churchill's Minister of Fuel and Power, Geoffrey Lloyd, fretted about 'our remaining indefinitely at the mercy of the miners'. In public, however, the talk was of promoting consumer choice between coal, oil and nuclear.[50] Though Macmillan was fond of recalling the heroism of the Durham miners in the First World War, his closure programme hit the Great Northern coalfield hard. Selwyn Lloyd, Heathcoat-Amory's replacement at the Exchequer, cautioned that without greater aid for mining communities, 'public anxiety might mount quickly and force the government to slow down the contraction process.[51]

Lloyd hailed from the professional classes of suburban Wirral, a self-help Methodist Liberal by upbringing. When offered the Treasury by Macmillan, Lloyd recalled telling the prime minister that 'he was wrong if he expected any originality. I had v. orthodox ideas about taxation and public expenditure.'[52] True to his word, on 25 July 1961, as sterling came under renewed pressure and the Bank of England's gold and dollar reserves ran low, Lloyd imposed another credit squeeze and a moratorium on state investment at the behest of bank governor Rowland Bearing, third Earl of Cromer. The *Economist* broadly welcomed 'the biggest immediate cut in demand that has been deliberately imposed by a British government on any single afternoon in peacetime history', on the grounds that higher unemployment would curb trade-union pay claims.[53] Once again, the economy was brought spluttering to a halt. There was a rash of redundancies in the North East's cramped and outmoded shipyards. The collapse of William Gray and Co. in Hartlepool, where the Conservative majority was wafer thin, threw 1,400 men out of work and brought shipbuilding in the town to an abrupt end. 'The national industrial recession, so slightly felt in the bustle of the South East districts, has hit hard round the Tees, the Tyne and the Durham hinterland', noted *The Times*.[54] The situation was by no means as desperate as in the thirties, but popular expectations cut less slack for laissez-faire. According to the *Newcastle Journal*, people had begun to wonder 'why the regional difficulties should recur in what was supposed to be the affluent society'.[55]

Lloyd's July measures attracted opprobrium from all quarters. The Conservatives suffered a string of dismal by-election results across the country, beginning on 14 March in Orpington, Kent, lost to the resurgent Liberals. On 6 June they were felled in Middlesbrough West on a 13 per cent swing to Labour – 'just about as bad as it could be for the government', commented the town's *Evening Gazette*.[56] Many Tory voters had either switched to the Liberals or stayed at home. A month later, in a sudden loss of nerve, Macmillan sacked a third of his cabinet. The chaotic reshuffle saw Lloyd's deputy, Henry Brooke, promoted to Home Secretary. Brooke had been a trenchant critic of National Government laissez-faire during the Great Depression, penning the newspaper articles on 'places without a future' from which Chamberlain's special-areas legislation had sprung. Freed from the constraints of a Treasury brief, he now urged Macmillan to impose a levy to curb the runaway growth of new offices in London, warning about a widening rift between North and South. Macmillan's younger self, the 1930s backbench radical, would have been the first to agree. Like Brooke, the prime minister had seen the ravages of the slump at first hand, railing against his own party's reliance on out-migration to ease the distress of depressed areas. What was needed, Macmillan had then argued, was 'some idea of the location of industry and some machinery for using its resources in a useful and proper way'.[57] But the problems of Teesside receded into the distance once the Second World War catapulted him from the parliamentary back benches to Eisenhower's Allied Forces Headquarters. When Stockton was lost in 1945 he retreated to Bromley, a safe seat in the London commuter belt, and acquired a completely new set of political coordinates. The early fifties saw him agitating for greater investment in South East new towns whose expansion came at the expense of the development areas.

Little wonder that in Downing Street, Macmillan turned out to be too orthodox by half, priding himself on his 'determination to defend sterling and stability by all means in our power'.[58] He could summon no enthusiasm whatever for Brooke's proposal. 'The government should not attempt to reverse trends deriving from such fundamental forces as were drawing population towards the South East,' he concluded, throwing a sop to Brooke that it was, at the same time, 'out of the question to allow Scotland or the North East or any large area to be abandoned to decay'.[59] In lieu of office controls, he created the Location of Offices Bureau, a harmless publicity outfit which ran adverts on the London Underground urging commute-weary executives to move their businesses out of central London, though few were prepared to go further than satellite towns like Reading and Basingstoke. Meanwhile shipbuilders were given a temporary boost by means of a credit scheme and Lord Hailsham was despatched to the North East, sporting a flat cap, to consult local notables on plans for regional development – part of a bigger show of corporatist planning in response to protests from industry groups at Conservative stop-go. Hailsham was greeted by entreaties for the entire region to be scheduled as a development area and for the

Treasury to loosen its clampdown on industrial credit.[60] Cobbling together a number of development districts between Tyneside and Teesside, he conjured up the mirage of a 'growth zone' which he assured journalists would radiate prosperity to the whole region and become a 'London of the North'.[61]

By the time Hailsham's proposals came before the Cabinet, Macmillan had retired on ill-health grounds, replaced by Mayfair-born aristocrat Alec Douglas-Home: an arid figure with none of his predecessor's talent for political evasion. Douglas-Home gave his stamp of approval to a much-anticipated White Paper which made no effort to hide the Whitehall view that the North East was in for 'a painful process of adjustment'. The paper also made it perfectly clear that there were strict limits to the amount of external assistance that the Tyne, Wear and Tees could expect from London. Economic growth depended in the main on local enterprise, not government assistance. 'In short', responded the *Newcastle Journal*, 'our people still have to work out their own salvation.'[62]

A mantra of self-help was never likely to aid the Conservative electoral cause in the region. The number of Tory MPs returned by voters in the North East dropped by nearly a third in the 15 October 1964 general election, a loss of position from which the party wouldn't fully recover until 2019. All the way up the coast, constituencies reverted to Labour. In Sunderland South, the winning candidate denounced the Tories for 'thirteen years of slapdash rule'.[63] There was an above-average swing against the Conservatives in south-east Lancashire as well, where the prosperous future that Macmillan promised the cotton industry had never materialised. The ceilings for Commonwealth imports were 'substantially higher than any of us had ever contemplated', confessed the chair of the Cotton Board. Import penetration had leapt from 35 to 47 per cent since 1959.[64] Further west, Labour seized four Conservative seats in Liverpool and increased its majorities in the three it already held, as the break-up of Protestant and Catholic districts through slum clearance removed the sectarian basis for Tory predominance.

❧

On the campaign trail in Liverpool, Labour leader Harold Wilson blamed Conservative economic mismanagement for holding back industrial expansion by burdening the South with congestion while starving the North of investment. To correct these imbalances, Labour would set up a Department for Economic Affairs to wrest control of policy from the deflationist Treasury. The DEA would raise business expectations about future growth through an indicative National Plan. There would also be a Plan for the Regions 'to check the present drift to the South and to build up the declining economies in other parts of our country'.[65]

If the North of the early sixties felt a world away from Wilson's rhetoric of white-hot industrial modernisation, could the first northern Labour prime minister bring the region up to speed? He was really less of a break with tradition than he pretended. A former mentor, Nye Bevan, pointed out the potential double-meaning in Wilson's boast of having been 'forged in Yorkshire'.[66] Proud of his Yorkshire pedigree he certainly was, pointing to a string of male ancestors born in the neighbourhood of Rievaulx Abbey near Helmsley. But his immediate family hailed from the other side of the Pennines and they baptised him in their old Congregationalist chapel in Openshaw, a heavy-industrial suburb of Manchester. The family later moved away from Yorkshire for good as Harold's father, an industrial chemist, took on jobs in various dye works. Harold finished his schooling on the Wirral before going on to Oxford on a minor scholarship. A wartime civil servant, he remarked on his good fortune, 'as someone with developing political ambitions, to obtain such intimate knowledge of the governance of Britain before I was even thirty'.[67] It was Merseyside, not the West Riding, which then provided the springboard for his parliamentary career. He won the Ormskirk constituency in 1945 and was immediately appointed to ministerial office by Attlee. The two men both had connections to University College Oxford, and 'college loyalties are strong,' Wilson explained.[68] Perhaps his strong footing in Whitehall is what gave him the confidence to shake up its departmental structure. On the other hand, early and prolonged exposure to the official mind acculturated him to the innermost impulses of the British state, instilling a reverence for the monarchy, for centralisation and for the pound sterling.

Hard on the heels of Labour's victory at the polls, with the financial markets hostile to the incoming government's taxation policies, another run on the pound got under way. Wilson, Chancellor of the Exchequer James Callaghan and Secretary of State for Economic Affairs George Brown refused to countenance devaluation, fearful of party-political embarrassment and of inflicting damage to the sterling area. 'To turn our back on the sterling area would be a body-blow to the Commonwealth and all it stands for,' Wilson told an audience of bankers at the London Guildhall.[69] The new prime minister was also desperate to keep on the right side of the Lyndon Johnson administration in Washington, which treated the pound as the dollar's first line of defence and wanted to forestall a bout of competitive devaluations which might disrupt the US's alliances, just as its assault on Vietnam intensified.[70]

Once again, the domestic economy would have to take the strain of problems on the external account. Wilson kicked against demands from Lord Cromer for spending curbs and policy U-turns, but consented to another hike in interest rates. The Bank of England governor extracted further concessions when pressure on the foreign exchanges resumed the following summer. On 27 July 1965, Callaghan announced deferrals to capital expenditure, reductions to departmental spending and further tightening of consumer credit. He pledged not to apply the full rigour of these measures in areas of high unemployment, but the general dampening effect was unavoidable.

Labour went to the polls in a snap general election on 31 March 1966 promising 'no return to stop-go'. Soon afterwards, amid more heavy selling of sterling, a troika of powers – the markets, the Americans and the Bank of England – demanded another 'stop'. US Treasury Secretary Fowler telephoned Callaghan insisting on measures to depress the economy and restrain wages. The same day, Cromer contacted his opposite number at the Federal Reserve to advise him to decline British requests for extended borrowing facilities until Wilson had been forced into 'a display of resolute policy'.[71] On 20 July, to a round of applause from London's financial quarter, the Labour prime minister unveiled a package of tax rises, hire-purchase restrictions and a statutory wage freeze. 'The government has endorsed the City's order of priorities. It has put sterling first', celebrated the *Banker* magazine.[72] In the North East, government-built factories stood empty for want of private-sector tenants.

Slavish monetary orthodoxy nullified the ambitions of Labour's national and regional plans. Wilson had promised substantial devolution of powers from Whitehall and an attack on vested interests. In the event, George Brown's regional planning councils had neither executive powers nor democratic legitimacy, consisting of hand-picked business leaders and local-government representatives such as T. Dan Smith, the Labour municipal boss of Newcastle, a leading advocate of slum clearance and high-rise flats who would receive a prison term for corrupt business dealings over the award of housing contracts.

With economic planning kaput, Wilson reverted to ramping up subsidies for the private sector. In opposition, he had condemned the Tories for relying 'on sporadic bribes to private industry' to set up branch plants in the North.[73] All that really changed was that the bribes got bigger. Regional industrial aid rose tenfold, with mixed implications for employment levels. Jeremy Bray, the Labour MP and former ICI man who had captured Middlesbrough West from Macmillan's Tories in 1962, complained, 'On Teesside which I know best, many millions of pounds of public funds have been poured into the development of capital-intensive industry without increasing employment. At the same time higher education, lighter industry and service employment were neglected, leaving an unbalanced and unstable local economy.'[74] To rebut this line of criticism, Labour introduced a direct labour subsidy, the Regional Employment Premium, shaving about 8 per cent off manufacturers' payroll costs in assisted areas. The party also ventured where Macmillan had feared to tread, extending distribution-of-industry controls to office-block developments, though most of the white-collar jobs dispersed from central London continued merely to fetch up on the fringes of the metropolitan area.

Despite these policy departures, regional aid represented only a tenth of expenditure on industrial subsidies, the bulk of state support going on tax incentives for manufacturing employment regardless of location, with a premium for jobs connected to scientific research.[75] What most engaged Labour's attention were corporate mergers and acquisitions, through which it hoped to see the emergence of internationally competitive entities – 'national champions'. In reality, when London conglomerates snapped up their provincial rivals they simply converted the newly acquired factories into storage depots or closed them down altogether.[76] The government's Industrial Redevelopment Corporation bolted together the two major British-owned auto firms, Lancashire's Leyland Motors and the British Motor Corporation of Long-bridge, Birmingham, to create one of the signature lame-duck firms of the seventies. Meanwhile the cotton industry was gobbled up by multi-fibre producers Courtaulds and ICI. At the end of 1968, cotton ceased to be traded in Manchester's Royal Exchange. 'There are fewer traders, and fewer kinds of traders, to whom membership of the Exchange could be an advantage,' reported the *Guardian*, 'and it had been clear for some time that a much smaller marketplace would be adequate.'[77]

Like Macmillan's Conservatives, Labour under Wilson also used regional policy to cushion the effects of a government rundown of the coal industry. Wilson believed that greater emphasis on nuclear technology bolstered Britain's status as a Great Power. An accelerated programme of colliery closures would also demonstrate the party's willingness to take tough decisions in the national interest, counselled George Brown.[78] Minister of Power Richard Marsh, later to switch his allegiance to Thatcher's Conservatives, told the Commons that the country couldn't afford to deny itself the advantage of cheap alternative fuels. 'The Marsh statement was really devastating, since it meant that literally scores of pits would be closed down in a year of high recession and unemployment,' observed Richard Crossman, leader of the House. But NUM president Sidney Ford, a right-wing Labour loyalist, warned his members against rocking the boat, so Wilson was secure in the knowledge that coalfield MPs weren't likely to contest the rundown. Crossman arranged a late-night sitting of the Commons to allow them to vent their spleen. 'It is clear that provided they can make their protest these miners felt that they were bound to support the government in an action which really meant the destruction of the mining industry,' Crossman confided to his diary.

> What these miners' MPs showed was a not very edifying loyalty, because people should not be as loyal as that to a government which is causing the total ruin of their industry. As the night went on I was pleased that they were so pleased to have me there but I was also shocked by their pathetic lack of fight.[79]

Wilson bought off resistance through enhanced pay-offs and aid packages for pit villages deprived of their livelihoods. 'Experience has shown that we shall obtain a more reasonable settlement from Labour than from a Tory administration', judged the NUM high command.[80] Under Labour, the number of miners in the North East and Cumbria fell by half, producing a net loss of overall regional employment of 14,000 jobs.[81] By the time coalfield discontent bubbled over, it was Edward Heath who reaped the consequences.

For all his bluster, Wilson proved a conventional prime minister. In his own retrospective gloss: 'As a government, we were ready to sacrifice a great deal in political terms to put sterling on a sound foundation, honoured and respected.'[82] Like Macmillan, he held his party's vote in the North steady by means of side payments to the party faithful: encouraging private-sector manufacturers to site overspill plant in the regions, and introducing statutory redundancy pay for workers displaced by industrial decline. Government policy accomplished no more than this. Promises of a more balanced distribution of industry are belied by the facts. In the course of the fifties and sixties, the North's share of national output fell from 28 to 25 per cent while that of London and the South East increased from 34 to 36 per cent – the gap between them virtually doubling.[83] In relative terms, the North didn't even tread water during the 'golden age of capitalism'. When the going got rougher in the seventies and eighties, its industrial economy would be forced below the waterline, never to re-emerge.

7

Freedom of the City

Five days into 1972, a peak year as it turned out for industrial militancy, workers at Fisher Bendix, a factory making domestic appliances on Merseyside's sprawling Kirkby industrial estate, stormed the administration building and invited senior executives assembled in the boardroom to leave the premises. Fisher Bendix was under new management, they announced. Parent company Thorn Electrical, headquartered in a handsome London office tower on Upper St Martin's Lane near Covent Garden, intended to close the unprofitable plant, only recently acquired, with the loss of 700 jobs. Trade-union convenor Jack Spriggs of the amalgamated engineers told the press, 'We will continue the occupation until something is done about protecting the jobs of all the people employed here.'[1]

Fisher Bendix was a product of Harold Macmillan's panicked efforts to disperse new jobs in the auto industry to areas of relatively high unemployment. The British Motor Corporation of Longbridge, Birmingham, which had a side interest in household consumer durables, agreed in 1960 to expand into a government-built facility at Kirkby on the eastern fringes of Liverpool, where overspill council estates clustered around a former Second World War munitions complex. But the large plant never generated sufficient throughput to cover its overheads. Depressed consumer demand attributable to the Wilson government's economic policies didn't help. The management was stand-offish; the shop floor recalcitrant. 'Over a period of time', complained Spriggs, 'it's been a stamping ground for people just to go down to sit in the boardroom drinking scotch and not care what happens in the factory.'[2] BMC offloaded the business in 1968. Three years later it was picked up by Thorn, purveyor of brands such as Kenwood and Tricity, who carried through an existing plan to outsource production of spin driers to Franco's Spain, leaving the Kirkby factory without a future.

The threatened workers took soundings from factory occupiers north of the border, at Upper Clyde Shipbuilders and Plessey electronics in Dumbarton, about ways to thwart Thorn's closure plans. 'We decided that the UCS-type operation of a work-in was impracticable for us,' explained Spriggs. 'Plessey's was more effective. A work-in involves problems of supply to keep production going, sales of products and payment of workers. At Plessey's a strike-in is tying up the movement of machinery, breaking the company's contracts and causing widespread disruption – it is a more effective weapon.'[3] They impounded the spare parts needed to service Fisher Bendix customers and threw open the factory to the press, to heap public-relations pressure on Thorn and constituency MP Harold Wilson, still leading Labour from the opposition benches.

Desperate to be rid of Kirkby, Thorn sold the factory from under the feet of its workforce to an obscure real-estate company, International Property Development Ltd (IPD), through a series of tax-haven transactions which netted around £1 million for financier Ivor Gershfield. 'Once his business was done', quipped the *Liverpool Free Press*, 'Mr Gershfield went home to the Alpine health resort of Crans-sur-Sierre, where his condition has been described as "extremely comfortable".'[4] Wilson, however, stepped in to broker an arrangement whereby the manufacture of radiators and storage heaters would remain at Kirkby under IPD's control until at least the end of 1973. Spriggs and his supporters had gained their point, after a sit-in lasting twenty-five days. Something *was* done to protect employment, though it proved only a temporary fix.

As these events unfolded, the number of UK unemployed topped one million for the first time since Attlee's 1947 sterling crisis. All the conurbations had begun to leak jobs in the sixties as the locus of manufacturing activity shifted to roomier premises in outlying settlements, stranding the blue-collar inhabitants of inner boroughs. The *Economist* lamented how London had become 'a disaster area losing 100,000 people a year (mainly skilled workers), where more businesses fail than manage to get out in time, and pockets of unemployment are as severe as in the depressed areas'.[5] The industrial exodus from the big cities was then superseded by a broader crisis of British manufacturing, uncompetitive in most product lines in an overstocked world market. Mass redundancies generated by the collapse of the long post-war boom came on top of existing regional disparities, so that the unemployment rate was three times as high in the North East and Cumbria (7 per cent) as in the South East (2 per cent). 'The whole country is sinking while the South East is just beginning to get its feet wet. In the North West and in other areas they are already well aswim,' commented a Conservative MP for Manchester as the economic crisis intensified.[6] The trend toward ever-larger container ships cost the narrow Manchester Ship Canal most of its business, with knock-on effects on Trafford Park, where activity tailed off rapidly.

National manufacturing employment dropped by a tenth in the course of the seventies. Those economic sectors still growing – clerical, retail, some light industry, schools, hospitals and local government, as well as part-time occupations – were not like-for-like replacements for heavy-industrial work and tended to draw new entrants into the labour market. A fall in male activity rates ensured that dole queues continued to lengthen. Chief beneficiaries of the urban–rural shift, and likeliest survivors of the decimation of the productive sector, were greenfield regions bordering England's south-eastern heartland. The South West, East Anglia and the East Midlands not only put on service-sector jobs at the fastest rates but also recorded modest manufacturing employment gains, bucking the downward trend.[7]

How would Edward Heath's Tories react to the gathering storm? Like his Labour predecessor, Heath came to office with direct experience of the regional-policy portfolio. As Secretary of State for Industry, Trade and Regional Development in the Douglas-Home administration, he had laid the groundwork for major house-building projects in the South East, his home region, assuring colleagues that 'the arrangements to be made for this purpose would not diminish the priority which the government had already accorded to the development of central Scotland and the North East region of England'. According to the Cabinet minutes, ministers found his draft White Paper 'not wholly convincing' on this point.[8]

A policy review conducted by Heath prior to the 1970 general election concluded that a vigorous regional policy was 'politically essential'.[9] One-fifth of Tory MPs were voted in by northern constituencies and Heath wouldn't have enjoyed a Commons majority without them. But he was convinced that there was fat to trim from Labour's subsidy regime. His government promptly reduced the differential on investment incentives in assisted areas; replaced regional grants with tax allowances only of use to profitable firms; phased out Wilson's payroll subsidy, the Regional Employment Premium; and relaxed location controls over factories and offices. New office space in central London was soon being added at twice the previous rate.[10]

Upon running into trouble over rising jobless figures, however, early in 1971, Chancellor Anthony Barber was prepared to concede that 'to a considerable extent the problem of unemployment is a problem of balance between the regions.' To fend off a Labour motion of no confidence in the government's industrial policy, he conferred special development area status – conceived by Labour to placate mining communities devastated by its pit closures – to Tyneside and Wearside and more of South Wales.[11] A year later, amidst a programme of general economic reflation, and to jeers from the Labour benches, he reintroduced regional investment grants for industrial modernisation without strings attached as regards job creation. An intermediate form of assisted-area status was created to placate opinion in previously overlooked towns and cities such as Sheffield, where the Tories briefly held municipal control in the late sixties. The whole of northern England, Scotland and Wales was now eligible for special assistance at one level of need or another.

Barber was the Oxford-educated son of a Doncaster company director, and sat for Altrincham and Sale in the Greater Manchester commuter belt. While preparing his March 1972 budget, he was buffeted by news that the country's largest machine-tool producer, Alfred Herbert, was closing its Altrincham works and would retreat to its Coventry base in response to tumbling sales. Shop stewards in Altrincham protested about 'the plundering of North West industry', to no avail.[12] Shaking off that local difficulty, the Chancellor assured the Commons that his budget would enhance the competitiveness of British firms as the country entered the European Economic Community and mount 'a new and intensified assault on the deep-seated problem of regional imbalance, which involves so much hardship and waste of resources'.[13]

The former objective took priority. For as in the Wilson years, general state aid to British industry put dedicated regional-policy measures in the shade. Public subsidies for industrial innovation were targeted at southern regions which accounted for two-thirds of jobs in research and development. The M4 corridor between London and Bristol, 'Britain's California within the Home Counties', saw new ventures in computing and microchip design, building on older specialisms in electronics and precision engineering.[14] Barber had no intention of emulating Macmillan by despatching a corporate cavalry from the South East to keep Merseyside and other depressed areas busy with branch-plant work. The number of manufacturers looking to move or expand their operations into assisted areas dwindled in the economic gloom.[15] Instead he further eased location controls over new factories. The system of office-development permits was retained solely for the purpose of distributing new floor space *within* the South East in ways that chimed with an updated strategic plan for the region.

In London itself, manufacturing decline met financial resurgence. Barber lifted lending restrictions on the banks, which devoted themselves to a furious bout of speculation in stocks and real estate. A White Paper on industrial and regional development assured the City that the Conservatives would take special account 'of the importance of enhancing the prospects of London as an international financial and commercial centre'.[16] Mergers and acquisitions had by now yielded an upper tier of blue-chip industrial outfits big enough to avail themselves of its markets and services. But the interpenetration of large-scale financial and industrial capital didn't so much reorient the City towards the home economy as distract manufacturers away from it. Geoffrey Ingham would shortly note that British multinationals had 'begun to rely more on their overseas operations, and are less concerned with the contraction of the domestic industrial base'.[17] Insulated from the travails of the domestic industrial sector, the Square Mile even turned to good account the OPEC price shock that poleaxed much of the global economy, recycling the petrodollars amassed by oil-rich states.

Less than a fortnight before Britain joined the Common Market on 1 January 1973, the Heath Cabinet signed off on a ten-year development strategy for the state-owned steel industry to improve its international competitiveness. Bulk production would be concentrated at half a dozen sites including a new complex at Redcar on Teesside. The strategy imperilled the Consett steelworks in County Durham. 'Consett is very isolated and already seriously affected by closures in the Durham coalfield,' Employment Secretary Maurice Macmillan, son of the former prime minister, warned his colleagues. 'The jobs at risk amount to 24 per cent of male employment in the area. A steel closure at Consett would represent a miniature social disaster, given the problems of nearby Tyneside and Teesside.'[18] Industry Secretary Peter Walker, a millionaire businessman, steadied Cabinet nerves by pointing out that the British Steel Corporation had dispensed with 20,000 steelworkers in Yorkshire 'without serious industrial unrest or widespread hardship'.[19]

Such managerial insouciance would eventually be dispelled even in the steel sector, where the unions were far from militant. It had no place at all in the coal industry. The first national coal strike since 1926 was largely an after-effect of Wilson-era policies: the gathering pace of colliery closures; declining pay relative to other industrial workers; and the introduction of a uniform wages structure, which supplied a countrywide platform for industrial action. The miners went into battle in 1972 under the generalship of NUM president Joe Gormley, an unlikely figure to lead a working-class insurgency. He hailed from a pit village halfway between Wigan and St Helens. Authoritarian by instinct, he was completely out of sympathy with 'the so-called militants, the fighters for this, that and the other', and confessed that 'even as a democratic socialist, I have a feeling that sometimes you can choke on democracy.'[20] He tried to become a Labour parliamentary candidate in 1959 but Burnley wouldn't have him on account of his hostility to CND, so he threw himself back into mining politics instead. The Lancashire coalfield was gutted in the course of the sixties from a workforce of 38,000 to less than 13,000. Gormley maintained that it wasn't for the union to determine the size of the industry, only to fight for the best wages and conditions for those miners who survived the cull. 'Our role in society is to look after our members, not run the country,' he argued.[21] But Gormley won the NUM presidency because he pledged tough action to reverse his members' slide down the industrial wages league. He *had* to take the fight to the National Coal Board, not least to find a safe outlet for militant energies within his union.

At the time of the General Strike, South Wales had been both the largest coalfield and the most radical. These epaulettes now belonged to Yorkshire, an efficient, low-cost inland coalfield accounting for over a quarter of national manpower and output. Barnsley left-winger Arthur Scargill stressed 'the tremendous power of the Yorkshire coalfield in relation to the national picture'. Yorkshire had done badly out of the national wages agreement and growing rank-and-file frustration enabled the left to gain control of the district union in the course of unofficial stoppages involving extensive use of mobile, 'flying' pickets. Scargill, responsible for picketing operations in south Yorkshire, delivered the *coup de grâce* to the Tories in Gormley's national strike when with the help of Birmingham engineering workers he forced the closure of a strategic fuel depot. 'We had to declare war on them,' Scargill explained, 'and the only way you could declare war was to attack the vulnerable points. They were the points of energy: the power stations, the coke depots, the coal depots, the points of supply.'[22] News that the battle of Saltley had been lost shattered Heath's confidence, only the fig leaf of a court of inquiry concealing capitulation to the miners' demands.

When Gormley looked for further gains in 1973–4 as the quadrupling of world oil prices put coal burning back into the commercial frame, he brought down a government without in the least meaning to – such was the forward momentum of the country's leading trade union in these heady days. He blamed Heath for boxing himself into a corner: 'As I had said all along, it was *not* a political dispute but an industrial one, and if the government had taken it upon themselves to interfere with normal negotiating machinery, forcing us to deal directly with them – well, that was their decision, not ours.' Heath dismissed the idea of trying to sit out a second national stoppage, fearing a run on the pound.[23] Instead he called a general election on the question 'who governs?', which he narrowly lost. It was a remarkable victory for the industrial ranks of Outer Britain. Senior Tory Reginald Maudling despaired that 'organised labour has the power to bring our economy to a halt and this power cannot be taken away from them.'[24] Unless, of course, one was prepared to dismantle the coal industry in Yorkshire, the North East and its other strongholds in order to destroy its trade union: the policy that future Conservative governments were to pursue.

A consumption boost resulting from the rising wages of coal miners and other manual workers helped to slow the deterioration of the North East economy relative to other regions. Its jobless rate fell from 172 per cent to 128 per cent of the UK average between 1974 and 1976 despite a rise in the number of people unemployed, because other parts of the country had also begun to feel the chill of deindustrialisation. Other factors rendering the North East less of an outlier were an above-average increase in public-sector employment linked to local-government and health-service reorganisations, a relatively small loss of mining jobs on an already much-reduced coalfield, and the lack of direct exposure to the deepening crisis in the auto trade.[25]

How long would this narrowing of regional disparities last? The economic reflation set in motion by Barber continued for a brief time under his Labour successor, Denis Healey. Scraping back into Downing Street on 4 March 1974, Wilson and Healey settled the miners' dispute and signed off a National Coal Board plan for major capital spending to reverse a contraction of the industry for which his previous administration had been largely culpable. Colliery closures in high-cost areas would be more than counterbalanced by fresh capacity in new or upgraded pits, Yorkshire gaining the massive Selby complex. Gormley swung his members behind the government's incomes policy and sponsored a return to local pay negotiations on incentive schemes which broke the NUM's fledgling unity on wages issues. As working-class unrest surged in virtually every other economic sector, the coalfields under ironclad Gormley went quiet.

Labour's left-wing National Executive Committee had signed up a wholly unenthusiastic leadership to an extension of state industrial control through planning agreements and nationalisation intended to achieve, among other things, 'decisive progress in eliminating regional disparities'.[26] The shipbuilding sector, brought to the point of collapse by global overcapacity and soaring oil prices, was one of the few areas in which Wilson was prepared to countenance an extension of public ownership. The new public corporation, British Shipbuilders, was officially headquartered in the North East, but senior figures enjoyed the use of an office in Knightsbridge and a private jet to shuttle them upcountry. Wilson was otherwise scornful of the idea of capturing the commanding heights of the British economy for socialism. His fall-back position, as far as regional policy went, was once again to increase industrial subsidies. The Regional Employment Premium was reprieved and its real-terms value restored. Expenditure on regional policy briefly exceeded the level of the late sixties. Industry Secretary Tony Benn tightened factory-location controls, granted special development area status to Merseyside and hit the pause button on steel closures. One of his deputies, Lord Beswick, intimated to steelworkers in Hartlepool that the town's threatened works, officially given only a two-year stay of execution, might not have to close at all.[27]

This expansionist posture was soon reversed. Overloaded by national economic problems – prices and wages soaring, corporate profitability falling, financial-market pressure intensifying – both the Labour government and Conservative opposition broke away from their formal commitments to full employment and a balanced distribution of industry. It turned out that sound money and an open market economy mattered more than the well-being of industrial communities. They probably always had, indeed the stop–go sterling crises of the fifties and sixties suggest as much, but rising prosperity previously kept the edge off the dilemma.

Criticism of regional industrial assistance had been bubbling away for years in banking-sector periodicals, think tanks and the Conservative right. 'Must we always take work to the workers?' despaired a couple of Newcastle economists in *Lloyds Bank Review* in 1964. 'To aim at steady inter-regional development may involve the old choice of having to sacrifice growth for stability,' they warned, no longer willing to accept such a trade-off. In the same year, Enoch Powell described regional policy as being in 'essential conflict with our party's belief in a free economy'. He urged greater reliance on market pressure to drag people to where work was more likely to be had.[28] The reproaches became more pointed in the seventies as the wider economy deteriorated. 'Regional policy for ever?' despaired the Institute for Economic Affairs, while UCL geographer Gerald Manners assured readers of the *Three Banks Review* that there was a 'growing realisation that the problem of unemployment, and the associated defects of the national, of regional and of local labour markets, cannot be solved by resort to the printing press and deficit finance'.[29]

Certainly this became the settled conviction of Labour Chancellor Denis Healey. One of the party's more remarkable figures, a man of culture and yet brusque and bullying, to this day he is feted by Establishment commentators for his economic 'realism' because he held the pass against Bennite industrial interventionists while allowing liberals and monetarists through the gates. Born in Kent, he moved north at the age of five when his father – a second-generation Irish immigrant whose politics, according to Denis, were limited to a romantic Irish nationalism – became principal of Keighley technical school. Like Wilson, therefore, Denis proceeded from Yorkshire grammar-school beginnings to an Oxford scholarship. But whereas Wilson's politics were tepid and parochial, Healey possessed fierce ideological views based on a reading of the international situation. He started out aggressively left-wing before swinging to the right with equal belligerence. At Oxford in the late thirties he joined the Communists – the only party, he explained, which 'seemed unambiguously against Hitler' – only to leave after the Nazi–Soviet pact and the fall of France. He fought in Italy, shared in the Labour-leaning camaraderie of the forces and was adopted as the Labour candidate for Pudsey and Otley, a safe Tory seat in west Yorkshire. Still in army fatigues, he urged the 1945 Labour conference 'to protect, assist, encourage and aid in every way' socialist movements in liberated Europe, then under threat from 'the armoured cars of Tory imperialism and counter-revolution'.[30] Churchill's crackdown on Greek communist partisans had just tilted the political balance in the Aegean from hard left to hard right.

The rapid division of Europe into rival Cold War camps caused Healey, without a moment's hesitation, to ditch hopes of 'third force' socialist autonomy for unswerving devotion to the American cause. In his memoirs he confessed, 'Like most Western observers at this time, I believed that Stalin's behaviour showed he was bent on the military conquest of western Europe. I now think we were all mistaken.' Appointed Labour's International Secretary, he channelled anti-communist propaganda from a covert Foreign Office unit to amenable Continental socialists.[31] His best friend was a US diplomat stationed in London. Wilson alleged that some of Healey's acquaintances 'took him in hand [and] sent him to the Rand Corporation of America, where he was brainwashed and came back very right-wing'.[32] This was evidently not a problem for Wilson, who would entrust his fellow Yorkshireman with key governmental positions.

Healey won a parliamentary seat in a 1952 by-election. Biographer Edward Pearce emphasises the size and vitality of the local Labour Party organisation in Leeds East, which made the constituency invulnerable to hard-left infiltration – what Pearce prefers to call, with a trenchancy Healey at least would have admired, 'a bedsitter infestation'.[33] The electoral ballast was provided by faithful Labour-supporting council estates such as Gipton and Seacroft. Healey would comfortably retain the seat until his elevation to the House of Lords forty years later, by which point the hostility he had voiced in 1945 toward a 'selfish, depraved, dissolute and decadent' upper class had presumably somewhat mellowed.[34] Despite this solid electoral base in his adopted northern county, Healey shared with Portsmouth-born Callaghan a taste for the southern pastoral, eventually buying a house near the South Downs big enough, he explained, to accommodate an extensive library and a grand piano.

A reliable Atlantic man, Healey served as Defence Secretary from 1964 to 1970 while Labour pursued colonial wars in Aden and Borneo. Ultimately obliged by the weakness of the domestic economy to cut back on military deployments east of Suez, he and Wilson ensured that the British nuclear-weapons programme survived this period of reluctant imperial retreat. He took the finance brief in 1972 while Labour was in opposition and entertained the rank and file with talk of squeezing property speculators until the pips squeaked. 'It was all high-class Healey Beelzebub,' says Pearce indulgently, 'but not a prelude to the guillotine in Trafalgar Square'. Corporate taxes went up when Healey took over the Treasury, only to come down again after howls of protest from industry and the City. Healey later boasted that British companies were 'the most lightly taxed in the developed world'.[35]

Loath to balance the books by soaking the rich, Healey found that a rising public-sector borrowing requirement exposed him to the adverse opinion of City markets and international creditors. He quickly tired of trying to counter the effects of the world-economic recession through Keynesian deficit financing. But a scapegoat was required for the government's worsening financial difficulties. In a speech at East Leeds Labour Club on 10 January 1975 he rounded on the trade unions, switching the blame for unemployment from weak aggregate demand to inflationary wage pressure. *The Times*'s economics editor Peter Jay, son of Labour minister Douglas Jay, hailed it as 'the most controversial inversion of post-1944 conventional economic vision about the management of the economy.'[36] Healey proceeded to impose cash limits on public expenditure – 'a noose round everybody's neck', commented Tony Benn after lunch with a senior Treasury official – in part to rein in the wage ambitions of Britain's expanded public-sector workforce.[37]

But the financial-market pressure didn't abate. A run on the pound got under way shortly before Wilson announced his retirement on 16 March 1976. Oil-producing states previously content to bank in UK currency began to ditch their sterling receipts. Trouble spread to the gilt markets as investors declined to finance government borrowing. What to do? The Labour left clamoured for selective import and capital controls: a siege economy to create room for national economic reflation. The Bank of England and the City, on the other hand, wanted further spending reductions to appease the markets. So did the Treasury, which once again sharpened the axe of austerity by exaggerating the size of the public-sector borrowing requirement. On 22 July Healey stripped £1 billion out of public expenditure for the coming financial year. The Regional Employment Premium would be cut, along with capital investment in the nationalised industries. Still it wasn't enough, and during negotiations with the Washington-based International Monetary Fund over a record-breaking loan to stabilise sterling, ministers returned to the Heathite question of how to save money on regional subsidies: should they abolish the Regional Employment Premium, restrict eligibility to investment grants or shrink the geographical extent of the assisted areas? The new prime minister, Callaghan, was firmly on the right of the party and had only narrowly missed out on the top job at the IMF a few years earlier. According to the Cabinet minutes, 'he was not personally wedded to all the expenditure in aid of regional policy, and was prepared to believe that over time its value reduced. Nevertheless it would be very difficult simply to abolish it; the need was to wean the public gradually away from it.'[38] Well in advance of Thatcher's arrival, regional assistance was already associated in Whitehall with a dependency culture.

Deficit hawks made inroads into public opinion even in the North East and Cumbria, where 40 per cent of regional service-sector employment was in education, health or public administration. On 4 November, Labour lost Workington for the first time since the constituency was created in 1918. It fell to a thirty-five-year-old Conservative company director from Guildford whose pitch to voters was that 'the right approach to Britain's problems is to stop spending and borrowing now. Public expenditure must be cut. There is no choice.' Similar voices were raised in Leeds. According to Healey, 'my own constituency party, which I had found far to the left of me on almost everything, voted by a large majority in favour of lower taxes rather than higher spending.' Opinion in west Yorkshire was far from unanimous, however. The

Leeds Weekly Citizen warned that capitulation to the IMF 'will be tantamount to a rout for the Labour party' and called for the Chancellor to be dismissed.[39]

But Callaghan was determined to allow Healey to finish what he had started. In return for IMF assistance, on 15 December the Chancellor outlined to MPs another package of cuts totalling £2.5 billion over two years. 'The backbenchers behind him showed that they knew he had abandoned, on the bidding of the IMF, the socialism in which they had marched to victory at the polls and that they were listening to budget measures of the kind that the opposition had been advocating', commented *The Times*.[40] The Regional Employment Premium was summarily abolished. It was the least cost-effective job-creation measure in the regional-policy toolkit, but its withdrawal was nevertheless expected to deprive the Development Areas of up to 45,000 manufacturing over four years.[41] Some of the £320 million saved went towards a new Selective Investment Scheme favouring southern and eastern regions, which also benefited from a further loosening of location controls. Environment Secretary Peter Shore green-lighted speculative office development to revive London's commercial-property market, while the dispersal of government jobs to the provinces ran into the sands amid civil-service opposition. A White Paper tentatively setting out options for some measure of devolution to the English regions warned that 'any proposals for a regional structure would have to take account of the dominance of the South East in relation to the rest of England, and of London over the rest of the South East.'[42] As far as the Callaghan government was concerned, the possibility of challenging these hierarchies no longer existed.

The IMF episode had seen a financial crisis resolved on City terms at the cost of a lingering recession in Outer Britain. The British Steel Corporation (BSC), loaded with additional losses by the Treasury through a change to its financing arrangements, now pushed ahead with plant closures. BSC announced the suspension of steelmaking at Hartlepool's South Works on 1 December 1977, then bought off shop-floor opposition to a permanent shutdown through enhanced redundancy payments. 'No other country would close it down,' despaired Bill Sirs, the Hartlepool-born general secretary of the Iron and Steel Trades Confederation.[43] Any optimism

generated by the earlier narrowing of regional economic disparities had to be put on ice. The Tyne, Wear and Tees entered the
1980s almost as far away from national norms as they had been
a decade earlier.[44] But at least Healey was happy. Enforcing the
worst spending squeeze since the Second World War burnished his
credentials within the policy-making fraternity. 'Even the British
correspondents described me as "walking on water",' he fondly
recalled of his appearance at the IMF's annual conference. 'My
own international reputation was secure.'[45] For a vainglorious
Labour figure so attuned to the balance of power in world politics,
nothing could be more important.

Wilson and Callaghan were just as porous in their dealings with
the rich and powerful. At Callaghan's request, his predecessor at
Number 10 headed an inquiry into the workings of London's
financial institutions: a device to ward off pressure from the
Labour left for nationalisation in this most sensitive area of international capital. Wilson had been delighted to receive the Freedom
of the City of London, 'which he did not feel at all inappropriate
to a Labour leader', recounts official biographer Philip Ziegler. His
review ruled against a significant overhaul of the financial sector.
'Some of his best friends were bankers,' Ziegler explains. 'By the
time of his retirement he felt that there was more that deserved to
be preserved than to be destroyed in the present system.'[46] Between
them, these Labour men defended the freedom of the City against
left-wingers within their own party in a period of working-class
militancy to rival anything seen since the twenties.

How were Merseyside's Fisher Bendix workers faring, all this
time? The property-development outfit Wilson had helped to
install in Kirkby was fronted by Harold King, a thirty-something
Liverpudlian soft-drinks entrepreneur whose major innovation
was to introduce a fruit-juice product line into a works otherwise
concerned with the manufacture of radiators and storage heaters.
Unsurprisingly he failed to turn the business around. When Tony
Benn at the Department of Industry declined to provide a stop-
gap loan, King suggested that he nationalise the factory instead,
hoping to get a good price. Instead Benn invited the shop stewards
to come up with their own solution to save the plant. He cited the

example of Triumph motorbike workers in Solihull who had successfully pitched the idea of converting their factory, also slated for closure, into a workers' cooperative.

The impetus for the Kirkby Manufacturing and Engineering (KME) cooperative thus came from West Midland manufacturing via the Labour front bench. 'No one would take us on,' said convenor Jack Spriggs. 'It was nice to become part of history, but it was Hobson's choice.'[47] Spriggs hastily worked up an application for selective financial assistance under Edward Heath's 1972 Industry Act in order to get the co-op off the ground: hardly the purpose for which the Tory legislation had been intended. To a chorus of disapproval from business, the City, Fleet Street and his own civil servants, Benn agreed to provide the requested £3.9 million. It was only a fraction of the bail-out funds thrown at the City that year to rescue banks caught up in a commercial-property crash.[48] Nevertheless, it marked a potential new departure in Whitehall industrial policy. A factory originally laid on by a Conservative government for the convenience of a private-sector conglomerate would now bear witness to an experiment in industrial self-management. Aghast, Tory industry spokesman Michael Heseltine, not yet ready to assume the mantle of saviour of Merseyside, damned the scheme as an irresponsible concession to militancy which would only encourage other workers 'to follow these illegal precedents'.[49] Wilson had no more truck with Bennite workerism than did the Conservatives, but he was implicated in the IPD failure and anxious to put off more redundancies in his political backyard.

The new workers' cooperative, the largest in the country, commenced trading on 15 January 1975. Effective control at KME lay with two worker-directors, Spriggs and his TGWU counterpart Dick Jenkins. They were reluctant to rationalise if it meant shedding the jobs that the co-op had been formed to save. Having underbid to Benn on account of pressure from hostile civil servants, they were never going to get out of the red without additional support. Further assistance, however, was not easy to come by. Their Whitehall patrons were scattered to the four winds. Benn was reshuffled after the Common Market referendum on 5 June, replaced by right-winger Eric Varley. Wilson departed the following year. His successor had no truck with left-field business models and fewer ties to the Merseyside area. An unnamed minister told the *Sunday Times*, 'Anti-Bennery is a favourite sport in Whitehall these days and there is uniform hostility to KME.'[50] The Cabinet did grant KME another £860,000 in April 1977 since, according to Benn, 'they could not risk killing it off in the middle of the pay negotiations with the TUC.'[51] Beyond that, the Kirkby pioneers were on their own.

After losing £1.5 million in the course of 1977, Spriggs and Jenkins hired management consultants favoured by Whitehall to draw up a turnaround plan. In spite of its difficulties, KME had cornered 10 per cent of the domestic radiator market and the consultants were confident that with strengthened management and fresh investment it could yet turn a profit. On this basis, the directors applied for £2.9 million from the Department for Industry to implement a rescue package. The application came before the Cabinet on 11 May 1978. 'It was a most unpleasant discussion,' Benn recorded in his diary. 'Jim interrupted every speaker, basically to deny that Merseyside was a disaster area.'[52] But Merseyside plainly *was* a disaster area, with thousands of redundancies announced at the branch plants of Bird's Eye, Courtaulds, General Electric, Lucas Aerospace, Meccano and Plessey, and on the waterfront at Cammell Laird and Western Ship Repairers. The Mersey docks had been left stranded by the shift in UK trade from the Commonwealth to Europe, to which Heath had added the spur of Common Market membership. Before the UK joined the Six, Liverpool enjoyed a bigger share of imports and exports (10 and 14 per cent respectively) than Dover and Felixstowe combined. By the early eighties, Dover and Felixstowe commanded 21 per cent of imports and 19 per cent of exports, and Liverpool's shares had dropped to 3 and 5 per cent.[53]

Industry secretary Eric Varley wanted to pull the plug on KME despite 'the admittedly powerful social arguments that the government could not allow a further 645 redundancies in an area where unemployment was already in the region of 20 per cent'. Plenty of businesses were going to the wall on Merseyside without attracting a state rescue. Amidst such an avalanche, a few hundred additional job losses wouldn't be too embarrassing. Employment

Secretary Albert Booth, leftish MP for Barrow, retorted that the government 'had to decide whether it was better to spend money on keeping workers unemployed or on maintaining them in productive jobs'. The cost to the Exchequer would be much the same either way, an irony even Varley acknowledged. Callaghan was in the middle of watering down a draft White Paper on industrial democracy, not to mention administering the austerity programme that Healey had agreed with the IMF. The discussion found him in full tough-guy mode. 'To give more help would be to take the soft option,' whereas his administration didn't shy away from taking 'very difficult and harsh economic decisions'.[54]

Industrial unrest had created an aura around Liverpool, Callaghan complained. Heavily engaged in three massively strike-prone sectors – car manufacture, shipbuilding and dock work – the city had been a thorn in the side of successive Whitehall administrations. Stevedores battling containerisation were first in the firing line of Heath's short-lived National Industrial Relations Court. Walkouts on the waterfront and at Ford had earlier attracted Wilson's ire. Speaking in his Huyton constituency in 1969, the year of his abortive 'In Place of Strife' proposals to curb union power, Wilson bemoaned 'strike after strike frustrating the effort of government; signalling the question mark to those industrialists who are attracted to the inducements and are considering establishing themselves here'.[55] Callaghan authorised the state-owned British Leyland to shut its car-assembly factory at Speke, Liverpool's other main industrial suburb, and move production of its TR7 sports car to Coventry. *The Times* suggested that the British Leyland closure, coming after a seventeen-week strike at the plant, was *pour encourager les autres*.[56] Coventry in fact had an even higher strike rate than Liverpool, but manufacturers had never been enthusiastic about setting up shop on Merseyside, and as shop-floor tensions rose, they headed for the exit.[57] The British Leyland factory was doomed and so, it seemed, was KME. The Cabinet resolved that no further financial assistance was to be made available.

Trouble was brewing within Merseyside Labour, however. After a period of relative calm on the industrial-relations front, members from Wavertree were about to overturn Callaghan's

5 per cent pay policy at the 1978 party conference in Blackpool. TGWU delegates had already slipped the leash, voting for a return to unfettered collective bargaining. General secretary Jack Jones, a former teenage shop steward on Liverpool's waterfront, maintained that he 'never doubted' the utility of the social contract, even as it degenerated into a straightforward wage-dampening device. It was in workers' interests to maintain the Labour administration, despite its obvious 'lack of socialist outlook'. Jones was concerned about a backlash from the financial markets, as well as from voters, should the unions bring the government down: 'In the end I felt we should not take the risk of a catastrophic run on the pound and a general election.'[58]

To avoid another bust-up with his party, Callaghan put the Kirkby cooperative on life support and appointed Professor Douglas Hague of the Manchester Business School – soon to become a Downing Street adviser to Thatcher – to chair a working party that would decide its fate. Hague recommended that KME surrender its cooperative structure and submit to a private-sector takeover. Although unwilling to invest further in KME as a mutual, the government was prepared to throw money at a private firm to make the co-op go away. This was the final straw for junior industry minister Bob Cryer, a West Riding MP formerly responsible for government policy on cooperatives, who resigned on 20 November. 'Every energy went on handing KME over to private enterprise,' he complained.[59]

KME might just have been prepared to swallow a takeover, but talks with a Midland engineering company collapsed amidst mutual recriminations. The worker-directors made a last-ditch plea for help from Whitehall only to meet another rebuff. Varley's deputy, Alan Williams, visited Kirkby on 11 December to account for the government's position. 'He cut a far from festive figure as he mounted the canteen stage to address the workforce among the Christmas lights and streamers,' reported the *Guardian*. 'In contributions from the floor, Mr Williams was accused of being a Tory and there was loud applause for claims that the government was no longer Labour.'[60]

The obvious alternative to privatisation was for the government to nationalise the plant through its National Enterprise

Board (NEB). Callaghan had set up regional NEBs in Liverpool and Newcastle after a back-bench Labour revolt over devolution to Scotland and Wales. But the NEB had funded only one venture in the Merseyside special development area and wanted nothing to do with the Kirkby cooperative. 'We are not a panacea for all ills,' insisted one official.[61]

At the start of 1979 Dunlop tires – squeezed by low-cost East European competition – selected its Speke plant for closure, making 2,300 workers redundant. Liverpool Garston MP Eddie Loyden cited the closure as 'another example of Merseyside being the cut-off point when rationalisation came along'.[62] That, of course, was one of the problems with regional policy: it supplied branch plants at the price of a loss of corporate control. The biggest manufacturing firms in the North West were all externally controlled: the likes of ICI, Courtalds and GE were headquartered in London, General Motors and Ford in Detroit. In the second half of the seventies, outsider firms shed a quarter of their manual workforce whereas companies with head offices in the region, less quick to cut and run, let go only a tenth.[63]

Despite the crushing news at Dunlop, the Conservative opposition in the Commons demanded that KME call in the receivers forthwith. Callaghan endorsed this position to Tory cheers. He told Parliament, 'The Cabinet believes that to put the cooperative into receivership at present is more likely to preserve the jobs of those concerned and the interests of commercial organisations than to continue putting in money on the present basis.'[64] NatWest took its cue from the politicians, terminating support, and KME fell into liquidation on 27 March. Spriggs told the *Echo*, 'We are terribly upset and cannot believe a government which is supposed to be socialist can take this action. We admit we are not lily white – we have made mistakes, but KME would have made it with more help.' A Labour government formally committed to a radical extension of industrial democracy had just killed off the UK's flagship worker's cooperative. Contrary to the prime ministers' assurances, no jobs were saved. 'The people who are facing the axe have no chance at all of immediate employment,' warned the manager of the Kirkby jobcentre. 'Many will face a very long wait if they wish to be employed in this area. We have nothing new in the jobs line coming in.'[65]

Industry minister Alan Williams pontificated to the *Liverpool Daily Post* that cooperatives should never again be established from what were already sinking ships. Bob Cryer's response was forthright: 'Of course, we would prefer not to have to support a co-operative which started off in crisis,' he told the Commons. 'However, we face an economy which is dominated by private-enterprise capitalism, and in those circumstances private-enterprise capitalists are not likely to give their profitable plums to work-people who want to investigate the possibility of a co-operative endeavour.'[66]

The day after KME collapsed, Labour lost a vote of confidence, triggering the general election that would bring Thatcher to power. Callaghan was politically as dead as the cooperative he had buried, discredited by his Treasury-inspired attempt to hold the unions to another year of wage restraint below the rate of inflation. The 1978–9 strike surge occurred at the peak of national trade-union strength, but membership density in the North was still nearly twice that in the South, and it was appropriate that the 'winter of discontent' should begin on Merseyside, at Ford's Liverpool Halewood plant, opened in 1963 under another of Macmillan's industrial-dispersal deals. Initial cut-price wages at Halewood 'created worse labour relations than at Dagenham' – no small achievement.[67] Voters in Liverpool Edge Hill gave Callaghan a parting blow by handing a by-election win to the Liberals on a 32 per cent swing. The seat had been Labour since 1945. The Liberal winner, deputy council leader David Alton, said he was fighting two Tory candidates, the official Conservative contestant and his Labour counterpart. Redundant Dunlop workers from Speke felt much the same, campaigning against the Labour man.[68]

The Fisher Bendix/KME story could stand for the seventies in miniature: spare capacity and a crisis of profitability at the end point of the post-war boom; the outsourcing of production to low-wage, anti-trade-union economies; corporate retrenchment versus working-class militancy; financial chicanery; rising unemployment; and the squelching by a right-wing Labour leadership of grass-roots pressure for workers' control and an alternative economic strategy. All things considered, these processes represented a thorough softening-up exercise for the destruction of the Thatcher years.

8

———

Enemy Damage

A new regional journal, *Southern History*, appeared in 1979 just as the long economic downturn brought Thatcher to power in Whitehall. Editor John Lowerson, a historian of the leisure pursuits of the English middle classes, hailed from a Doncaster mining village and had studied at the University of Leeds during *Northern History*'s gestation period. However, his academic career swiftly removed him from this Yorkshire milieu. He taught in Lincoln and Northampton before finding a congenial berth at Sussex University, where he stayed until retirement. Immersion in the culture and society of the South Downs not only elicited from him a history of the county of Sussex but also nurtured a grievance that southern England had 'been treated as a pale shadow of the other regions, despite its earlier social, economic and political predominance and its return to that state after the comparatively short-lived shift in gravity produced by the Industrial Revolution.'[1] A hint of the triumphalism that would characterise the Thatcher years may here be discernible.

Under Thatcher's rule, the Conservatives tightened the austerity introduced by Callaghan's Labour, carried through the industrial shake-out Heath had attempted a decade earlier, broke the back of a labour movement responsible for bringing down the last two administrations, and completed the transformation of the City of London from a British into a freewheeling international oligarchy. With an electoral coalition firmly based in England's lower half – three-quarters of Tory seats won in the South and the Midlands, as the 'wealth generated by London's booming financial-services

industry turned neighbouring regions a deeper shade of blue' – the
New Right would see off inner city riots, steel and coal strikes,
and protests against cuts in northern and inner London municipalities.[2] Scargill's Yorkshire miners, seeking to fight the idea that
'any industry inside capitalist society – whether public or private
sectors – has the right to destroy the livelihood of men and women
at the stroke of an accountant's pen,' went down to complete
defeat, demonstrating that Whitehall at least had the power to do
so.[3] The legitimacy of bottom-line capitalism would not be challenged in like fashion again.

When Tory Chancellor Geoffrey Howe, a monetarist wolf in
sheep's clothing, began to turn the screws in his June 1979 budget,
he was able to point to 'common ground' with his Labour predecessor over the need to cut public spending in order to rein
in price inflation.[4] Healey had bowed to pressure from the Bank
of England during the IMF crisis to publish official estimates for
annual growth in the money supply. Interpreted as hard targets
by the financial markets, the forecasts were likened by a senior
Bank of England official to a 'rope round the chancellor's neck'.[5]
The Labour heavyweight had also helped to clear the ground for
the Conservative assault on organised labour, berating workers
who abused their industrial power to 'scoop the pool' in pay
negotiations.[6] He could have few complaints when Howe proceeded to squeeze corporate profits in order to stiffen managerial
resolve when faced with inflationary wage demands from the
shop floor.[7]

While Healey was beating the Labour Cabinet into submission
to IMF austerity, a constituency neighbour of his converted the
Thatcher opposition to Friedmanite monetarism. Keith Joseph had
represented Leeds North East since 1956. Born into the Bovis construction empire in London and educated at Harrow, 'he had no
particular connection with Leeds, and he made it clear that he had
no intention of moving to Yorkshire if he was elected.'[8] He could
afford some complacency. Leeds was better hunting ground for
the Conservatives than heavy-industrial Sheffield to its south. Its
North East division boasted a good spread of Tory villadom in the
upmarket suburbs of Roundhay and Alwoodley, although increasing numbers of student, Asian and black voters in the terraced

streets of Harehills, closer to the city centre, created the outside chance of a Labour upset.

In the early phases of his ministerial career, Joseph was an unremarkable One Nation Conservative. 'The objectives of the government have been clearly stated,' he advised a Commons debate on regional development during the Douglas-Home premiership. 'They are to achieve the fuller use of national resources and a more even spread of prosperity. These purposes march with the purposes of modernisation which are the theme of government policies.'[9] It was a perfect sample of Macmillanite rhetoric and nothing Wilson could have disagreed with either.

Only when the miners toppled Heath did he break with the post-war consensus around maintenance of near-full employment. In a September 1974 speech at Preston's Bull and Royal Hotel, he alleged that successive governments had been spooked by rising jobless figures into injecting excessive amounts of money into the economy. 'The effect of overreacting to temporary recessions has been to push up inflation to ever higher levels, not to help the unemployed, but to increase their numbers.' Callaghan would make the identical argument at the Labour Party conference in Blackpool two years later. The number of genuine jobseekers in Britain had been greatly exaggerated, Joseph continued: it was necessary to make a large subtraction from the headline figure to account for the unemployable and the fraudulent, the drifters and the hippies. Lengthening dole queues were not, by implication, cause for alarm. The task for the next Conservative government was to tighten the money supply and hold its nerve while unemployment rose. 'In due course, and without any artificial stimulus or reflation, spontaneous in-built correctives will begin to make themselves felt.'[10] This argument failed to sway the voters of Leeds North East, who produced a rare swing in Labour's direction in the 3 May 1979 general election. Healey likewise saw his majority fall. Thus neither harbinger of the Thatcherite dawn was ringingly endorsed by the Yorkshire public.

But Joseph had other, more powerful, resources on which to draw. *The Times* printed his Preston speech in full and London's banking fraternity was increasingly of his persuasion. One stockbroker described the City as 'the spiritual centre of British

monetarism'.[11] To appease its bond markets, Howe hoisted interest rates to an unprecedented 17 per cent in November 1979 after
overshooting his money-supply forecast. Rates were held at this
'punitive' and 'fearsome' level – the words of Thatcher's biographer Charles Moore – for seven months, ushering in the worst
recession since the 1930s.[12] 'The strategy is to make all lines less
profitable and kill off the marginal ones altogether in the process.
It is a strategy an enemy might seek to force on us in wartime,'
protested Sheffield economic historian Sidney Pollard.[13] A soaring
pound sucked in foreign goods and priced commodities produced
in the UK out of world markets. For the first time in its history,
Britain imported more manufactured goods than it exported.

This baleful trend was pushed further along by industrial
multinationals as they rebalanced their global operations. The
thirty-odd biggest manufacturers in the North West, including
the likes of Pilkington and Tootal, stripped out 87,000 jobs in
the region between 1975 and 1982 while creating twice as many
jobs abroad. 'As the recession has cut a swathe through domestic earnings, the comparative success of overseas subsidiaries has
often kept companies in profit overall and obviated the need for
embarrassing dividend omissions,' the *Financial Times* noted.[14]
On 23 October 1979 the Conservatives announced the removal of
exchange controls dating back to the Second World War, freeing up
British investors to buy as many foreign-currency securities as they
pleased. 'The financial markets were being stifled,' claimed Howe.
'Competition was stunted. Pension funds and institutions were
being prevented from getting the best return on capital.' Within
two years, the amount committed to direct investment overseas
and outward portfolio investment had jumped from £3.7 billion
to £9.2 billion. Domestic manufacturing investment, on the other
hand, fell from £7.5 billion to £4.8 billion.[15]

Although by no means sufficient to cover the loss of capital
abroad, a new wave of foreign direct investment in the UK was
seized on by the Conservatives as a riposte to their critics.[16] Branch
plants operated by foreign multinationals accounted for a third of
remaining jobs in the North East's shrunken manufacturing sector
by the mid-1990s, as the deepening of European economic integration attracted US and Asian producers seeking a foothold in

the Single Market. One analyst coolly notes how the Tyne, Wear and Tees 'possessed a number of attractions for inward investors, including a pool of industrial labour made quiescent by their experience of high unemployment'.[17] Thatcher donned a hard hat and safety goggles for the official opening of Nissan's assembly plant in Sunderland on 8 September 1986, at which the company unveiled plans to base a new European R & D facility in Britain and create another 2,300 jobs, in return for a further £100 million of state aid. It turned out that the new Nissan European Technology Centre would not be located anywhere near Wearside but rather in rural Bedfordshire, on a site adjacent to the business-friendly Cranfield Institute of Technology heavily patronised by the Ministry of Defence.[18] If only Wearside's state-owned shipbuilding industry had enjoyed the sort of political patronage lavished on the Japanese carmaker. The last Sunderland shipyard, Pallion, was shut down on 7 December 1988 in return for European Commission funding toward one of Howe's enterprise zones. 'There is a bloody great steamroller moving towards Sunderland. I don't like it but there may not be much I can do about it,' British Shipbuilders chairman John Lister reportedly told Sunderland North MP Bob Clay.[19]

Other industries in the state sector were given similarly short shrift. The British Steel Corporation had been ordered by the outgoing Callaghan administration to eliminate its budget deficit by the end of the 1979–80 financial year. 'It is no kindness to struggle to defer the necessary increase in the competitiveness of the industry,' said Joseph, appointed Industry Secretary by Thatcher. He refused to fund the corporation's operating losses even as Labour cavilled from the opposition benches.[20] American union buster Ian MacGregor, fresh from battering the auto unions at British Leyland on Callaghan's behalf, was brought in to oversee the jobs cull. As demand for British-made steel plummeted because of the recession and the overvalued pound, McGregor announced plans to dispense with a third of BSC's 160,000 workers. The closure of Consett in County Durham on 26 September 1980 sent the local unemployment rate soaring to 22 per cent by the year's end, the worst figure in the North East. 'The real prospect for Consett will come when the country becomes more competitive,' said Joseph on a visit to South Shields.[21]

With a virtual pay freeze adding insult to injury, the ISTC steel union was left with no alternative but to break with its conservative traditions and mount a national stoppage. The three-month steel strike beginning on 2 January 1980 centred on south Yorkshire, not so borne down by closures as other areas and with Scargill's example close at hand. After conferring with the miners, Rotherham steelworkers despatched flying pickets hither and thither to spread the strike. They also carried a divisional vote of no confidence in the ISTC's cautious-minded general secretary Bill Sirs, reluctant to drag private steel firms into the dispute. On 14 February, a mass picket forced the temporary closure of Sheffield's largest private producer, Hadfields, owned by Tiny Rowland's Lonrho conglomerate. In Downing Street, Thatcher thought she heard the echoes of Saltley. An improved pay offer was conceded to help her administration win the larger battle over closures.[22] National union negotiators recommended a return to work once they had secured an 11 per cent wage offer, against the urging of the Rotherham militants. Enhanced redundancy payments averted further unrest.

Predictably, the blows inflicted by the interest rate squeeze, the flight of large corporate producers and the dismantling of state-owned manufacturing landed heavily on Britain's older industrial regions. Over the course of the first Thatcher administration, manufacturing output dropped by 16 per cent in the North East and Cumbria, 18 per cent in Yorkshire and Humberside, and 19 per cent in the North West. Wales and the West Midlands recorded even steeper drop-offs. By contrast, production fell by only 6 per cent in the South East, 5 per cent in the South West and 3 per cent in East Anglia.[23] Industry in southern regions was the prime beneficiary of remaining corporate and state investment. More than half of national expenditure on research and development passed through the Ministry of Defence, which parcelled it out to electronics and aerospace contractors along the M4 corridor where 'the recession passed almost unnoticed.' Defence expenditure supported one in ten manufacturing jobs in the South East and South West compared to only one in a hundred in Yorkshire.[24]

Retracing J. B. Priestley's footsteps for her sequel to *English Journey* in summer 1983, Liverpool novelist Beryl Bainbridge found Bristol to be flourishing through financial services and defence-related advanced engineering – British Aerospace, Rolls Royce. 'I was right in thinking Bristol was rich. Firms from all over the country have built their head offices here, mostly insurance companies,' she noted. 'The prosperity shows in the superior design and quality of the new office blocks.' Tyneside offered a marked contrast. Although there were signs of consumer bustle in central Newcastle as the unemployed cashed their redundancy cheques, the city's heavy-industrial hinterland was a wreck. 'The past was laid out on the banks of the Tyne like exhibits in a museum – Palmers, Vickers Armstrong, the Baltic Flour Mills, Dunston's Yard and the Coal Staithes. All in ruins with weeds growing, or about to be demolished, or else rotting in the water.'[25]

Accelerated deindustrialisation brought mass unemployment to the North, but not to large parts of the South. When the national jobless figure surged above three million at the start of 1982, the regional unemployment statistics ranged from 9 per cent in the South East to almost twice that figure in the North East. Tyneside's largest engineering group, Northern Engineering Industries, shed 1,300 jobs at Heaton and Hebburn in the first twelve months of the squeeze, prompting pleas from the shop floor for assurances about job security. 'We are haunted by the spectre of redundancy all the time,' complained staff-side chairman Matt Straughan. No sooner had the unions spoken up than the company announced a further 1,500 lay-offs.[26]

Contrary to Joseph's assurances, the dire employment prospects of industrial Britain weren't eased by automatic market mechanisms. Only southern and eastern England would put on enough service-sector jobs during the Thatcher period to offset their (relatively minor) losses in manufacturing. In the North, on the other hand, the total employment base contracted by half a million.[27] No relief could be looked for from Joseph's ministerial office. He instead put the last nails in the coffin of post-war distribution-of-industry policy, cutting the regional-policy budget by a third, abolishing office development permits and suspending factory location controls 'until further notice' to placate West Midland Tory MPs and regional business groups who blamed Whitehall red tape for their economic woes. 'There has to be self-help in the assisted areas,' Joseph lectured the Commons. 'There has to be enterprise, competitiveness, high productivity and a reputation for co-operation between management and the workforce in the assisted areas if they are to reach the level of employment that we all want them to reach'. Teesside MP Ian Wrigglesworth dismissed his sermonising, coming in the midst of an economic slump, as a bad joke.[28]

In the context of these glaring regional disparities, policy discussions in the international-development arena rebounded on the troubled English scene. A report by a commission convened at the World Bank's prompting by former West German chancellor Willy Brandt provoked passing interest in Westminster in the gulf between the global North – the US and Canada, Europe, the USSR – and underdeveloped South: Africa, Asia, Latin America. 'In general terms, and although neither is a uniform or permanent grouping, "North" and "South" are broadly synonymous with "rich" and "poor", "developed" and "developing",' the commission noted. With Britain mired in a self-inflicted recession, MPs representing industrial constituencies took up the idea and ran with it. The North–South divide entered the political lexicon on 20 November 1980 when Lancashire Conservative John Lee, seconding the loyal address in reply to the Queen's speech, told the Commons,

> Those of us who represent the regions are increasingly aware of the North–South divide [cheers from the Labour benches], as twenty-first century industry is increasingly sucked towards the South-East – the Channel tilt. Unless that trend is positively corrected, we shall in future years need a United Kingdom version of the Brandt report.[29]

Whereas Thatcher prudently disallowed the existence of such a divide, one of her key allies, Lord Young, eagerly endorsed it. 'The two present growth industries – the City and tourism – are concentrated in the South,' he said. 'It's our turn, that's all.'[30] Few of the government's supporters were as indiscreet. 'Boom and decay can be found in nearly all Britain's regions, which is why the

so-called North–South divide is no help when it comes to devis-
ing policies to create more jobs,' insisted the *Sunday Times* under
Murdoch appointee Andrew Neil, a Scots-born metropolitan who
would subsequently declare that 'England, for me, is London.'
The editorial tersely added that 'Britain's dole queues could be cut
dramatically if those who wanted to work were able to move to
where jobs are available.'[31]

This drew a polite but firm riposte from the paper's own economics editor, David Smith, whose *North and South: Britain's
Growing Divide* (1989) was the pick of a crop of books which
emerged around the time of Thatcher's departure from Downing
Street, intersecting with the socio-economic crisis that had marked
her tenure. Smith patiently documented the worsening regional rift
in employment, output, health outcomes and house prices, which
further European economic integration and the opening of the
Channel Tunnel on London's doorstep would further compound.
The concentration of so much business activity in one corner of
the country was detrimental to national economic performance.
Thatcher's manufacturing rundown had aggravated the UK's
overseas trade deficit, which the City's foreign earnings – dipping
in the wake of the 1987 stock market crash – might not always
be able to compensate for. It was disingenuous to explain away
statistical averages by pointing to pockets of prosperity in otherwise disadvantaged regions. 'There must be something about the
South which results in its having more than its fair share of thriving towns and well-to-do individuals,' Smith mused. The answer
lay in its monopoly of political and corporate decision-making
power. Though there was little likelihood of any change on this
score, London ought at least to acknowledge the existence of the
regional problem, and re-engage with policy ideas for its ameliora-
tion. 'The longer the problem is swept under the carpet, the more
difficult it will be to solve.'[32]

However bad the general unemployment picture, Liverpool stood
out. The proportion of unemployed workers may have been higher
in Consett and a handful of other depressed areas – the East
Midland steel town of Corby, Mexborough on the south Yorkshire
coalfield, Hartlepool and Sunderland on the North East coast – but

the dole queues on Merseyside, a much bigger conurbation, were longer than anywhere else. Behind closed doors, Environment Secretary Michael Heseltine echoed a popular suspicion that 'it took a riot' to interest the Conservatives in Liverpool's economic collapse.[33] In fact, Thatcher's attention had been drawn to the Mersey well before the Toxteth disturbances. While the party was still in opposition, Joseph had toyed with the idea of turning Liverpool into a laboratory for free-market experimentation after reading an *Economist* feature urging unorthodox, but pro-business, local initiatives. 'The idea would be to establish our practical interest in a region which, as Anthony Steen says, has been poisoned by socialism and which contains a number of marginal seats,' he explained to Thatcher. 'At the same time, we would be preparing our thinking for what we would need to do by way of dismantling the myriad interventionist bodies and applying our general policy of encouragement and reduced controls to a region.'[34]

Thatcher scotched the idea of setting up a Tory task force on Merseyside, but once in office had to respond to a political furore surrounding Tate & Lyle's announcement on 22 January 1980 that it was closing its Love Lane sugar refinery with the loss of 1,600 jobs. Although there were many other instances of corporate disinvestment from Merseyside, sugar processing was a historic portside industry and Tate & Lyle one of the few industrial firms left in the inner city. Love Lane also had a good productivity record and harmonious industrial relations: so much for Joseph's sermonising about the advantages of shop-floor cooperation with management. Thatcher instructed her Central Policy Review Staff to devise acceptable countermeasures to Liverpool's difficulties. The CPRS concluded that 'it would be short-sighted to let major city regions like Merseyside go into irreversible decline particularly when this is likely to mean further overstrain, e.g. on land and infrastructure resources, in the South East.' A policy of controlled decline was neither politically feasible nor strategically sensible, since outmigration would leave behind a residue of 'socially inadequate' people.[35] But the CPRS could come up with only minor policy suggestions to slow Merseyside's descent – a strategy to promote tourism, for example, along with a call for renewed emphasis on small businesses, since these had a freer hand to drive down wages than branch plants constrained by national pay frameworks. Howe created an 'enterprise zone', where firms could obtain tax breaks, on the site of the former British Leyland and Dunlop factories in Speke, but it never filled up.[36] The Merseyside Development Corporation, a quango, successfully took over spluttering municipal attempts to renovate the Albert Docks – shut down by the Heath government in 1972 – as a visitor attraction, but levered in just 8 per cent of the private-sector investment that the London Docklands UDC attracted to the Isle of Dogs, converted into an overspill site for City banks.[37]

Unsympathetic policy deliberations within Whitehall were swiftly overtaken by the wave of inner-city riots spreading north from Brixton in summer 1981, triggered by racist policing against a backdrop of worsening socio-economic deprivation. Birmingham, Leeds and Manchester were all affected, but the disturbances on Merseyside were fiercest of all. The black community in Toxteth was heavily discriminated against in access to jobs and housing. The backlash there began on 3 July after a heavy-handed police attempt to detain a young black man wrongly suspected of stealing a motorbike. Eight police vehicles were deployed to effect the arrest, an instance of public-sector overmanning which drew no criticism from Whitehall.[38] Among the targets for arsonists was a racquet club frequented by judges and barristers.

Thatcher set the tone for the security response, treating the riots as instances of wanton delinquency. In the early hours of 6 July, tear gas was used by UK security forces for the first time outside Northern Ireland. The high-velocity CS cartridges fired into a Liverpool crowd by police marksmen were designed to penetrate barricaded buildings. One of the manufacturers, Smith and Wesson, complained, 'If you're going to fire them directly at people you might as well fire live ammunition, because you'd have the same effect.'[39] Several people were left in need of hospital treatment. Nevertheless, speaking in the Commons later that day, Home Secretary Willie Whitelaw – an advocate of 'short, sharp shock' treatment for young offenders, who dispensed with trial by jury for terrorist suspects in Northern Ireland – offered the Merseyside constabulary his unequivocal support. Thus encouraged, Chief Inspector Kenneth Oxford, formerly of the Metropolitan Police, ordered his officers to drive their vehicles directly at rioters. 'They can see the vehicles coming and they know what will happen if they get in the way,' said Oxford brusquely.⁴⁰ On 28 July, a twenty-two-year-old disabled bystander, David Moore, was knocked down and killed in a police hit-and-run. Two officers were tried and acquitted of manslaughter.

Amidst the tumult, Heseltine joined the Tory Wets in urging Thatcher to call off the fiscal squeeze. 'Reducing taxes has nothing to do with problem of Merseyside,' he argued. 'Colleagues don't understand how bad it is.' He called for the reversal of 'some, at least', of the cuts made over the past decade to the housing budget and the bending of government spending programmes towards the conurbations.⁴¹ But Howe and Joseph were firmly against throwing Liverpool a lifeline. On 11 August, shortly before setting off on his summer holiday, the Chancellor wrote to Thatcher, 'I cannot help feeling that the option of managed decline, which the CPRS rejected in its study of Merseyside, is one which we should not forget altogether. We must not expend all our resources in trying to make water flow uphill.'⁴²

Of course, the whole idea behind post-war regional policy, however much tokenism there had been in its actual application, was precisely to canalise national economic growth so that it irrigated outer regions and not just the Thames basin. Howe soon repented of his forthrightness, counselling the prime minister that managed decline was 'not a term for use, even privately. It is much too negative.'⁴³ Downing Street now reluctantly consented to Heseltine's breezy suggestion that he lead a task force staffed by civil servants and seconded business executives, despite concern among the prime minister's advisers that such an initiative 'might arouse expectations which could be difficult to fulfil, and lead to claims for similar treatment from other hard-hit parts of England, notably Tyneside'.⁴⁴ Howe would not provide the task force with a dedicated budget and it achieved little more than the staging of a garden festival on derelict dockland in Dingle, to local protests of 'jobs, not trees'.

A wrecking-ball industrial strategy caused the Conservative vote in northern England to fall by 8 per cent in the 9 June 1983 general election. Although Thatcher had reason to express grudging admiration for Heseltine's 'skilful public relations', Liverpool didn't return a single one of the party's candidates.[45] However, support for the Labour opposition also fell sharply in other parts of the region. The loss of Bradford North to a twenty-something Tory PR executive was emblematic of the party's difficulties. Official Labour nominee Pat Wall, a member of Militant, leaked support not only to a former party agent representing the SDP but also to the constituency's previous MP, Labour right-winger Ben Ford, deselected by the constituency party and standing as an independent. In addition to a smattering of such gains in the North, the Conservatives swept the board in the South East, where one in six employees worked in financial services. They had everything to lose from a Labour Party formally committed to a 'programme of socialist reconstruction' and much to gain from Howe's loosening of the monetary squeeze in the run-up to the poll. The Chancellor had eased interest rates to 10 per cent, deregulated consumer credit and lifted 'corset' restrictions on bank lending, allowing the high-street banks to enter the mortgage market. The strings attached to mortgage finance were loosened and the modern spiral of house price rises got under way, generating substantial wealth effects for homeowners in the South East where the total value of housing stock was ten times higher than in the North.[46] The pre-election consumer boom, disarray within Labour and a flukey colonial triumph in the South Atlantic ensured Thatcher a landslide victory, in her assessment 'the single most devastating defeat ever inflicted upon democratic socialism in Britain'.[47]

The ramparts of Westminster unbreached, it fell to leftist currents in coalmining trade unionism and inner-city municipal politics to confront the Thatcherite ascendancy. Joe Gormley had earlier forced the Conservatives into a tactical retreat on the subject of pit closures. Thatcher privately conceded that she was prepared 'go along, to a large extent, with whatever Mr Gormley proposed in order to ensure that the militants did not regain the ascendancy'.[48] Upon his retirement in 1982, however, the prime minister's worst fears were realised. The new NUM president stood for everything the market fundamentalists despised. 'History is littered with abortive attempts to reform capitalism,' said Scargill. 'You cannot reform this system out of existence. What we need is a complete and utter change in this society. What we must create is a new socialist society.'[49] His was the pivotal coalfield, accounting for a third of the industry's remaining staff. 'Yorkshire had to be broken,' observed John Saville in *Socialist Register*. 'Scotland and South Wales could remain on strike for five years and the NCB and Whitehall could and would have forgotten that there were miners still living in those parts; and the shortfall in output would have embarrassed no one.'[50] Thatcher and her National Coal Board hatchet man Ian MacGregor, recruited from British Steel, provoked Scargill into untimely industrial action by announcing 20,000 redundancies, including the unexpected closure of Cortonwood in the NUM leader's south Yorkshire powerbase, in violation of industry consultation procedures. The fightback began at Cortonwood on 5 March 1984.

In the midst of the miners' strike, Liverpool voters propelled the city onto the front line of local-government resistance to Conservative efforts to force retrenchment of public services. The Liverpool Labour group had split in the early seventies after council leader Bill Sefton reneged on a commitment to fight the housing legislation of the Heath government, which imposed large rent rises on council-house tenants. It resumed majority control of the recession-wracked city in May 1983 on an anti-austerity platform. The political balance within the district party had tilted the way of Militant, a Trotskyist entryist group active in the Walton constituency party since the fifties. The new town-hall administration, headed by Sefton's successor as Labour leader, the quietly spoken John Hamilton, with Derek Hatton of Militant as his deputy, refused to impose severe Whitehall spending cuts on a deprived urban population with a high and growing needs base, instead kick-starting a council-house building programme and reducing housing rents – hugely important in a city with one of the country's longest waiting lists for council housing and the highest charges outside London. On 29 March 1984 the administration tabled an unbalanced budget for the coming year, demanding that central government make up the difference. Deficit financing was illegal for local authorities, Whitehall reserving this Keynesian prerogative to itself. A rump of six right-wing Labour councillors prevented the budget's passage, but Militant was then bolstered by gains in local elections – 'an enormous "thumbs up" from the electorate over the fight with Thatcher and the government', acknowledged the *Liverpool Post*.[51]

Patrick Jenkin at the Department of the Environment prepared draft legislation to replace the elected city council with central-government appointees and privately canvassed names for would-be commissioners, the list headed by right-wing northern Labour MPs Joel Barnett and Roy Mason. Downing Street policy adviser Oliver Letwin, later a key figure in the Cameron administration, suggested empowering the commissioners to levy a local poll tax, 'which would bite on everybody in Liverpool, and thereby penalise those who voted the present council into office'.[52] Any sort of municipal annexation by Whitehall was a risky proposition, let alone one with a poll tax tacked on. Instead, with the miners drawing Thatcher's fire, and to the consternation of Fleet Street, Jenkin struck a deal with Liverpool's councillors, conceding around £30 million of additional funds.

In a speech to Conservative MPs on 19 July, Thatcher famously grouped the NUM with Liverpool and other left-wing local authorities as 'the enemy within' – 'just as dangerous' as General Galtieri and 'in a way more difficult to fight'.[53] Run by area ballot, the miners' strike was solid in Yorkshire and the coalfield periphery – the North East, South Wales, Scotland, Kent – but Scargill couldn't emerge victorious from a do-or-die confrontation with the British state unless he achieved a fully national stoppage, and this required solidarity from Midland coalfields. The Thatcher administration organised an unprecedented national paramilitary policing operation to drive Scargill's picketers out of the Midlands and keep them on the back foot. Only a third of miners came out in Nottinghamshire, which had the largest number of coalworkers after Yorkshire. Nottinghamshire was profitable and highly productive, and had a history of right-wing trade unionism. 'If we could keep Nottingham going, we could keep the lights on in Britain,' recalled MacGregor. Nottinghamshire miners maintained supplies to coal-fired power stations along the Trent, extending the endurance of the national grid, although the primary boost to electricity generation came from increased oil burn in South East power stations located beside the Thames and Medway that were difficult for picketers to get at.[54] Scargill hoped to break the impasse with a repeat of his Saltley triumph at the Orgreave coke works outside Sheffield, but what ensued was closer to a Yorkshire Peterloo. On 18 June 1984, over 4,000 riot police, including several dozen on horseback, weighed in on picketers with truncheons and riot shields in the worst industrial-relations confrontation since the war. This carefully planned police operation was the beginning of the end for the NUM, which eventually conceded defeat on 3 March the following year.

With the NUM overcome, and the national Labour leadership under Neil Kinnock urging acceptance of Whitehall austerity to burnish the party's 'respectability', Ken Livingstone's Greater London Council initiated a climbdown on the part of soft-left councils, allowing Thatcher to despatch her Merseyside opponents with ease. Militant's Peter Taaffe and Tony Mulhearn bitterly note how 'many Labour councillors in other authorities who had pledged to resist the Tory government ran for cover at the first whiff of grapeshot'.[55] A formal Conservative takeover on Merseyside proved unnecessary, though Kinnock had been willing to endorse it. In the event the government could leave it to district auditor Tim McMahon, appointed by the National Audit Commission, to initiate legal proceedings to surcharge, dismiss and disbar the forty-nine Labour councillors in Liverpool who had approved another deficit budget. 'McMahon came down on us like a ton of bricks,' recalls Hatton.[56] Running out of money, on 22 November 1985 the council retreated, setting a legal budget. Kinnock then denounced Militant at the Labour Party conference, winning praise from The Times for his 'courageous speeches'.[57]

A third general-election victory for Thatcher on 11 June 1987 caused local authorities to throw in the municipal-socialist towel for good. Labour's popular vote in the North recovered from 2.9 to 3.5 million, not far off its historic norm, yielding 96 out of 163 seats, a net gain of 7. But the Conservatives retained their grip on southern and eastern England, where they held 294 out of 359 seats. As Doreen Massey dejectedly commented, Labour's strongholds in northern England, Scotland and Wales constituted 'a base which is electorally too small to win from'.[58] Seeing how matters stood, Manchester City Council under Graham Stringer shifted from outright hostility to free-market urban policy to a warm embrace of the enterprise culture, eagerly bidding for public and private investment against what it now termed 'competitor cities'.[59] John Major subsequently contracted-out the problem of Liverpool to the European Commission, its structural funds intended to help lagging local economies catch up with the rest of the community. But GDP per head merely fell further behind EU and UK averages under the Commission's supply-side measures. A consultant's report for Brussels noted concern amongst Liverpudlians about the efficacy of 'spending money on training for jobs which did not yet exist'.[60] As for the miners, even collaborationist Nottinghamshire saw its workforce halve in the aftermath of Scargill's defeat. Heseltine and Major announced the short-notice closure on 13 October 1992 of the majority of the country's remaining deep mines on the advice of merchant bank Rothschild, tasked with preparing the remains of British Coal for privatisation. On this occasion, a greatly weakened NUM opted – against Scargill's wishes – for a coalition-building public-relations campaign. It achieved an outpouring of public sympathy, but negligible political effect.

Rothschild was among the few London finance houses to withstand takeovers by super-profitable US competitors following the Conservatives' 'Big Bang' deregulation of 27 October 1986. Cecil Parkinson, one of Joseph's successors at the Department for Trade and Industry, said he feared that the London Stock Exchange would have become as outmoded as its Mancunian equivalent if it weren't opened up to the world's biggest financial operators.[61] Tom Nairn had forecast in 1981, 'The underlying trajectory of the state is towards the eversion of the British political economy. The metropolitan heartland complex will become ever more of a service-zone to international capital – the conveniently offshore location for investment or reinvestment, insurance and speculation.'[62] So it proved, as a remodelled Square Mile bid adieu to the sinking ship of British industry. 'It is true that investment in financial-service activity tends to create less jobs [sic] than, say, a comparable investment in manufacturing,' conceded Bank of England governor Robin Leigh-Pemberton in 1984, hastily adding that 'our primary concern must be to ensure that new areas of wealth-generating activity develop to take the place of those that are actually or prospectively in decline.'[63]

Regional disparities eased for a spell in the 1990–2 recession, as an overextended London unwound from the Lawson credit boom. 'There's a whiff of satisfaction in the air as the North of England watches the South's economic troubles,' observed Emma Duncan, regional affairs correspondent of the *Economist*, writing in the *Sunday Times*. What also entered into the changed regional calculus, Duncan insisted, though this has been ignored amidst the *Schadenfreude*, were the beneficial effects of the structural changes wrought under the Thatcherite settlement, creating nothing less than a 'new North'. Redundancy had forced more people into self-employment – up by a quarter since the mid-1980s. There were now over twenty-five Japanese companies in the North East, Kellogg's was moving into Trafford Park and the driveways of *nouveau riche* Wilmslow on the Cheshire fringes of Manchester were filling up with Porsches. Even though regional prosperity remained 'patchy' – financial-services growth in Manchester and Leeds leaving Liverpool, Bradford and Sheffield behind; unemployment in South Tyneside still over 14 per cent, the worst figure outside Northern Ireland – things were definitely on the up. 'The place has begun to see its way out of a century of decline.'[64] In vain did David Smith, returning to the fray in the second edition of *North and South* (1994), point out that the downturn had merely reduced the South's lead over the North in output per capita to the already very high level of the mid-1980s. 'The recession's main effect', he observed, 'has been to push the problem of regional economic disparities a long way down the political agenda'. There it would remain, until the Brexit upset of 2016.[65] For when the Major administration suffered a national electoral drubbing on May Day in 1997, the beneficiary was the aggressively pro-City New Labour.

9

The Bank of South-East England

'It was in this constituency that we created New Labour,' said a jubilant Tony Blair at Trimdon Labour Club in Sedgefield, County Durham, on election night in 1997.[1] This was not, of course, strictly true. With good reason Thatcher claimed New Labour was her greatest achievement – its essential strategy, according to party ideologue and insider Peter Mandelson, MP for Hartlepool, was 'to move forward where Margaret Thatcher left off'.[2] Blair had been selected for the coalfield seat in the early eighties on the strength of boyhood connections and support from right-leaning party and union branches. He also had up his sleeve an endorsement from party leader Michael Foot, grateful to the future New Labour standard-bearer for previously mounting a thankless by-election campaign in Tory Buckinghamshire. For Blair, Sedgefield was simply a stepping stone to the capital. Life revolved around the gentrifying north London borough of Islington, where he sealed his leadership compact with Brown. 'Don't worry,' Blair reportedly told a Labour Londoner lined up to contest a northern constituency. 'I only have to go up once a month. You can do the same.'[3]

Making his way at Westminster in the eighties, Blair had levelled the usual criticisms about widening regional disparities on One Nation grounds. 'Our regions are our manufacturing base, and in our manufacturing base lies our capacity to create wealth,' he declared in response to Thatcher's abolition of automatic regional capital subsidies. 'A narrowing of the gap between the North and the South is in the interests not only of the North but of the South.

It is part of the interests of the whole country.' But he slipperily added, 'it is not a case of being wedded to the old-fashioned traditional ways of doing it and we are perfectly able to take on board and realise the need to change the means of industrial assistance.'[4]

In office, New Labour would in fact concur with Keith Joseph that post-war controls over the location of factories and offices had wrongly stifled market forces. 'I certainly do not think', Industry Secretary Patricia Hewitt declared to MPs, 'that we can ban business from locating in the South East'.[5] Instead business interests and local authorities were invited to pull together in development agencies through which the regions could promote competitiveness and 'ameliorate their own weaknesses'.[6] New Labour also introduced a morass of pro-market initiatives at neighbourhood level, including a swingeing 'pathfinder' programme intended to spread the house-price boom into less salubrious locales by boarding up and demolishing homes to choke off supply.

Blair extolled a forward march to economic globalisation that gave short shrift to laggards – 'Those who will live with decline. Those who yearn for yesteryear' – who might resist it in his party's working-class base. New Labour rode the long credit-driven boom centred on Wall Street and the City with delight. Brown's first act at the Treasury was to burnish his credentials with the financial markets by handing control of interest rates to the Bank of England. For the *Economist* this was a Mandela moment: the bank was 'free at last'. Threadneedle Street promptly raised rates from 6.25 to 7.5 per cent to moderate inflationary pressure in London and the South East, further overvaluing the pound to the detriment of industrial exporters. 'We were trying to bring about a slowdown', the bank's governor, Eddie George, told provincial lobby journalists over lunch, explaining that 'unemployment in the North East is an acceptable price to pay to curb inflation in the South'.[7] Naturally there was uproar. Sunderland council leader Bryn Sidaway dubbed Britain's central bank the 'Bank of South East England'. The North East Chamber of Commerce said it felt betrayed. Brown expressed his confidence in the governor, and support for the difficult decisions he had been obliged to make, George promising to be more discreet in future.[8]

The North East was hosting a Labour prime minister for the first time since Ramsay MacDonald abandoned the party in 1931. By now manufacturing accounted for just over a quarter of economic output in the region, and Bank of England deflation and assorted capitalist dynamics – competition on the British high street, market stresses from the Asian financial crisis, continued corporate outsourcing – were combining to put the sector under renewed strain. Clothing production declined as Marks & Spencer, the UK's largest retailer, instructed suppliers to source more material from sweatshops overseas.[9] There were also problems in foreign-owned high-tech ventures. Electronics multinationals Siemens and Fujitsi shed 1,700 jobs as they walked away from microchip plants in Newcastle and Newton Aycliffe because of a glut in the world market. 'Britain has earned itself an unenviable reputation as a country where it is agreeably cheap to close factories', complained the *Newcastle Journal*. Newton Aycliffe fell within Blair's Sedgefield constituency, but the prime minister initially had only cold comfort for the Fujitsu shop floor: 'We can't, as the government, do much about the twists and turns of world markets in an increasingly globalised economy'.[10] Only after being jeered by workers facing redundancy at an American crane manufacturer in Sunderland did Blair offer £5 million to a Yorkshire electronics firm to take over the Fujitsu factory.

Under New Labour, financial-services output would increase at twice the overall growth rate, while the contribution of manufacturing to UK gross value added dropped from a little under a fifth (19 per cent) to just a tenth. In the North, manufactures declined from 24 to 15 per cent of regional output, with an even bigger drop in the metal-bashing West Midlands, tumbling from 27 to 13 per cent.[11] The demise of Birmingham's MG Rover, the last British volume carmaker, was followed by Peugeot's withdrawal from its Ryton plant in Coventry as the French auto giant shifted production to Slovakia. In November 1999, with a slew of statistics pointing to widening regional disparities, Downing Street acted to bury bad news concerning what chief press secretary Alastair Campbell – Yorkshire-born, but an old Fleet Street hand – privately termed 'North–South stuff'.[12] Thatcher had dismissed the North–South divide as a myth. Very well, Blair would do the same. But first he had to fix his own County Durham voters. For purely local consumption, he told the *Northern Echo*, 'There is a North–South divide. That it exists there is no doubt. We do have to bridge it, we have to narrow the gap.'[13] A week later, Campbell orchestrated national headlines that, as far as his boss was concerned, the regional divide was in fact 'over', 'dead' and indeed a 'myth'. In public, a mealy-mouthed Blair merely had to hazard the view 'what we actually found when we looked into it was that some of the differences between regions and within regions were every bit as great as the difference that people traditionally talk about as the North–South divide'. Even in the capital, few were impressed.[14] The left-field *Guardian* columnist George Monbiot urged New Labour to 'signal unequivocally that the government takes the North of England's problems seriously' by switching the capital to Newcastle.[15] But metropolitan opinion was against him. A round table of political and cultural worthies in *Prospect* magazine returned a negative verdict. 'Create a new capital if you like', shrugged historian Linda Colley, who lectured for Blair on Britishness in the twenty-first century. 'London', she insisted, 'will keep growing.'[16]

From this point on, accelerated deindustrialisation would be buffered by the stimulants administered by New Labour to hollowing regional economies in the shape of higher public spending, which increased by over 6 per cent a year in real terms between 1999 and 2006, flooring the opposition parties – 'Labour investment versus Tory cuts' – and subduing resistance to the marketisation of schools and hospitals. 'It is reform in return for resources', the Chancellor intoned, or in Blair's inimitable version, 'a spoonful of sugar helps it all go down.'[17] On one estimate, public bodies and state-funded jobs in the private sector accounted for 73 per cent of employment growth in the North East over the pre-recession decade, 67 per cent in Yorkshire and the Humber and 62 per cent in the North West.[18] The gap in employment rates between the North and the rest of England, which had widened from five to six percentage points in the deflationary late nineties, closed to two points by the end of 2004, and relative output per head in northern regions rallied.[19]

Whitehall could point out that job losses in North East

manufacturing were more than offset by growth in services. At the time of the interest-rate row, there were 2,500 promised new openings at call centres in Sunderland run by telecoms firm BT and Barclays Bank. But these were not the same kind of jobs as privileged classes in the capital were enjoying. A shift to low-level service activity wasn't welcomed by the North East arm of the CBI business group: 'call centres could be located on the Moon for the amount of good they do to the regional economy.'[20] Journeying from Outer Britain to the City took the traveller from relative famine to outrageous feast, where the bonus pool for London's 350,000 wholesale financial-services workers peaked at £11.5 billion on the eve of the credit crunch. 'And boy, is all that felicitous, filthy lucre affecting London life,' thrilled the *Telegraph*. 'It has fed a salivating atavism that makes the Beckhams' lifestyle look positively spiritual.'[21] Writing at the tail end of the boom, Doreen Massey denied that London had functioned as a 'simple transmission belt for neoliberalism', pointing to the frictions created by grass-roots campaigns against it and the two-term mayoralty of Ken Livingstone, a soft-left bugbear of Thatcher and Blair. Still, she conceded, 'the contest in and over London' was 'at present subdued'. The City actually thrived under a neutered Livingstone. 'There isn't a great ideological conflict any more,' said the mayor defensively, and in any case 'I don't have any powers for the redistribution of wealth in London.'[22]

As nemesis approached, in June 2007 Gordon Brown used his last Mansion House speech as Chancellor to congratulate the assembled bankers on 'an era that history will record as the beginning of a new golden age for the City of London'. James Cayne, chairman of Bear Stearns, told the *Financial Times*, 'London is no longer the second city. Right now it is as fast as New York.' Thatcher's deregulation had exposed dowdy British merchant banks to takeovers by much larger and more profitable US competitors, hard-wiring the City into a lucrative Wall Street system of speculative proprietary trading, extreme leverage, and a shadow-banking sector of hedge funds and privately traded 'over-the-counter' (OCT) derivatives. It had become not just as fast as New York, but in some senses a good deal faster. Two-fifths of the surging turnover ($2,544 billion daily) in OCT derivatives

were booked in London, thanks to its especially complaisant reg-
ulators and tax collectors. Brown essentially tasked his new UK
banking supervisor with touting for extra business for the City,
one hedge-fund tycoon describing the Financial Services Authority
as 'a pleasure to work with'.[23]

New Labour made a virtue of its sponsorship of casino capitalism by having down-at-heel Blackpool and Beswick in east
Manchester argue over the awarding of the UK's first super-casino
licence, a money-grubber blocked by Anglican clergy in the House
of Lords.[24] Fittingly, when the crisis came, its first casualty was
a swollen mortgage bank in north-east England. Newcastle's
Northern Rock, one of only two FTSE 100 companies headquartered in the region, was the weakest link in the golden chain of
finance. At the prompting of Conservative ministers, City financiers and carpet-bagging investors, it had joined the nineties rush
to convert itself from a mutual building society into a publicly
listed bank. To compensate for a small retail deposits base, this
try-hard out-of-towner plunged into securitisation, borrowing
against packaged-up mortgages in the wholesale money markets.
On this basis, the bank ballooned into the country's fifth-largest
mortgage provider, expanding into southern England, where ultimately half its lending was placed.[25] When the markets seized up,
the Rock crumbled. Fearing for the stability of Britain's finance
capitalism, a Bank of England and New Labour regime famously
relaxed about job losses in North East manufacturing sped to the
rescue, providing emergency loans and a deposit guarantee followed up by a rushed-through nationalisation bill. Still, as the
Economist lamented, the collapse of Northern Rock 'undermined
confidence in the ability of one of Britain's poorest regions to build
a post-industrial future'.[26]

New Labour could continue to coast to victory as long as the
credit boom lasted, retaining its grip on Westminster even as
its share of the vote fell and turnout dropped to a historic low,
thanks to Britain's winner-takes-all electoral system. Politically,
Celtic fringe nationalism dominated the domestic front during the
early years of the Blair regime: pacification of Northern Ireland
and devolution in Scotland as well as Wales. Concession of a
parliament in Edinburgh, spiking the SNP's guns, would – it was

thought – settle the Scottish question. Labour voters in northern England required no such special attention. 'They have nowhere else to go,' Blair's advisers would at one point counsel the front bench.[27] As early as the year 2000, the *New Statesman* reported 'significant falls' in party membership across the North East, Sedgefield included. The region 'elected a third of the Cabinet to their seats, but gets, locals say, "bugger all" in return'.[28] In 2002 Labour lost inaugural mayoral contests in Hartlepool and Middlesbrough to a football-club mascot and a zero-tolerance detective respectively, the latter at least previously much admired in Blairite circles. Two years later the party was swept from power in its regional citadel of Newcastle, losing nearly half its council seats to the Lib Dems, and a referendum in the North East met a Brexit-like riposte from voters, dismissing the government's proposal for a toothless regional assembly. Over three-quarters of opinion-poll respondents agreed that New Labour 'looks after some parts of England more than others'.[29] By the time New Labour was ousted, its vote in the three northern regions had dropped from 4.1 to 2.6 million.[30]

On entering office in 2010, the leaders of the Conservative–Liberal coalition spoke with one voice. 'This country has been too London-centric for far too long,' remonstrated Cameron. 'I can see the risk of our capital city's dominance. It is not healthy for our country or our economy,' warned George Osborne. 'We can never rely on only one part of the country, sectorally or geographically. We have to spread our bets,' declared Deputy Prime Minister Nick Clegg. The new administration stood for balanced economic growth 'across all regions and all industries'.[31] Cameron, Osborne, Clegg: three more typical specimens of the *haute bourgeoisie* of the South of England would be difficult to find. The two Tories were born in the capital; the Lib Dem grew up close by in affluent Buckinghamshire. Cameron profited from his stockbroker father's offshore trust in Panama and while in office defended the anonymities of such tax-haven investment vehicles. Clegg is a merchant banker's son, Osborne the heir to a genteel fabric and wallpaper company and an Anglo-Irish baronetcy. All three were privately educated at elite London-area institutions – Eton, St Paul's, Westminster – and went seamlessly on to Oxbridge. Cameron and Osborne kick-started their careers as Whitehall apparatchiks. Clegg, more European-ist, worked as a trade-policy aide in Brussels and an MEP before taking the suburban constituency of Sheffield Hallam, 'similar to Bristol West or Cambridge', noted a *Telegraph* reporter taking his bearings, 'wealthy, open-minded ghettoes of the highly educated bourgeoisie who don't like what the Tories have become but also haven't been historically attracted to Labour's working-class poli-tics'.[32] Cameron didn't have to stray further than Oxfordshire for his own parliamentary seat and when he did venture north, he was caught on microphone joking that people in Yorkshire hated each other and everyone else.[33] These were unlikely champions of greater regional equity.

Plunging tax receipts in the wake of the 2008–9 downturn provided the occasion for a groundswell of organised neoliberal opinion in the capital pressing for the opposite. Initial dismay at emergency extension of the state into high finance was soon dis-placed into strident demands for a rollback in less strategically sensitive areas. If the City was on life support, the North should have its plug pulled. 'Public subsidies to failing areas undermine the adjustment process needed for their economies to recover,' solemnly declared the Institute for Economic Affairs, as a collaps-ing banking sector received £130 billion in government loans and share purchases, and £1,030 billion in guarantees and indemni-ties.[34] 'The state now looms far larger in many parts of Britain than it did in former Soviet satellite states such as Hungary and Slovakia as they emerged from communism in the 1990s,' fulmi-nated Murdoch's *Sunday Times*.[35] New Labour largesse, having pump-primed the privatisation of core public services, could now be dispensed with.

In this climate, the three main Westminster parties converged on spending cuts as the primary means to tackle a record peacetime budget deficit. Britain had 'become far too dependent on the public sector', complained Cameron. 'You can't revive the regions just through handouts from Whitehall,' lectured Clegg. A White Paper on regional development published by the coalition announced that 'places are unique and have different potential for growth.' In other words, the North could lag all it liked. Chancellor George

Osborne intensified a fiscal squeeze that the outgoing Labour Chancellor Alistair Darling had already pencilled in for the post-election period. The new-look opposition under Ed Miliband and Ed Balls – former Brown advisers levered into a couple of Yorkshire constituencies – prevaricated for a time, then fell into line. This was bad news for Outer Britain: one in four people in employment worked in the public sector in north-east England, Scotland and Wales; one in six in London and the South East.[36] Public spending was equivalent to 52 per cent of economic output in the North East, 47 per cent in the North West and 44 per cent in Yorkshire and the Humber, compared to a national average of 38 per cent.[37]

The UK's cross-party fiscal tightening, as a proportion of national income, was on a par with that pursued in France under Sarkozy and Hollande and in Italy under Monti. It differed in tilting towards cuts in expenditure rather than tax rises, by a ratio of four to one.[38] At the Treasury, Osborne slashed average departmental spending by 10 per cent in real terms between 2010–11 and 2015–16. High-need, mainly Labour-controlled, municipalities bore the brunt of swingeing cuts to local government services; the Tory shires came away relatively intact. By March 2015 net public-service spending per person by local authorities had dropped by 27 per cent in both the North East and London, compared to 16 per cent in the South East.[39]

The Chancellor also went directly after surplus industrial workers – including the younger generation of miners and steelmen discarded by Thatcher and Major – vilifying them as shirkers 'sleeping off a life on benefits'. Ken Loach's 2016 Palme d'Or winner *I, Daniel Blake*, set in Newcastle, dramatised the Kafkaesque torments of the capability test and sanctions regime introduced into the social security system by New Labour and extended by the coalition. Ex-industrial communities such as Bradford, Oldham and the Rhondda were losing twice as much money per working-age adult from curbs to disability and other state benefits as southern market towns like Guildford and Wokingham. Observed two analysts for Sheffield Hallam's Centre for Regional Economic and Social Research, 'This is an economic geography that overlaps strongly with Britain's political geography: the coalition government is presiding over national welfare reforms that will impact principally on individuals and communities outside its own heartlands.'[40]

The heartlands staged a swift recovery. The financial crisis had been expected to trigger a white-collar recession in the City, as when Nigel Lawson's asset-price bubble burst over yuppie heads in 1990. But too much was at stake to permit a repetition of that. The financial and insurance industry accounted for nearly a fifth (19 per cent) of economic output in the capital, slightly more than Wall Street contributed to New York. City-type high finance had spread itself from east to west, big banks overspilling from the Square Mile into reclaimed dockland on the Isle of Dogs while hedge funds and other discreet operators preferred Mayfair and St James's. Second place in the London economy went to real-estate activities (13 per cent). After that came professional, scientific and technical activities (11 per cent), including City-dependent legal and accounting services.[41]

To keep all this afloat, the Bank of England had already reduced interest rates to 0.5 per cent and launched a £200 billion pro-gramme of quantitative easing (QE). Further rounds of bond purchases followed under the coalition, blowing up another asset-price bubble. By May 2012, QE had run to £325 billion and pushed up the value of assets held by the richest 10 per cent of households, clustered in and around London, by as much as £322,000 per household. The *Spectator* uneasily called it 'the biggest transfer of wealth to the rich of any government policy in recent documented history'.[42] The first three years of QE saw house prices jump by 17 and 15 per cent in London and the South East, compared to rises of 2 and 4 per cent in the North West and Yorkshire–Humber respectively. In the North East, prices didn't move.[43] 'Feelgood factor returns to the City of London,' celebrated the *FT* in October 2013. 'Animal spirits have awakened in board-rooms and even the private-equity dealmaking machine has kicked into gear.'

The general slump saw manufacturing shed jobs at twice the rate of financial and business services, and London survived it largely unscathed, growing strongly in 2008, suffering a smaller decline in output in 2009 than anywhere else, and in 2011 once again posting faster growth in output than the rest of the country.[44] Cameron's enterprise tsar Lord Young – a bow-tied London businessman left over from the Thatcher government – was forced to resign in November 2010 after candidly telling the *Telegraph* that, from where he sat, people 'have never had it so good' than during the 'so-called recession'.[45] In fact, London posted twice the total growth rate (17 per cent) of any other UK region or nation between 2010 and 2014, the coalition's last full year in power. Northern Ireland (1 per cent) and the three northern English regions (3–4 per cent) brought up the rear.[46] London now consistently out-produced the three northern regions combined, and by an increasing margin, despite having not much more than half the number of residents.

Not surprisingly, the spring 2014 elections for the European Parliament saw above-average drop-offs in Conservative support in the North West and Yorkshire–Humber. With a Westminster election only a year away, Osborne changed his prospectus. The new Treasury line was that 'successful rebalancing will not be achieved by pulling down the capital city, but by building up the Northern Powerhouse.'[47] The NP was a public-relations device to highlight Conservative good works in the still largely pro-Labour North. After the 2010 election the Tories held 43 out of 158 northern constituencies, a modest haul but important in a finely balanced Parliament. New Labour had presented its regional development agencies as 'economic powerhouses for sustainable growth'. Cameron and Osborne abolished these quangos but retained the rubric, with its tellingly Victorian air tacitly acknowledging industrial antiquation while formally disavowing it. The Chancellor unveiled the NP in a speech at Manchester's Museum of Science and Industry, surrounded by working steam engines, and went on to dangle the prospect of £6 billion investment in the northern transport network (under the coalition, transport spending per head was two and a half times higher in London than in the North).[48] He also entered into negotiations with local authorities over devolution of policy and regulatory – but not fiscal – powers, beginning in Manchester.

Delivering his pre-election budget in March 2015, Osborne was at pains to stress 'a truly national recovery'. But the fiscal squeeze on fragile regional economies, combined with quantitative easing for international finance, had predictably distorted effects.[49] Between 2009 and 2015 the number of employee jobs in London rose by 18 per cent, compared to increases of between 4 and 6 per cent in northern regions. The North East lost 14 per cent of its public-sector workforce under the coalition. The South East shed less than 3 per cent, as did London, where town-hall cuts were cushioned by a more diverse public-sector base and a civil service readier to slash jobs in provincial outposts than in White-hall.[50] 'The South is seeing recovery and the rest of the country is being left behind,' complained a Keynesian former member of the Bank of England's monetary policy committee in February 2014. He was echoed by the bank's chief economist, in an extraordinary outburst a week after the Brexit vote. 'Whose recovery? To a significant extent, those living in London and the South East of England.'[51]

Under the Cameron coalition, median household wealth in London increased by 14 per cent, while it fell 8 per cent in Yorkshire and the Humber.[52] The real average jobless rate was clocked at over 11 per cent in the two most northerly English regions, rising above 16 per cent in the worst blackspots, compared to just 3 or 4 per cent in large parts of the South. At the bottom end of the income ladder, very high deprivation loomed largest in a quintet of northern boroughs: Middlesbrough, Knowsley, Hull, Liverpool and Manchester. 'I'll tell you what's at stake,' warned Osborne, a millionaire Londoner, in the run-up to the referendum: 'the prosperity of the British economy, people's incomes would be hit, the ability to provide for their families would be hit. We've not even talked about unemployment.'[53] His parliamentary seat was a Tory constituency in leafy east Cheshire, one of only four out of thirty-eight areas across northern England where household income per head was above rather than below the national average. London, of course, had problems of its own, as the Grenfell fire would show. Out in the sticks, meanwhile, Jaywick on the Essex coast was England's single most destitute neighbourhood.[54] But as finance boomed, the London commentariat failed to fully register the extent of regional and local area economic degradation.[55]

❧

In the space of less than a year, the established political order of the United Kingdom received two successive, jolting blows – a referendum in which a population voted, against the express will of the leadership of all three major parties and an overwhelming majority of the country's Parliament, to leave the European Union, followed by a general election in June 2017 in which a 20 per cent lead in opinion polls for the sitting government vanished overnight, and the most radical opposition programme since Thatcherism, presented by the most vilified leader in the history of the country's media, came close enough to victory to generate a hung parliament – one then confronted with fraught negotiations over the terms of departure from the EU. The dismay of bourgeois opinion at the plight of the state is the best register of the effect of these temblors. 'Chronic instability', lamented the *Economist*, 'has taken hold of British politics', and it 'will be hard to suppress'.[56]

To understand the dynamics that produced this situation, the starting point has to be a closer analysis of the pattern of Brexit. Like any popular poll, the 23 June 2016 referendum can be broken down in a variety of ways. As the dust settles, however, some facts stand out. Nationalist dynamics produced wins for Remain in Scotland and Northern Ireland, while Wales's 80,000 net votes for Leave amounted to only 6 per cent of Brexit's winning margin. Cameron met his Singapore closer to home: every part of England voted Leave with the single exception of London, the previous Conservative administration of John Major having designated the capital city – swollen in size, wealth and self-esteem – a region in its own right. There was more than enough support for the EU in London and Scotland to cancel out both the modest surplus of Leave votes in southern England and the strong Euroscepticism of eastern counties. But coming on top of these setbacks, the six million Leave votes cast in England's historic industrial regions proved indigestible. Out of seventy-two counting areas in the North, fewer than a dozen answered the call from the Conservative government, the Labour opposition, Obama, Merkel and the IMF to support the European status quo. Had England's three northern regions – North East, North West, Yorkshire and the Humber – and the West Midlands been excluded from the count, Remain would have scraped home by 200,000 votes instead of finishing 1.3 million short. In 2014 Cameron's old Oxford tutor, Vernon Bogdanor – a TV regular on the mysteries of the British constitution – confidently declared there was little regional feeling in England, assuring the *New York Times* that 'the regions are ghosts.'[57] If so, could the UK still be haunted by them?

The Brexit poll exposed a set of interlinked fractures: national, regional, social, ideological. National: the contraflow 'In' verdicts of Scotland and Northern Ireland. Regional: London and the South East boast the UK's highest economic output per head and delivered the best numbers for Remain – 60 and 48 per cent respectively – outside the devolved nations. The Midlands, in sharp relative decline over the past two decades, voted most firmly the other way.[58] Social: the 'Out' vote correlated with lower levels of education, income and occupational grade. At the same time, a racially charged Leave campaign denied Brexit the support of most black and minority-ethnic voters and many socialists of all backgrounds.[59] Ideological: not regions, which were alive, but memories were the real ghosts abroad in England, ghosts of industry and of empire. Like the leading Brexiteers, affluent retirees in the Tory shires prefer their shareholder capitalism wrapped in a Union Jack.

But though the North–South divide is not England's only fault line, it's no accident that the deindustrialised periphery ranged itself against the London establishment in the referendum, sealing Remain's fate. For just as Asa Briggs wrote of the nineteenth-century Chartist campaign for working-class suffrage, 'All the social grievances of a discontented Britain were poured into the political vessel.'[60]

Brexit's margin of victory climbed to an unequivocal 56:44 across northern England. The strongest Out vote in the North West came in the deprived seaside resort of Blackpool, which had suffered the greatest financial loss from government welfare cuts of any local-authority district. Leave swept through the Pennine mill towns – at either extremes: Burnley 67 per cent; Bradford and Bury both 54 per cent – and the former heavy-industrial and coal-mining communities of west Lancashire and south Yorkshire (Wigan 64 per cent, Doncaster 69 per cent). The Tyne, Wear and Tees also registered strong protest votes, particularly Hartlepool

(70 per cent) and Redcar–Cleveland (66 per cent). Redcar had lost its steelworks – including the second-largest blast furnace in Europe – and 3,000 jobs the previous October, when Thai multinational SSI pulled out and the Cameron government refused to renationalise the former British Steel facility. 'It's just not something that is going to happen,' said James Wharton, Minister for the Northern Powerhouse.[61]

Towns where the number of EU migrants had been rising quickly were more inclined to vote Leave – for example, farm-working and food-processing Boston in the East Midlands, which posted the strongest 'Out' vote in the country (76:24). But many others that leant heavily towards Brexit had seen few arrivals from the Continent. Only 2 per cent of residents in Hartlepool were born elsewhere in the EU; in Stoke-on-Trent, centre of the decimated Staffordshire ceramics industry, 3 per cent.[62] Yet these depressed localities, like Jaywick's district, voted about 70:30 for Leave. In the eviscerated West Midlands, only affluent Warwick bucked the Brexit trend. Much of the rhetoric of Leave was anti-immigrant; the anger that powered it to victory came from decline.

Most of the pro-EU holdouts in the North were located in the central service areas or wealthier fringes of the major conurbations. Leeds and Newcastle voted 'In' by a whisker. Whereas the student-heavy and commuter-village constituency of Leeds North West is estimated to have voted 65 per cent for Remain, on the council estates and terraced streets of Leeds East disaffected working-class voters are reckoned to have been almost as vehemently for Leave.[63] Liverpool and Manchester, on the other hand, posted impressive municipality-wide Remain wins – 58 and 60 per cent respectively – and each brought with them a couple of fairly prosperous adjacent local authorities. Manchester, however, offered an extreme example of the coolness of pro-EU sentiment, its turnout 12 percentage points below the national average. Furthermore, the Greater Manchester conurbation overturned its core municipality to produce an overall majority in Leave's favour. The only other Remain islands in northern England were the Yorkshire spa and university towns of Harrogate and York and a prosperous patch of rural Cumbria. Sheffield, the former Steel City and the North's third-largest primary urban area, followed the rest of south Yorkshire into the Brexit camp by a margin of 5,000 votes. 'For a lot of people it was a vote against London, "them down there",' explained Clegg, who represented Sheffield Hallam while living in Putney.

The referendum defeat tipped Cameron and Osborne out of office, to be replaced by a couple of low-profile Remainers. Theresa May and Chancellor Philip Hammond came from a less stratospheric social orbit than their predecessors, but they were just as narrowly bounded by the comfortable Home Counties. One progressed from a Cotswold vicarage to an analyst's job at the Bank of England; the other was a jack-of-all-trades entrepreneur in Thatcher's Essex. Contemporaries at Oxford, they sit for well-off constituencies in the London commuter belt, though May did prior national service in the Tory cause by contesting a Labour seat in County Durham.

On the face of it, a Labour opposition led by two veteran London MPs, neither of whom had ever shown much concern at the party's centralist mould, might have seemed little better placed than a government of shire Tories to rally public opinion against the dominance of the capital, even if Shadow Chancellor John McDonnell was born in working-class Liverpool and represented a pro-Brexit Outer London seat. Proposing the introduction of regional development banks to improve lending to small busi-nesses, McDonnell pledged at best to divert some infrastructure spending from London to the provinces so 'that no government can ever again bias its own investment plans so heavily against the majority of the country';[64] while the centre-right leader of Labour in Scotland, Kezia Dugdale – championed by Brown – got the party to accept a constitutional convention to examine options for 'extending democracy locally, regionally and nationally', to ward off another SNP bid for independence. Of course, if Labour's regional policies were modest or studiously vague, the Conserva-tives' hardly figured at all. Depressed areas reduced to reliance on volunteer food banks were offered circuses in place of bread: a 'Great Exhibition of the North' echoing not so much the impe-rial Victorian pageant of 1851 as the compensatory Festival of Britain promoted by Attlee in bomb-damaged austerity London a century later.

With no choice but to heed the Brexit result, May attempted to make a virtue of necessity by rhetorically placing herself at the service of the struggling low- and middle-income voters in the regions who effected it. At the 2016 Tory Party conference, she acknowledged the widespread anger at London's soaraway wealth and admonished the Bank of England for the divisive effects of its emergency monetary policies: 'People with assets have got richer. People without them have suffered'. The new prime minister was committed to 'shifting the balance of Britain decisively in favour of ordinary working-class people'. While Cameron had peddled his own fairness agenda and tried in vain to repackage the Tories as the real workers' party, agreeing a truce with the unions ahead of the referendum, May's oratory had a conflictual bite to it absent from her predecessor's. She would be Brexit's guarantor against backsliding by 'the privileged few'. The mass-market end of the bourgeois media hailed a clean break with metropolitan elitism: the lessons of the referendum had been learnt.

In practical terms, there was less to differentiate the first May government – holding office prior to the 8 June 2017 general election – from Cameron's regime, beyond the rupture of Brexit. Whitehall was at a near standstill, its energies consumed with the technicalities of EU withdrawal. As for what passed for regional policy, the Northern Powerhouse fell out of favour when May sent a disgraced Osborne packing, but a New Labour plan for a high-speed rail link between London and the provinces – allowing corporate managers to shuttle between headquarters in the capital and back-offices 'near-shored' to lower-wage areas – was retained.

Osborne had threatened voters with a punishment budget if Leave won the referendum. Instead May indicated that austerity might have to be scaled back in the interests of national economic stabilisation. By postponing elimination of the budget deficit to 2025, a delay Osborne himself had conceded was inevitable, Hammond created headroom for extra borrowing to boost infrastructure spending and meet the costs of any future slowdown. The administration also called a halt to Osborne's public flogging of working-class welfare claimants, ruling out further cuts to allowances beyond those already planned, softening a £3 billion reduction of universal credit – an amalgamation of six existing means-tested benefits, including the dole – and pledging 'full support' for people with the most severe chronic health conditions and disabilities, no longer compelled to undergo regular medical re-examination in order to qualify for Employment and Support Allowance (ESA), the sickness-related unemployment benefit depicted in Loach's *I, Daniel Blake*.

But since the economy weathered the initial referendum shock better than anticipated – borrowing costs held down by extra credit loosening, including another dose of QE; the Bank of England assuring the financial markets that it would take 'any additional measures required' to protect their interests – Hammond pressed on with implementation of Osborne's spending settlement of November 2015. This had scheduled a further 18 per cent decrease in most day-to-day departmental expenditure by 2020 and taken another £12 billion out of the welfare system. The benefits payable to new ESA recipients deemed capable of some work-related activity were docked by 28 per cent at the start of the 2017–18 financial year, one of a raft of Osborne-era cuts waved through by the sponsors of a supposedly more compassionate Conservatism.

Still, following the capture of the Brexit surge for the right by the dissident Tories who dominated the Leave operation, and with Labour seemingly paralysed by a rolling Blairite coup attempt, the option of a snap general election proved irresistible. For the first time since taking Britain into the Common Market in the name of economic modernisation, the Conservatives stood on a platform of unadulterated Euroscepticism. Bowing to the logic of the Leave campaign, May prioritised immigration controls over membership of the single market and customs union, espousing a civic gospel with overtones of anti-globalisation nationalism: 'if you believe you're a citizen of the world, you're a citizen of nowhere.' Her berating of would-be saboteurs of Brexit on both sides of the Channel put British patriotism into fuller use than at any time since the late-imperial spasm of Thatcher's foray into the South Atlantic. One year on from the referendum, support for complete severance from the EU implied a vote for the country's traditional party of government.

If hostility to Brussels and immigrants from any point of the compass had been the true underlying drivers of the vote for Brexit,

May's hard-line posture would have merited a Conservative land-slide when the vote was held on 8 June 2017. And the general election did demonstrate a large constituency of opinion for her position. Despite a shaky campaign she increased the Conservatives' share of the popular vote by six percentage points compared to that achieved by Cameron two years earlier. At 42.4 per cent, May's performance equalled Thatcher's in 1983, and exceeded Major's in 1992, when the absolute size of the Tory vote hit an all-time high. Conservative confidence in a spectacular victory rested in good part on the collapse of the United Kingdom Independence Party, a right-wing anti-EU protest vehicle which lost its *raison d'être* with the previous year's Brexit success. Its eclipse released 3.3 million ballots into the electoral mix, to which May had prior claim. More UKIP voters had defected from the Tories than from Labour, and in 2017 more of them decamped to the former – 57 per cent switching to May's Conservatives, her consolidation of the political right around the promise of a hard Brexit gaining traction as intended in strongly pro-Leave constituencies.

A 4 per cent swing was sufficient to enable the Tories to over-take Labour in Middlesbrough South and Cleveland East, a mixed urban–rural constituency at the bottom of a red bloc stretch-ing up the ex-industrial North East coast – where two in three people voted 'Out' the previous summer. Swings of 6 to 7 per cent secured from Labour the deprived West Midland seat of Walsall North – the constituency estimated to contain the highest propor-tion of Leave voters (74 per cent) after Lincolnshire's Boston and Skegness, already in Tory hands – and Mansfield in the former Nottinghamshire coalfield which had always been a bastion of right-wing trade unionism. Having launched her manifesto in a former carpet factory in the west Yorkshire town of Halifax, which voted 55 per cent for Leave and where the Labour incumbent had a majority of just over 400, May bet on replicating such gains across the Midlands, the North and Wales.[65] Her expectations were comprehensively dashed. In Halifax, Labour increased its slender majority tenfold, elsewhere wresting three other mill-town constituencies from the Tories. In the depressed east-coast fishing town of Hull, a constituency where 73 per cent had voted Leave in the referendum – the highest of any northern seat – awarded the Tory candidate 5,000 more votes than in 2015, but support for the Labour incumbent also rose; less so, but enough to preserve his seat comfortably. In all, May gained a grand total of only two seats in the North and four in the Midlands.[66]

The central fact of the election was the counterperformance of Labour, whose share of the vote under Corbyn surged by a third, rising to a full 40 per cent – three to four points more than Cameron when he won the elections of 2010 and 2015, and five points above Blair when he was re-elected in 2005, as turnout rose to its highest level in two decades.[67] Seats were captured from the Conservatives in all regions of England, but it was the North that yielded most – a third of the total. In Stockton South, Labour ousted Cameron's minister for the Northern Powerhouse. The major northern cities went completely red for the first time, Labour toppling Clegg in Sheffield and another Lib Dem in Leeds. Cameron's old coalition partners were left with only one seat in the North, Clegg's ineffectual successor as party leader, Tim Farron, clinging on in the Cumbrian countryside. While the Tory shires held fast for May, Corbyn picked up southern constituencies from Plymouth in the west to Canterbury in the east – both districts having large student populations – as well as four seats in the capital. He won twenty-seven English seats in all, largely at May's expense, achieving a net gain of twenty-one. There was also some Labour revival in the central belt between Glasgow and East Lothian, where Blairite Scottish Labour had been deservedly routed by the SNP. May needed a dozen gains from the SNP, mostly in north-east Scotland and the Borders, to mitigate a dismal showing in England, where, as in Wales, Labour's vote share increased by twice that of the Tories. The prime minister suffered a net loss of thirteen seats to leave her party with 318 MPs, four short of a working Commons majority.

Labour under a socialist-inclined leadership, distinctly radical by recent British standards and backed by a growing non-parliamentary left, had made its first Commons gains in a general election in twenty years. The key to Corbyn's success lay in the platform on which the party ran – a rollback of regionally inflected Conservative–Liberal austerity, to be funded through redistributive taxation falling squarely on the London elite: higher income tax on the wealthiest 5 per cent, a levy on City financial transactions and reversal of Osborne's giveaways to cash-rich corporations. Corbyn's acceptance of the referendum verdict had drawn a barrage of protests from pro-Remain media in London, but stemmed a potential outpouring of aggrieved Leave voters.

Three parallel voter insurgencies left their mark on the post-2008 distemper: a Brexit revolt that originated in opposition to Maastricht among City mavericks and Tory voters in the market-town South, but then pivoted to attract northern working-class communities left behind by the New Labour boom and reeling from Conservative–Lib Dem austerity; the left-inclined 2014 Yes campaign for Scottish independence, 'as much a social movement as a national one'; and a Corbynist upsurge pitting a millennial precariat against a still largely Blairite Parliamentary Labour Party.[68] In 2017, Corbyn managed to hold together an electoral coalition drawing to varying degrees on the energies of all three. What would happen if Labour and the Brexit movement began to get in each other's way?

10

Taking a Stand

The crisis provoked by the rustbelt vote for Brexit and Westminster's unwillingness to implement it dominated British politics until the close of the decade. Labour had performed strongly at the 2017 general election on an anti-austerity platform, neutralising the European issue by promising to respect the vote whilst seeking as close ties as possible with the EU-27. Its subsequent obstruction of a Conservative-brokered withdrawal process drove one prime minister from office and fractured the governing majority of another. But the impasse also gave Remain diehards in the parliamentary party and activist base, obeying Lord Salisbury's dictum that 'delay is life', time to wear down Corbyn's resolve to respect the verdict of 2016, and Labour shifted slowly but inexorably towards demanding a second referendum to overturn the first.[1] Tactical successes in the Commons masked a deep-seated strategic failure to reckon with popular feeling in the party's deindustrialised northern heartland, where voters watched the parliamentary goings-on stony-faced.

The stalemate was broken on 12 December 2019, more than eight months after the UK had been due to depart from the EU, when a reconfigured Conservative Party under the country's chief advocate of European withdrawal secured a crushing general-election victory by capturing Labour citadels in the North and Midlands whose aggrieved voters had powered the original Brexit upset. The outcome made a severing of ties with the Continent inevitable, but even the Remain wing of the bourgeois press could

sigh with relief that Downing Street, 'having lost control of Parliament for years', was 'once more in charge'.[2]

After the general-election reversal of 2017, May's enfeebled
government had been propped up by the defenders of the Union
on the troubled Celtic fringe. Her Commons majority hinged
on the 13 seats won by the Scottish Conservatives and the ten
supplied by Northern Ireland's Democratic Unionist Party, a
Free Presbyterian–Orangeist grouping combining anti-Catholic
bigotry; all-round social conservatism, and low-tax, free-market
economics.[3] The threat to the Union from a weakened SNP had
temporarily receded but the politics of Irish partition loomed
larger, as May's DUP allies baulked at Europe's insistence on a
'backstop' arrangement to guarantee an open border on the island
of Ireland, potentially keeping Northern Ireland in the EU customs
territory and common regulatory area long after the UK mainland
had left the bloc.

While the withdrawal negotiations proceeded, the Labour conference in September 2018 opened the door to a 'public vote'
on their outcome, despite the misgivings of Corbyn and at this
stage also Shadow Chancellor John McDonnell. 'Nobody is
ruling out Remain as an option', declared Brexit spokesman Sir
Keir Starmer to rapturous applause from delegates. Labour had
traditionally been sceptical towards European integration for a
mixture of nationalist, sovereigntist and socialism-in-one-country
reasons. A special party conference had voted by a margin of two
to one against the Common Market ahead of the 1975 referendum, powered by the block votes of the transport and engineering
unions and by the left, with rising European imports blamed for
industrial unemployment. But union affiliates then embraced the
Social Chapter of Commission president Jacques Delors – his tran-
quilising adjunct to the Single Market – during Thatcher's third
term. The marginalisation of social policy in a European arena
governed by the fiscal constraints of the Stability Pact and Six-
Pack and the monetary and sovereign-debt management of the
central bank in Frankfurt has passed largely unnoticed.[4] The membership favoured adoption of the single currency in the 1990s, and
today it has a Remain demographic: 77 per cent drawn from the
ABC1 social grades and 57 per cent university-educated, though

earning fairly modest incomes.[5] Even in Leave-voting regions, activists overwhelmingly favoured a referendum rerun.[6] The pro-Remain broadsheets, having by now recovered from the shock of 2016, urged them on.[7]

At this point, Labour had slipped back in the polls following a renewed media onslaught accusing Corbyn and his supporters of anti-Semitism.[8] Besieged once more as the electoral success of the previous year receded from view, the tiny band of socialists sitting atop the parliamentary party were in no position to resist the tug of opinion within the party in favour of staying in the EU at all costs. Starmer's 'six tests' that May's withdrawal agreement would have to meet before Labour would support it included retention of the 'exact same' economic benefits as continued EU membership: ample pretext to reject whatever deal the prime minister was likely to bring back from Brussels and force a reference-back to the people.

The magnitude of the electoral miscalculation wasn't immediately obvious. Although 60 per cent of seats won by the party in 2017 had voted Leave, in nearly every one of them, the bulk of Labour support had come from the Remain minority. Remain voters were chiefly to thank for the wider Corbyn surge, and there were plenty of untapped reserves within this camp. According to polling commissioned by the People's Vote campaign group – bankrolled by PR executive and socialite Roland Rudd with the involvement of New Labour's Peter Mandelson – the party might lose 200,000 voters if it committed to a second referendum, but gain 1.7 million new ones: enough to yield 66 more Westminster seats and catapult Corbyn into Downing Street if – a heroic assumption – the surplus was evenly distributed across the country.[9] Another anti-Brexit group, Best for Britain, backed by insurance tycoon Clive Cowdery and hedge-fund financier George Soros's Open Society Foundations, reported that many Labour Leave voters were having second thoughts about EU withdrawal, that support for Remain had strengthened in nearly every Labour seat, and that over 100 parliamentary constituencies which had voted 'Out' in 2016 – in north-west England in particular – now had majorities for staying In.[10] Separate sampling which indicated that the party had already shed a quarter of its Leave-voting supporters since 2017 could be set aside in the name of Labour values. 'Sometimes, in politics, you just have to fight for what you believe in,' argued Paul Mason in the *Guardian*. Labour existed to represent progressive opinion in the cities, along with like-minded souls in towns otherwise given over to petty nationalists and xenophobes. The danger of a voter backlash from the latter had to be weighed, but by the time another referendum was held, 'the moral authority of the old result will have evaporated'.[11]

To avoid a backstop arrangement severing Northern Ireland from the rest of the UK, in November 2018 Theresa May conceded a protocol placing the whole country in a default customs union with the EU-27, terminable only by co-decision. Still unacceptable to the DUP on account of additional regulatory burdens placed on the territory to manage traffic of goods across the Irish border, the protocol also ran afoul of the larger number of Tory backbenchers wanting a clean break with EU institutions. Labour, of course, opposed the deal, citing its conference position. The backstop protocol ceded too much power to Brussels, argued Corbyn, but at the same time not enough power to prevent a Conservative government in Westminster from tearing up environmental and labour standards. When the text was brought to a Commons vote at the beginning of 2019 it fell by 230 votes, the heaviest government defeat in the modern party era.

Twice more the prime minister tabled it, to no avail, and cross-party talks foundered – May backsliding on the promise of a customs union under pressure from her own side, Corbyn and McDonnell seeing little reason to cut a deal with a Tory administration on its way out, and anyway hamstrung by demands for a second referendum from senior figures, including Starmer, Shadow Foreign Secretary Emily Thornberry and Deputy Leader Tom Watson, a conduit for the Blairite wing of the party. The prime minister announced her resignation on 24 May after European Parliament elections in which the Conservatives finished a lowly fifth. The Brexit Party of ex-UKIP leader Nigel Farage topped the poll, on a turnout of 37 per cent, rekindling Tory fears of an electoral eclipse on the right.

Labour came third in the Euro elections, beaten by the Brexit

Party in the North and the West Midlands and by the hard-Remain Liberal Democrats in London. There was no question which way the party ought to jump to escape this bind. 'Our members are Remain. Our values are Remain. Our hearts are Remain,' said Watson, as if the referendum to Leave had never taken place. Europe, he added, was 'Good with a capital G'.[12] Watson's demand for a full-throated endorsement of another public vote was echoed by McDonnell and Shadow Home Secretary Dianne Abbott, both key Corbyn allies. Figures from Best for Britain indicated that Abbott's Hackney constituency was the most pro-EU seat in the country – Corbyn's neighbouring seat in Islington a close second – and that voter opinion in McDonnell's west London ward of Hayes and Harlington had swung in favour of Remain.[13] Overriding the concerns of party chair Ian Lavery, a former North East miner, as well as senior staffers Karie Murphy, Andrew Murray and Seumas Milne, Corbyn announced he was 'ready to support a public vote on any deal'. Two dozen northern and Midland Labour MPs warned in response that 'a commitment to a second referendum would be toxic to our bedrock Labour voters, driving a wedge between them and our party.' They urged Corbyn to wait for stage two of the Brexit talks, after the UK had departed, to contest the terms of the country's future relationship with the EU-27. The signatories to this letter represented various tendencies within the party – Dennis Skinner was a workerist veteran of Corbyn's socialist Campaign Group, Caroline Flint a former New Labour minister – united in apprehension of looming electoral disaster: half would lose their seats in 2019 or retire ahead of the poll, the rest holding on but in nearly all cases with sharply reduced majorities.[14]

Standing outside Number 10 on 24 July, Theresa May's successor, once the public face of the official Leave campaign, pledged to heed the views of Leave voters in left-behind towns and defy the naysayers who thought Whitehall 'incapable of honouring a basic democratic mandate'. The Conservatives would break the parliamentary logjam by quitting the EU on 31 October come what may. Shortly afterwards, on a goodwill tour of Outer Britain, Johnson borrowed from Osborne's playbook to announce, at Manchester's

Museum of Science and Industry, a new cross-Pennine railway to Leeds. If the new prime minister had only the standard mayoral placebos to placate a demand from a concert of regional media outlets for 'a fundamental shift in decision-making out of London', he could at least assert a bond, forged in the referendum battle, with the outlying mill towns which had 'voted for change, but for too long politicians have failed to deliver'.

Johnson brought with him into Downing Street the former campaign director of Vote Leave, Dominic Cummings, a Durham-born, privately educated Oxford graduate who had cut his teeth working for the Business for Sterling group, rallying opposition to the euro among City figures and the CBI, and on the 'No' campaign in the New Labour plebiscite for a North East Regional Assembly. In contrast to Farage's anti-immigrant Leave.EU group, Cummings had wrapped the official Vote Leave campaign in social-democratic colours, its battle bus sporting a promise to divert money from the EU budget into the NHS. Under his direction, the Johnson administration shifted to a middle-period Blairism, promising higher public spending – £4.6 billion per year for schools by 2022 to return per-pupil spending to 2015 levels, a one-off £1.8 billion cash boost for hospitals, a £3.6 billion fund for deprived towns, £1.1 billion to bring police numbers back to their 2010 strength as part of a broader law-and-order crackdown – accompanied by a warning to business leaders that they would have to forgo a planned cut in corporation tax to help pay for it all.

If the Conservatives were culpable for the deterioration in public-service provision that this additional expenditure was intended to correct, Johnson could nevertheless distance himself from his party's record in office. He had only returned to the Commons in 2015, criticising George Osborne's 'hair-shirt, Stafford Cripps' austerity measures while London mayor for holding up infrastructure spending and depressing business confidence. At the spending review in early September, Chancellor Sajid Javid, a Rochdale-born former investment banker, announced a 4 per cent real-terms increase in overall departmental spending for the coming year. Outside healthcare, spending would still be 16 per cent lower than in 2010, and 21 per cent lower per capita.[15] But enough had been promised to allow Javid to claim that he was 'turning the page on austerity and beginning a new decade of renewal'.

These measures brought a Conservative bounce in the polls. After dipping below 20 per cent at the end of May's premiership and being overtaken by the Brexit Party, by the end of the summer they had recovered to 33 per cent: a 10-point lead over Labour they would take into the general election. On 28 August Johnson prorogued Parliament until mid-October, a fortnight before the UK was to leave the EU, in order to reduce the time available for cross-party groups of Remain MPs to legislate for another extension to the negotiation period. The UK's uncodified constitution is notoriously pliable, and Major had made a similar gambit in 1997 to forestall publication of a report into parliamentary corruption, but the shutdown was ruled unlawful by the Supreme Court, a New Labour creation seeking to build its role. For Cummings, who had foreseen the decision, this was grist to Johnson's mill. The Commons still hadn't recovered from its loss of face in the 2009 expenses scandal, and most Leave voters felt the prime minister was more in tune with the public on Brexit. The stand-off boosted his personal ratings while Corbyn's remained atrocious.[16]

On 17 October, Johnson surprised his critics by sealing a revised withdrawal package in Brussels. Gone was the threatened UK–EU customs territory, replaced by a bespoke arrangement for Northern Ireland. The province would be *de jure* part of the UK's customs area, and de facto part of the EU's. The Democratic Unionists were appalled, but most Tory MPs swallowed a deal that kept the rest of the country clear of the backstop quagmire. Corbyn opposed the Withdrawal Agreement Bill, characterising it as 'a charter for deregulation and a race to the bottom', but it passed its second reading in the Commons on 22 September through the support of eighteen of the regional Labour MPs who had earlier urged the party to end its obstruction of EU exit.[17] Fewer of them were prepared to support the government's attempt to force the bill through the House in a matter of days, however, and defeat of the accompanying programme motion supplied the pretext for Johnson to go the country ahead of the Christmas recess.

❧

Despite Johnson's reputation in the liberal press for reckless populism, there was no cause for the Conservatives to mount a riotous 'people versus Parliament' campaign: a slogan of 'get Brexit done' implied as much. The election manifesto added another £3 billion to projected day-to-day public service spending with a few minor funding streams for struggling towns as well as more CCTV and an appeal to 'community spirit': enough on top of previous spending announcements to shake off the millstone of austerity, but hardly a game-changer without the Brexit factor.

Labour's plans were on an altogether different scale. The party needed another huge surge to deny Johnson a governing majority, and McDonnell went for broke: £80 billion of additional current expenditure compared to the £50 billion pledged at the last poll, plus £55 billion of investment spending. The programme was carefully costed, the Institute for Fiscal Studies reduced to muttering vague generalities about the implausibility of so much extra outlay while at the same time conceding that it would still leave public spending lower than in Germany as a share of national income. Though policies such as abolition of tuition fees and nationalisation of the railways were individually popular, there wasn't a compelling anti-austerity message to bind them, Cummings and Johnson having moved the conversation on.

Promise of 'real change' rang oddly for a party that had spent the past twelve months attempting to preserve the pre-2016 European status quo. McDonnell had devoted most of his energy to placating opinion in the City rather than popularising Labour's economic programme in the regions. 'When we go into government, we will go into government together,' he assured an audience of bankers at Bloomberg – as if a softer Brexit, or no Brexit at all, together with a pledge not to impose capital controls on the City, could dispel capitalist aversion to the prospect of a socialist-led Labour Party in government, especially one committed to raising taxes on earnings and financial transactions and appropriating up to 10 per cent of the equity of large companies.[18] Although Labour was generally distrusted on the economy, only a quarter of voters put this among their top three concerns, while a large majority cited 'leaving the EU'.[19] Strapped to a tortuous policy of reopening the withdrawal negotiations and holding another In/

Out referendum, Corbyn was exposed to Johnson's accusation that he wanted to 'argue about Brexit for years'.

Labour's blocking of EU withdrawal precipitated a general election in which the party was bound to leak support on both flanks. When the polls opened on 12 December, between 900,000 and 1 million Labour Leave voters plumped for the Conservatives or the Brexit Party, while 1.1 million Labour Remain voters moved over to other Remain parties, mostly the Lib Dems.[20] In terms of seats rather than votes, the election turned on a Labour collapse in the deindustrialised small towns and former pit villages of the Midlands and the North. In these 'red wall' regions, 750,000 Leave voters switched to the Conservatives while hundreds of thousands more stayed at home. Turnout fell by most in working-class constituencies where, as the saying goes, Labour votes are usually weighed, not counted.[21] The party's vote share plunged by 13 percentage points in the North East, 10 points in Yorkshire–Humber and 8 points in the North West and Midlands. It held up better in London and the South, but the promised Remain bounty – always a poor bet since Remain support was concentrated in fewer constituencies – failed to materialise. In the west London marginal of Kensington, the 9,000 votes accrued by the Lib Dems allowed the Tories to retake the seat by 150 votes. Labour's sole gain of the night came in Putney, on a 6 per cent swing.

Countrywide, Corbyn retained four-fifths (79 per cent) of the party's Remain voters despite competition from more stridently anti-Brexit parties – the SNP and Greens along with the Lib Dems – but only half (52 per cent) of those who had voted Leave in 2016.[22] The Conservatives had a modest night in their own heartland, adding just three seats to their column in southern England. The six they picked up in Wales were offset by defeats to a resurgent SNP in Scotland. But among pro-Brexit voters in northern England and the Midlands they overwhelmed a weakened Labour Party to post a net regional gain of 44 seats.

Johnson's progress through the English rustbelt mirrored that of the 2016 Leave campaign. The Conservatives swept heavy-industrial Barrow and Workington in Cumbria on swings of 7 and 10 per cent respectively; Blackpool South and Grimsby on either coast (9 and 15 per cent); mill town constituencies in Accrington,

Bolton, Burnley, Bury and Rochdale, and also across the Pennines in Dewsbury, Keighley and Wakefield; former steel towns Redcar and Scunthorpe (15 and 13 per cent); Crewe and Darlington, once famous for their locomotive works (8 and 7 per cent); and most stunningly of all, a dozen ex-coalfield seats, from Blyth Valley in Northumberland (10 per cent) and Sedgefield in County Durham, Blair's former constituency (13 per cent), down to Don Valley and Rother Valley in south Yorkshire (10 per cent in both); Dennis Skinner's Bolsover constituency in Derbyshire (11 per cent); and Ashfield and Gedling in Nottinghamshire (10 and 5 per cent). 'It's as if there's a new modern mindset in the region', commented the *Northern Echo*: 'people have not worked in mines for decades, so now there is no need to vote as if they still do'.[23] Farage's Brexit Party detached additional Leave voters from Labour, but by splitting the Eurosceptic vote it prevented the Conservatives carrying off even more seats, including Hartlepool and the two Barnsley constituencies.

Johnson secured 365 seats in total and the largest Conservative governing majority since Thatcher. Corbyn finished with just 202, the party's worst return since the Great Depression. Compared to 2017, when it was possible to walk through unbroken Labour-held territory from Clwyd and Liverpool on the Irish coast to Pontefract in west Yorkshire and Bassetlaw in Nottinghamshire, the red wall had broken into three major pieces: the Merseyside and Greater Manchester conurbations, linked by a narrow corridor through Warrington North; the Leeds–Bradford urban area; and a stretch of south Yorkshire centred on Sheffield and Doncaster. The party also retained a truncated strip of North East coast between Tynemouth and Middlesbrough, a trio of seats in Hull, and solitary enclaves in Blackburn, Lancaster, Preston, York, Chesterfield and Ian Lavery's Wansbeck constituency in Northumberland. In the old Lancashire pit town of Leigh the Conservatives overturned a Labour majority of more than 9,000 on a 12 per cent swing. 'I think I understand the hostility to Corbyn among some voters,' wrote Paul Mason on a pre-election despatch from his hometown. 'At root it stems from the same hunch that the Leave vote did: "nobody's listening to us".' Leigh had voted 63 per cent Leave in

2016, but Mason omitted to mention his urging of a 'progressive alliance' to overturn its decision.[24]

It is worth pausing to reflect on the historic scale of the Northern Question posed by the general-election outcome. In the 2016 referendum, the three official northern regions and two official Midland regions had returned Leave majorities of 900,000 and 990,000 respectively, enough in tandem to swing the national result. In Johnson's election landslide it was the North that made the weightier contribution, accounting for twenty-eight of the fifty-eight seats gained by the Conservatives, while sixteen changed hands in the Midlands. In other words, the shock to the political system from the North was still larger and more clear-cut in 2019 than in 2016. Nothing much changed in the electoral landscape of London, the South East, the South West or East Anglia; the concentration of Tory gains in Leave-voting, working-class areas of the North was overwhelming.

Why could Labour still attract three in four voters in working-class constituencies in the major conurbations – Gorton in south Manchester; Bootle, Knowsley, Riverside and Walton on Merseyside; Ladywood and Hodge Hill in Birmingham; East Ham in London – while losing support hand over fist in secondary urban centres like Barnsley and Doncaster?

Bishop Auckland in County Durham, Hugh Dalton's old seat, was carried by Johnson's Conservatives on a 9 per cent swing. It contains a mixture of moorland and farming country in the west, Barnard Castle – once a preserve of Richard III – in the centre, and former pit communities in the east on the approach to Durham city, including Coundon, Spennymoor and Shildon, whose railway works closed during the miners' strike. Most of the mines around Bishop closed under Wilson in the sixties. The textile industry moved into the area but the main plant, Courtaulds in Spennymoor, closed in 1979. There is now a railway museum at Shildon as part of the local heritage trail.

New Labour shed nearly half its support in Bishop between 1997 and 2010, but with turnout falling and the Tories and Lib Dems splitting the opposition vote it never came to grief. The constituency voted 61 per cent Leave in 2016. Labour's vote share rose

7 percentage points under Corbyn in 2017, barely enough to hold off a 14-point surge for May's Conservatives that cut Labour's majority to just 500 votes. In 2019 the contest wasn't close: the Labour vote fell back to its level under Brown and Miliband while support for the Tories rose again and they won an 8,000-vote majority. The victorious Conservative candidate, a working-class millennial from Sheffield privately educated on a scholarship from City bank HSBC, cited popular estrangement from the Labour incumbent – 'very well known locally for her Remain stance' – as well as the 'metropolitan London attitude' of the Labour leader. Voters canvassed ahead of the vote voiced their anger at Labour for reneging on the referendum.[25]

Gorton in Manchester followed a different path. The constituency is a jagged, densely populated rectangle lying just south and east of the city centre, taking in the tough inner suburb of Longsight and low-rise council estates in Gorton; tightly packed Edwardian terraces in Levenshulme and Fallowfield; and two wards built to house the Victoria bourgeoisie before being overtaken by urban sprawl, Rusholme and Whalley Range, the latter now re-gentrifying. Labour's majority in the constituency halved to 6,000 votes in 2005, its lowest for decades, as the Lib Dems gained ground on anti-war sentiment following Blair's invasion of Iraq. It swelled to 24,000 in 2015, Clegg's party punished for its participation in the Cameron austerity coalition. Gorton voted 62 per cent Remain in 2016. Labour's vote share increased by 9 percentage points in 2017, stretching the party's lead to 32,000 votes, and it lost only 500 votes in 2019.

What social determinants lie behind these divergent outcomes? Gorton and Bishop are both broadly working-class, C2DE social grades making up 51 and 60 per cent of the workday population respectively. Whereas Bishop is 99 per cent white, Gorton is 52 per cent white and 29 per cent Asian, mainly of Pakistani or Bangladeshi heritage. Gorton is home to more university graduates, in addition to a large student cohort. Manufacturing accounts for one in seven employee jobs in Bishop – a GlaxoSmithKline plant outside Barnard Castle, which dates back to the 1940s, employs around 1,000 people – compared to just one in twenty-five in Gorton, where General Electric closed its Long and Crawford engineering works in 1996, causing MP Gerald Kaufman to describe the area as an 'industrial graveyard'. Retail is now a leading sector in both constituencies, along with education and healthcare.[26]

Patterns of asset ownership differ markedly. In Bishop, where the median age has risen to forty-six years, up from forty-one in the early 2000s, 65 per cent of households are owner-occupiers and, of these, slightly more own their property outright than have a mortgage. Many of the miners around Bishop lived in terraced houses owned by the National Coal Board, which sold them off at discounted rates. In Gorton, by contrast, the median age is twenty-nine years and most households (58 per cent) are rented, the majority from private landlords.[27] The North East may be far removed from the giddy house-price inflation seen in London, but most voters are people of modest property.[28] Precariously employed young graduates and students in Gorton, on the other hand, are less likely than in previous generations to attain a material security commensurate with their accumulated cultural capital.

In short, Bishop and Gorton belong to worlds of labour that, while not without their intersections, are in many ways distinct. In London and to a lesser but still sufficient degree in the larger provincial cities, glass-plated office towers and affluent suburbs testify to the fact that the world's sixth-largest economy has enough wealth at hand to mitigate its social problems. 'What is true of London, is true of Manchester, Birmingham, Leeds, is true of all great towns', argued Engels in *The Condition of the Working Class in England*:

> Everywhere barbarous indifference, hard egotism on one hand, and nameless misery on the other, everywhere social warfare, every man's house in a state of siege, everywhere reciprocal plundering under the protection of the law, and all so shameless, so openly avowed that one shrinks before the consequences of our social state as they manifest themselves here undisguised, and can only wonder that the whole crazy fabric still hangs together.[29]

For the millennial left of today's great towns, brazen injustices don't deter but rather invite a challenge, and protest cultures galvanise their grievances. In smaller, older, more isolated working-class communities, on the other hand, it strained credulity that a degraded public estate and a labour movement in organisational recession for a generation could deliver on Corbyn's pledge for 'investment on a scale you have never known before'.[30]

In 2017 Corbyn had improved Labour's vote share across the North by an average of 10 percentage points. Two years later his support dropped by the same margin. Although Blair and his supporters accuse Corbyn's leadership and politics of causing a 'rupture with long-held loyalties', the party's malaise in its heart-lands dates as least as far back as their experience of New Labour rule.[31] Even in defeat, Corbyn polled more votes in the region than New Labour, once in power, ever attracted. Corbyn's personal biography hadn't changed from one election to the other, even if a Conservative whispering campaign on social media alleging ter-rorist sympathies proved more effective in 2019 than the frontal Fleet Street assault of 2017. But the Labour leader's position on Brexit, the signature political issue of the day, had deteriorated in the interval. To suppose that if Labour had moved more decisively to an anti-Brexit position it would have earned the respect and assent Leave voters seems fanciful. They were 'more despondent than in 2017', reported shadow cabinet member Angela Rayner, MP for working-class Ashton-under-Lyne on the outskirts of Manchester. 'They wanted one thing done and it's not happened – and they hate us all.'[32]

Although there were voices on the socialist left urging Labour to stop flirting with rearguard notions of 'Remain and Reform', the party was wedded to staying in the EU.[33] One-fifth of Labour MPs had defied the whip to vote against the Notification of Withdrawal Bill triggering the exit process in February 2017. Corbyn would have endured endless criticism, from MPs and members alike, if he had gone on to allow MPs a free vote on the withdrawal agreements according to their consciences, Leave or Remain as the case may be. But Wilson's decision to let everyone in the Labour Party, from his Cabinet downwards, take which side they wished in the 1975 referendum was a democratic precedent that did the party no harm. If Corbyn himself had stuck firmly to a position of personal neutrality from the start, on the Wilson model, he would have been assailed as a weak leader by the likes of the *Guardian* and the BBC, but by emboldening his Leave MPs, this approach would have made the systematic Labour obstructivism which sank the party very difficult, if not impossible. Had the Johnson deal secured its passage through the Commons by means of a little more Labour support, it would have allowed Corbyn to fight the next election in 2022, according to schedule, by which time implementation of the 2016 referendum would no longer have been an issue and its consequences would have taken effect, with Labour free to attack the government all along the line for its socioeconomic record and, as it turns out, its handling of the pandemic.

Instead Corbyn was dragged towards a policy of disregarding the 2016 popular vote, and the ideological polarisation between the governing Conservatives and Labour opposition was confined to a proxy debate about the technicalities of EU withdrawal. Johnson's Withdrawal Agreement Bill, said the Labour leader, would 'decide the future of our country, of our economy and of the economic model we follow'.[34] He and McDonnell pinned their economic programme to a Brexit stance indistinguishable from that of the London establishment against which a large part of the Leave vote had been directed. Johnson stepped into the vacated ground: 'get Brexit done' had the force of basic democratic principle.[35]

Since the Treaty of Rome, no popular referendum has been allowed to reverse the top-down, intergovernmental process of European integration.[36] The Danes voted down Maastricht but then accepted it with opt-outs; the Irish were sent back to the polling booths after rejecting the treaties of Nice and Lisbon; the French and Dutch torpedoed the EU Constitution only to have the same provisions foisted on them by intergovernmental compact. Other than derogations for Britain – negotiated by Blair, who pledged in 2005 to put the Constitutional Treaty to a refer- endum, and never did – the Lisbon Treaty was virtually identical to its rejected predecessor. 'The proposals in the original Consti- tutional Treaty are practically unchanged,' acknowledged Valéry

Giscard d'Estaing, author of the aborted Constitution. 'They have simply been dispersed through old treaties in the form of amendments. Why this subtle change? Above all, to head off any threat of referenda by avoiding any form of constitutional vocabulary.' Blair was, of course, a firm believer in a second Brexit referendum, brazenly insisting, 'It's not an outrage to go back to the people.'[37]

A triumphant Johnson arrived in Sedgefield on the Saturday after the election to thank voters for breaking with the habits of generations. The North East had become an election battleground for the first time since the 1950s, when the Tories last claimed a third of the region's seats.[38] Johnson quickly pledged £70 million towards conversion of the former Redcar steelworks into a private-sector business park. Redcar had become Bluecar, the prime minister joked with his aides: it needed to be looked after. The North East may benefit from open bidding between the major parties for support. In a sense this marks to post-war norms, the dispensing of palliatives to take the edge of structural economic change, although mill towns in Lancashire and Yorkshire that have been marginal seats for decades haven't much to show for their swings of opinion.

The social bloc behind the 2016 Leave vote weighed decisively on the Brexit crisis: Eurosceptic Conservatives in the South hoisting Johnson into Downing Street, northern Leave voters handing him a landslide. The Northern Question had assumed its most pressing form since the miners' strike. But party-political musings – whether the Conservatives can hold on to their gains, or Labour reclaim its former strongholds – are not the same as asking what the region itself wants. Voters in left-behind areas have, for the moment at least, settled for a junior place within a ruling coalition led by the country's traditional party of government, giving the lie to New Labour condescension that they had nowhere else to go. Those in the cities opted instead for a social-democratic alternative under Corbyn that would have patched up a dilapidated public realm but had little to say about the political-constitutional order at national or European level. Different parts of the North are presently facing different ways, though if this is a culture war then its opening salvo was fired by progressives' disregard of the outcome of a referendum generally held, until it went the wrong the way, to be a legitimate, if tedious, democratic exercise.

Responding to the election outcome, the *Economist* hoped that Conservative investment in the northern rail network might serve to bind Blackpool to Manchester as Brighton is bound to London, even if existing links – between Dewsbury and Leeds, for example – haven't achieved as much.[39] Spreading such a tarpaulin over an uneven social geography will not prevent the bumps from showing through. The UK's spatial inequalities persisted, a running sore, into the new decade.

Conclusion

There have been two strands to our reappraisal of the Northern Question in British history: the apportioning of blame for the region's long economic decline, of which there's more than enough to go around, and the weighing of its political influence within a national power structure 'anchored' from its earlier days in the South.[1] What answers are available on either score?

First, on the subject of decline. We have seen Conservative and Labour governments put aside rhetorical commitments to reversing the North's economic deterioration in pursuit of policies that keep London and the South riding high. The City of London takes precedence over domestic manufacturing, deflation is preferred to regional stimulus, and meaningful measures to divert economic activity away from the capital are eschewed. Allowing for period detail, there isn't much to distinguish the record of either party.

For Tom Nairn, the 'slow floundering' of the British state began in earnest after the Second World War, when Attlee and Churchill abdicated the task of economic modernisation and instead began to liquidate the smokestack inheritance of the Industrial Revolution, falling back on London's older comparative advantages in overseas trade, capital export and international financial intermediation. Stripped of its empire, outgunned by rival industrial capitalisms, the southern English bourgeoisie could nevertheless prosper through control of the world's money market, periodically deflating the domestic economy to maintain investor confidence.

In the sixties, Labour's first northern prime minister promised a course correction in favour of industrial renewal. When that came to nothing, the party resigned itself to the defence of past achievements: the welfare state, the NHS – as one might say, the whole spirit of '45. Unable to resolve the contradictions of the long downturn, Callaghan ultimately surrendered the initiative to Thatcher's Conservatives, whose hawkish monetary policies killed off domestic industrial producers while drawing a new wave of international capital to the City. 'The established pattern of southern parasitism acquired boisterous new life', observed Nairn amid the manufacturing recession of 1980–1. The remnants of northern industry, 'unnecessary to offshore success', could be disposed of, although the region might offer a landing strip for foreign multinationals seeking a point of entry into the Common Market. But EEC membership since 1973 had done nothing to arrest the galloping decline of industrial regions, and Europe was already the target for a popular mood of 'sour contraction' that would only strengthen as the years went by.[2]

Since the Conservatives are first and foremost creatures of the South, even when their national electoral hegemony is at its most complete, their contribution to the dramatic widening of the regional gap should come as no surprise: it is Labour's conduct that has to be accounted for. In office, the party has always followed J. R. Clynes's dictum of the 1920s, playing the part of 'a national government and not of a class government'. It has routinely swallowed a definition of the national interest that puts sterling and the City ahead of manufacturing and the North, submitting time and again to pressure from London's financial quarter – the dominant fraction within British capitalism. Financial market pressures undid the 1929–31 government, Macdonald and Snowden rushing into Baldwin's open arms; the post-war Attlee administration exhausted itself in the 1947 convertibility crisis; runs on the pound pulled the rug from under Wilson's National Plan and provided the occasion for Callaghan and Healey's rightward shift in 1975–6. This isn't just a historical concern. The *Economist* sketched out five reasons why a Corbyn government would have been met by capital flight.[3]

On the second point, how to categorise the power-plays through which northern social classes have rattled the bars of their subordination within what Nairn terms the 'kingdom of Crown and

Capital'?[4] Writing in *New Left Review*, the literary scholar Wang Chaohua deconstructed the 'island consciousness' of Taiwan vis-à-vis the People's Republic of China into a matrix of claims for national legitimacy: political/democratic, economic, cultural, religious and ethnic.[5] Below I apply the same typology to *regional* class claims and hegemonic initiatives.

To begin with, political enterprise in northern England lay with the feudal barons of the frontier, heirs to the drawn-out Norman conquest of the region, who first precipitated the Magna Carta revolt and later, inflated by their military role as border force against the Scots, became the kingmakers of the Wars of the Roses. Then came the Tudor reaction, a century of centralisation, briefly interrupted by the Pilgrimage of Grace – a religious mobilisation against the new faith, with an economic undertow ('Captain Poverty'). After the downfall of the northern earls, leadership passed to southern merchants and modernising landowners, although Royalist northern gentry were participants in, and beneficiaries of, the Restoration stabilisation.

The emergence of northern England as the world's first industrial-capitalist region, a century and a half later, saw the rise of two distinct classes, each undertaking a hegemonic project in the 1830s and 40s: the Charter, a political-democratic challenge uniting northern workers and a layer of intellectuals with London artisans and radical democrats, and the Anti-Corn Law League, an economic challenge led by northern industrialists with Whig/Radical support against the big landowners. The latter succeeded, but without landing the lasting political blow its leading figures had hoped for. Later in the century, with the absorption of northern industrialists into the general capitalist class, national political leadership was consolidated in the South. The northern, Scottish and Welsh working classes attempted another political breakthrough, the formation of the ILP/Labour Party, in alliance with southern Fabian intellectuals. But from the 1920s onwards, Labour proved a broken stick as far as they were concerned. Under national TUC auspices they resorted to an economic initiative, the General Strike, largely without external allies. Throughout the interwar period, they bore the brunt of the City's demands.

Post-1945, northern working-class rebelliousness – cultural and economic, if not political – was a real problem for Britain's rulers, the subject of daily newspaper headlines throughout the period. While the cultural challenge of provincial England's Angry Young Men was absorbed, the economic one was anathematised. In Gramsci's terms, industrial action by unions around wages was largely a corporatist offensive, without seeking allies among the upwardly mobile skilled Midlands workers who would be an important part of Thatcher's base. The alternative economic model linking Solihull's Meriden Workers Cooperative to Merseyside's KME, a last-ditch counteroffensive to corporate closures, broke on the rocks of market competition. It was easy for Wilson, Healey and Callaghan to join Fleet Street in castigating 'selfish unions' holding the country to ransom and driving up inflation with their wage claims. But again, in terms of consequences for the country, the North – or the northern-led working class – carried real weight: the civil strife of the 1970s was seen internationally as a problem for the country's rulers. This was one reason why the southern intelligentsia stood by as Thatcher launched her onslaught against an isolated northern working class – with Essex and the Midlands largely on her side – weaponising Manchester liberalism against them.

The bursting of the Thatcher–Major–Blair financial bubble in 2008 and subsequent bailout of the City intensified existing discontents among working-class voters in Scotland and the North, to which Cameron's referendums on Scottish independence and EU membership gave vent. Brexit handed a political weapon to a class and region that had been denied one by Labourist hegemony for so long. The Brexit challenge was both political – 'take back control' – and to a lesser degree ethnic: control immigration. The North was decisive in tipping the vote, creating another huge headache for the governing class. Rejection of the Lib-Lab establishment locked the region into an alliance with its Mancunian ideological nemesis, the neo-Thatcherite right. But northern England remained of consequence, and Labour under Corbyn committed electoral suicide in pressing for a second referendum, abandoning the party's ex-industrial regional heartland to Johnson's Conservatives.

Following the Brexit vote, the structures of the liberal–conservative centre were weaker than at any time since 1911–14, as the British state came under increasing cross-pressures: from Europe, from Scotland, from Ireland – and, not least, trigger of the political crisis, the northern and West Midland rustbelt. The UK had slid back into the situation Nairn described in the 1970s: beneath the surface crises of economic stagnation and peripheral nationalism, a generalised disequilibrium of class, nation and region. Johnson and Cummings managed to right the ship. Their back-to-back victories in the 2016 referendum and 2019 general election rested on a willingness to trade in the four freedoms of the EU single market – unhindered cross-border movement of goods, capital, services and persons – for an electoral compact with the UK's left-behind regions. In doing so, they kept Corbynism at bay while protecting market imperatives within the national economic arena.

But Scottish nationalism and regional grievance will continue to reverberate within the country's unitary framework. Alarmed by the politicisation of 'anti-London' sentiment, aghast at the projected cost of refurbishing the Palace of Westminster, in 2017 the *Economist* proposed moving the seat of the UK government permanently to Manchester. 'The point of the exercise should be to create two rival centres of the Establishment,' it explained. The experiment would be unlikely to get out of hand, since Manchester voted Remain in the referendum and its central quarter is nearly as metropolitan as London.[6]

Add a second fraction of a widely loathed governing class, or despatch the one we already suffer? Mary Wollstonecraft wrote, five years into the French Revolution: 'It appears very certain, that should a republican government be consolidated, Paris must rapidly crumble into decay. Its rise and splendour were owing chiefly, if not entirely, to the old system of government.' Change the system, and the problem of an overgrown capital takes care of itself.[7] Wollstonecraft ought to have added the proviso that the new ruling system needs to break with the spatial hierarchies of the old. Its *ancien régime* overthrown, nineteenth-century Paris boasted more bourgeois splendour than ever before: the neoclassical triumphal arches and modernised infrastructure of the First

Empire; the fashionable arcades of the Restoration and the July Monarchy; the barricade-proof boulevards of Baron Haussmann and Napoleon III; the Eiffel Tower of the Third Republic.

By endangering the City's frictionless access to Continental capital and markets, Brexit struck a blow. As Wollstonecraft would have said, the foundation of London's luxury has been shaken. A more thorough recasting of the political order on this side of the Channel would put 'Londonism' in the balance, even if a favourable outcome for the North has against it the entire weight of English history and nearly every vested interest in the country.[8]

Does the deep recession accompanying the pandemic contain its own levelling tendency? Before the virus, average household wealth ranged from £170,000 in the North East (mostly pensions) to £450,000 in the South East (a mix of property, pensions, and stocks and shares). The money sloshing around London and the Home Counties was not, of course, equally distributed. The first wave of Covid-19 struck cruelly in working-class Newham, Brent and Hackney, even as a quarter of a million Londoners of means fled the city ahead of the lockdown.[9] London's industrial mix proved relatively adaptable to home working, and the decampment of the professional classes may permanently alter the economic balance between town and country, complicating workplace-based measures of regional output.

A less congested London could become another Copenhagen or Amsterdam, but as the *Economist* scornfully remarks: 'those are hardly world-beating metropolises'.[10] Property wealth in London climbed by 51 per cent between 2008 and 2018 under the impetus of Bank of England quantitative easing. What goes up can come down, but the announcement of an additional £200bn of QE in March 2020 was intended to ensure that it does not. London declines to decline, and the continuing power of the City–Whitehall nexus illustrates why the allocation of economic activity across a small island is ultimately a political question.[11] Today, the North accounts for a quarter of the UK's population and parliamentary constituencies and a fifth of its GDP. All these indicators are trending downwards, but from a great height. The problem of the North isn't going away anytime soon.

Notes

Preface

1 'Theresa May's hubris robs Britain of stability', *Financial Times*, 9 June 2017.
2 'Britain turns its back on Europe', and accompanying editorial, 'Britain cuts itself adrift from the EU', *Financial Times*, 24 June 2016.
3 'If London were representative of the rest of the country, Labour would have won by a crushing landslide. Of course, it is not': Owen Hatherley, 'The Government of London', *New Left Review* 122, March–April 2020, p. 112.
4 Susan Watkins, 'Casting off?', *New Left Review*, 100, July–August 2016, pp. 23–4. For the polling data: Eleonora Alabrese, Sascha O. Becker, Thiemo Fetzer and Dennis Novy, 'Who voted for Brexit? Individual and regional data combined', *European Journal of Political Economy*, 56, January 2019, Figure 2.
5 Doreen Massey, 'Heartlands of defeat', *Marxism Today*, July 1987.
6 'England-without-London': Anthony Barnett, *The Lure of Greatness*, London, 2017, Chapter 10.

1. North and South

1 Combined totals for the North, North West and Yorkshire–Humberside standard statistical regions. Frank Geary and Tom Stark, 'What happened to regional inequality in Britain in the twentieth century?', *Economic History Review*, 69, 1, 2016,

Table 1; ONS data set, 'Regional gross value added (income approach)', 12 December 2018.

2 David Harvey, *Spaces of Global Capitalism*, London, 2006, p. 115; 'The geography of class power', *Socialist Register*, 34, 1998, p. 49. Emphasis in original.

3 'OECD regional outlook 2016', 11 October 2016, p. 19.

4 'Eurostat regional yearbook: 2016 edition', 14 September 2016, p. 118.

5 Philip McCann, *The UK Regional–National Economic Problem*, Abingdon, 2016, Section 1.1; 'Eurostat regional yearbook', p. 118.

6 UN National Accounts Main Aggregates Database, 'Value added by economic activity, percentage distribution (shares)', December 2017.

7 Martin Wainwright, *True North: In Praise of England's Better Half*, London, 2010, pp. 144, 243.

8 Christina Beatty, Stephen Fothergill and Tony Gore, 'The real level of unemployment 2017', Centre for Regional Economic and Social Research, October 2017; ONS, 'Regional gross disposable household income (GDHI): 1997 to 2014', 25 May 2016.

9 Wainwright, *True North*, pp. 142, 294. London 'has sucked colleague after colleague out of my working life without replacement, so that my august job title is now perilously close to becoming a fiction' (p. 12).

10 Keith Jeffery and Peter Hennessy, *States of Emergency: British Governments and Strikebreaking since 1919*, London, 1983, pp. 244–6.

11 Bruce M. S. Campbell, 'North–South dichotomies, 1066–1550', in Alan R. H. Baker and Mark Billinge, eds, *Geographies of England: The North–South Divide, Material and Imagined*, Cambridge, 2010, pp. 153–4.

12 Tony Blair, *A Journey: My Political Life*, London, 2011, p. 251.

13 Russell, *Looking North*, p. 273.

14 Adrian Green and A. J. Pollard, 'Conclusion: finding north-east England', in their edited volume *Regional Identities in North-East England, 1300–2000*, Woodbridge, 2007, p. 225; John K. Walton, *Lancashire: A Social History, 1558–1939*, Manchester, 1987, p. 1; 'David Cameron "in off-camera jibe at Yorkshire"', *Yorkshire Evening Post*, 11 September 2015. See also 'Sheffield first and then we'll talk Yorkshire', *Sheffield Star*, 15 December 2017.

15 S. J. D. Green, '*Northern History* and the history of the North: forty years on', *Northern History*, 42, 1, 2005, p. 23.

16 Green, 'Forty years on', p. 20 n. Musgrove, *The North of England*, p. 7, defines the region in like manner: 'Cheshire is something of a problem', he says, 'but there is no doubt about the other six'.

17 Asa Briggs, 'Themes in northern history', *Northern History*, 1, 1966, pp. 1, 5. See also Green's account of the journal's formation in 'Forty years on'.

18 'Regional development – and some sort of regional autonomy – is coming to Britain sooner or later,' Neil Ascherson anticipated in 1962: 'The divided kingdom', *Observer*, 11 November 1962.

19 Briggs, 'Themes', p. 4; M. W. Beresford and W. B. Stephens, 'Gordon Forster in Leeds and beyond', *Northern History*, 31, 1995, pp. 1–9.

20 Green, 'Forty years on', p. 24; David Hey, 'Reflections on the local and regional history of the North', *Northern History*, 50, 2, 2013, p. 169.

21 Frank Musgrove, *Dresden and the Heavy Bombers: An RAF Navigator's Perspective*, Barnsley, 2005, p. 79. Musgrove completed his tour of duty in the Second World War by flying in Britain and America's wanton firebombing of Dresden of 13–15 February 1945. Looking back, he said he had 'not the slightest regret for having flown to Dresden'. Nevertheless, 'the moral issues that surround the bombing campaign ... have come to haunt me more insistently as the years have passed' (pp. 71, 86).

22 Frank Musgrove, *School and the Social Order*, Chichester, 1979, pp. 7–10, 186.

23 Frank Musgrove, letter to the editor, *The Times*, 1 January 1992.

24 Frank Musgrove, *The North of England: A History from Roman Times to the Present*, Oxford, 1990, pp. 1, 16–25, 316, 319.

25 Frank Musgrove, 'Lost kingdom of the mining men', *Sunday Times*, 12 August 1984; 'Summer of discontent', *The Times*, 21 July 1984.

26 Patrick Joyce, *Visions of the People: Industrial England and the Question of Class 1848–1914*, Cambridge, 1991, pp. 9, 65. Engels to G. V. Plekhanov, 21 May 1894, in *Karl Marx and Frederick Engels on Britain*, 2nd edn, Moscow, 1962, p. 583.

27 Dave Russell, *Looking North: Northern England and the National Imagination*, Manchester, 2004, pp. 8–9.

28 Dave Haslam, *Manchester, England: The Story of the Pop-Cult City*, London, 1999; Paul Morley, *The North (and Almost Everything in It)*, London, 2013.

29 Morley, *The North (and Almost Everything in It)*, pp. 5, 383 ff, 75, 138, 555; Terry Eagleton, reviewing Morley in the *Guardian*, 13 June 2013.

30 George Orwell, *The Road to Wigan Pier*, London, 2001 [1937], p. 104.

31 Geoffrey Ingham, *Capitalism Divided? The City and Industry in British Social Development*, Basingstoke, 1984, p. 6.

32 Despite all these accumulated privileges, however, if Britain were to choose its capital afresh, London might lose out to Manchester: 'The origin of London', *Cornhill Magazine*, 43, 1881, pp. 180–2; Asa Briggs, *Victorian Cities*, Harmondsworth, 1971, p. 48.

33 J. A. Hobson, 'The general election: a sociological interpretation', *Sociological Review*, 3, 2, 1910, pp. 112–13.

34 Orwell, *The Road to Wigan Pier*, pp. 78, 105, 113.

35 Ascherson, 'The divided kingdom'.

36 R. Ross Mackay, 'Twenty-five years of regional development', *Regional Studies*, 37, 3, 2003, p. 306.

37 Stephen Armstrong, *The Road to Wigan Pier Revisited*, London, 2012, p. 151; *The Super-rich Shall Inherit the Earth*, London, 2010; 'The billionaire refugees', *Guardian*, 6 March 2010; Hobson, 'The general election', p. 113.

38 Henry Pelling, *Social Geography of British Elections 1885–1910*, London, 1967, p. 229.

39 Danny Dorling, 'Persistent North–South divides,' in Neil Coe and Andrew Jones, eds, *The Economic Geography of the UK*, London 2010, pp. 24–5.

40 Beatrix Campbell, *Wigan Pier Revisited: Poverty and Politics in the 1980s*, London, 1989, pp. 3, 4, 117, 176.

41 Mark Billinge, 'Divided by a common language: North and South, 1750–1830', in Baker and Billinge, *Geographies of England*, p. 99.

42 Eric Hobsbawm, *The Age of Revolution 1789–1848*, London, 1988, p. 48.

43 Hobson, 'The general election', p. 112.

44 The Staffordshire Potteries, equidistant from Manchester and Birmingham, and historically a 'completely isolated industrial region', had by the Second World War drifted into the latter's orbit. A. H. Morgan, 'Regional consciousness in the North Staffordshire Potteries', *Geography*, 27, 3, 1942, pp. 98, 102.

45 Helen Jewell, *The North–South Divide: The Origins of Northern Consciousness in England*, Manchester, 1994.

46 Raymond Williams, *Culture and Society*, London, 1993, p. 3. Gaskell's biographer Jenny Uglow describes *North and South* as 'an industrial *Pride and Prejudice*' and notes its 'network of inter-linked contrasts – between men and women, country and city, royalist and roundhead, evangelical, Anglican and freethinker,

Norse and oriental myth'. 'Gaskell, Elizabeth Cleghorn (1810–1865)', *Oxford Dictionary of National Biography (ODNB)*, 2004.

47 Elizabeth Gaskell, *North and South*, London, 2003, pp. 40, 60.

48 Green, 'Forty years on', p. 23 n., who stretches a point by also pairing Manchester with London. Gaskell, *North and South*, p. 82.

49 Gaskell, *North and South*, pp. 121, 158.

50 Gaskell, *North and South*, pp. 299–300.

51 Even if 'it had to be admitted that there was "pull" in programme production towards London, and a good many of the programmes produced by ATV Granada and ABC Television were, in fact, produced there': Bernard Sendall, *Independent Television in Britain*, vol. 1: *Origin and Foundation, 1946–62*, London, 1982, p. 303. Granada founders Cecil and Sidney Bernstein 'had hoped to be allowed one of the potentially lucrative London franchises, but accepted the North with good grace': Julia Hallam, 'The development of commercial TV in Britain', in John Finch, ed., *Granada Television: The First Generation*, Manchester, 2003, p. 20.

52 Danny Dorling argues that the North–South divide was basically ignored in the 1920s and 30s, buried by post-First World War British nationalism and the dearth of proper statistics. Economists were absorbed by general theories of unemployment while geographers worried more about suburban sprawl and the interplay between town and country. The travelogues of Priestley and Orwell were outliers; only in the 1980s did the regional divide really hit home. Danny Dorling, 'Distressed times and areas, 1918–71', in Baker and Billinge, *Geographies of England*, pp. 44–63.

53 Owen Hatherley, *Uncommon: An Essay on Pulp*, Winchester, 2011, p. 48.

54 Antonio Gramsci, 'Workers and peasants', *L'Ordine Nuovo*, 3 January 1920, reprinted in Antonio Gramsci, *The Southern Question*, trans. Pasquale Verdicchio, New York, 2015, pp. 47–9.

55 Antonio Gramsci, 'Notes on the Southern Problem', reprinted in Gramsci, *The Southern Question*, pp. 15–46.

56 Quintin Hoare and Geoffrey Nowell-Smith, 'General introduction', in Antonio Gramsci, *Selections from the Prison Notebooks of Antonio Gramsci*, ed. and trans. Quintin Hoare and Geoffrey Nowell Smith, New York, 1971, p. xix.

57 Antonio Gramsci, 'Notes on Italian history', reprinted in Gramsci, *Selections from the Prison Notebooks*, pp. 51–120.

58 Quoted by Selina Todd, *Tastes of Honey: The Making of Shelagh Delaney and a Cultural Revolution*, London 2019. Nick Bosanquet, et al., 'Whitehall's last colonies: breaking the cycle of collectivisation in the UK regions', Reform, July 2006; see also Bosanquet, 'The North, last outpost of the Empire', *The Times*, 1 August 2006.

59 Gramsci, 'Notes on Italian history', p. 93.

60 Anthony Eden came from landed stock in County Durham but was schooled at Eton and Oxford, early journalism for the *Yorkshire Post* giving way to a political career at the Foreign Office with a weekend home outside Chichester. Philip Ziegler describes Harold Wilson as 'provincial to the backbone, committedly *petit bourgeois*'. But like his predecessor as Labour leader, Hugh Gaitskell, Wilson was an Oxford economist who arrived at Labour via the London Fabians. Whitehall, not provincial England, quickly became his preferred locale. Ziegler, *Harold Wilson: The Authorised Life*, London, 1995, p. 366.

61 Tom Nairn, *The Enchanted Glass: Britain and Its Monarchy*, London, 1994 [1988], p. 243.

62 G. T. Lapsley, 'The problem of the North: a study in English border history', *American Historical Review*, 5, 3, 1900, pp. 440–66. An apology for Tudor centralisation from a Harvard-trained constitutional historian. 'The problem of incorporating the northern counties with the rest of England was yet unsolved at the accession of the house of Tudor. It cannot be said that Henry VIII reached a final solution of the problem. He crushed, however, a dangerous rebellion in his own time and submitted the northern counties to such a discipline, that they were able a century later to take their natural place in the kingdom' (p. 452).

2. Badlands

1 James Campbell, 'The United Kingdom of England: the Anglo Saxon achievement', in Alexander Grant and Keith Stringer, eds, *Uniting the Kingdom? The Making of British History*, London, 1995, p. 44.

2 Peter Godman, ed. and trans., *Alcuin: The Bishops, Kings and Saints of York*, Oxford, 1982, pp. 4–5, 114–27; Mary Garrison, 'The library of Alcuin's York', in Richard Gameson, ed., *The Cambridge History of the Book in Britain*, vol. 1: *c.400–1100*, Cambridge, 2011, pp. 633–64.

3 D. M. Palliser, *Medieval York: 600–1540*, Oxford, 2014, p. 297.

4   Michael Swanton, ed. and trans., *The Anglo-Saxon Chronicles*, London, 2000, p. 200.

5   Paul Dalton, *Conquest, Anarchy and Lordship: Yorkshire 1066–1154*, Cambridge, 1994, p. 19.

6   Helen M. Jewell, *The North–South Divide: The Origins of Northern Consciousness in England*, Manchester, 1994, p. 34.

7   David Rollason, ed. and trans., *Symeon of Durham: Tract on the Origins and Progress of This the Church of Durham*, Oxford, 2000, pp. 182–5. William M. Aird, *St Cuthbert and the Normans: The Church of Durham, 1071–1153*, Woodbridge, 1998, pp. 64–73. The Durham ecclesia was a transplant of the monastic settlement of Lindisfarne and known as the Church of St Cuthbert, after a seventh-century Lindisfarne bishop said by Alcuin to have had 'led the life of an angel while still on this earth'.

8   Aird, *St Cuthbert*, p. 75.

9   Swanton, *Anglo-Saxon Chronicles*, p. 204; Aird, *St Cuthbert*, p. 76; Marjorie Chibnall, ed. and trans., *The Ecclesiastical History of Orderic Vitalis*, vol. 2, Oxford, 1983, pp. 232–3.

10 H. C. Darby, 'The northern counties', in H. C. Darby and I. S. Maxwell, eds, *The Domesday Geography of Northern England*, Cambridge, 1977, p. 448; T. A. M. Bishop, 'The Norman settlement of Yorkshire', in R. W. Hunt, W. A. Pantin and R. W. Southern, eds, *Studies in Medieval History Presented to Frederick Maurice Powicke*, Oxford, 1948, pp. 1–14. Cf. D. M. Palliser, 'Domesday Book and the "Harrying of the North"', *Northern History*, 29, 1993, pp. 1–23.

11 P. G. Walsh and M. J. Kennedy, eds and trans., *William of Newburgh: The History of English Affairs*, Book 2, Cambridge, 2007, pp. 20–1.

12 G. W. S. Barrow, *The Kingdom of the Scots: Government, Church and Society from the Eleventh to the Fourteenth Century*, 2nd edn, Edinburgh, 2003, p. 299.

13 Daniel Defoe, *A Tour through the Whole Island of Great Britain*, ed. Pat Rogers, London, 1986, pp. 449–550.

14 Jennifer Kermode, 'Northern towns', in D. M. Palliser, ed., *The Cambridge Urban History of Britain*, vol. 1: 600–1540, Cambridge, 2000, pp. 657–79; Bruce Campbell, 'North–South dichotomies, 1066–1550' in Alan Baker and Mark Billinge, eds, *Geographies of England: The North–South divide, real and imagined*, Cambridge, 2010, pp. 159–60.

15 Campbell, 'North–South dichotomies', pp. 164–7.

16 Rodney Hilton, *The Decline of Serfdom in Medieval England*,

London, 1970, pp. 20–2, 30; and Edward Miller, 'Social structure: northern England', in H. E. Hallam, ed., *The Agrarian
History of England and Wales*, vol. 2: *1042–1350*, Cambridge,
1988, pp. 685–98.

17 E. A. Kosminsky, *Studies in the Agrarian History of England in
the Thirteenth Century*, Oxford, 1956, p. 135.

18 Hilton, *The Decline of Serfdom*, p. 30. On the energetic but ultimately futile seigniorial rearguard action mounted in Durham
by Bishop Thomas Hatfield, a protégé of Edward III, see R. H.
Britnell, 'Feudal reaction after the Black Death in the palatinate
of Durham', *Past and Present*, 128, August 1990, pp. 28–47.

19 Musgrove, *The North of England*, pp. 13–16; Jewell, *The North–
South divide*, p. 210.

20 Campbell, 'North–South dichotomies', p. 161.

21 J. C. Holt, *The Northerners: A Study in the Reign of King John*,
Oxford, 1992.

22 The need to turn out troops for the Scottish Wars also accounts
for royal toleration of lordly encroachment on prerogatives
usually reserved for the central power. The Durham palatinate,
recognised as 'a bulwark against the Scots', was permitted to
exclude the king's writ; appoint its own sheriffs and justices;
and maintain a private chancery, exchequer and mint. Similar
schemes of sovereign delegation would be applied by the English
state to its colonisation of Ireland and North America: Charles I's
charter of Maryland granted its lord proprietor, Cecil Calvert, all
the privileges and immunities enjoyed by the Bishop of Durham.
But even under the grandest of prince-bishops, Durham couldn't
hold a candle to the lords of the Welsh marches, who claimed
full sovereign authority by right of conquest. Edward I shattered
episcopal vanities by twice confiscating the bishopric from his
friend and servant Antony Bek, upbraiding him that he was the
king's minister and must submit to royal mandates, since 'royal
authority extends through the whole realm, both within the lib-
erties and without'. A. J. Pollard, 'The Crown and the county
palatine of Durham, 1437–94', in Pollard, ed., *The North of
England in the Age of Richard III*, Stroud, 1996, pp. 67–87; Tim
Thornton, 'The palatinate of Durham and the Maryland charter',
American Journal of Legal History, 45, 3, 2001, pp. 235–55;
Kenneth Emsley and C. M. Fraser, *The Courts of the County
Palatine of Durham*, Durham, 1984.

23 R. L. Storey, 'The North of England', in S. B. Chrimes, C. D. Ross
and R. A. Griffiths, eds, *Fifteenth-Century England, 1399–1509:
Studies in Politics and Society*, Manchester, 1972, p. 134.

24 'So many great lords, nobles, magnates and commoners, and even three bishops, were attainted that we nowhere read of the like even under the triumvirate of Octavian, Anthony and Lepidus. What great numbers of estates and inheritances were amassed in the King's treasury in consequence! He distributed all these amongst his northerners whom he had planted in every part of his dominions, to the shame of all the southern people who murmured ceaselessly and longed more each day for the return of their old lords in place of the tyranny of the present ones.' Nicholas Pronay and John Cox, eds, *The Crowland Chronicle Continuations: 1459–1486*, London, 1986, p. 170–1.

25 S. T. Bindoff, *Tudor England*, Harmondsworth, 1991, p. 107.

26 Eric Hobsbawm, *The Age of Empire 1875–1914*, London, 1989, p. 22; Austin Woolrych, *Britain in Revolution, 1625–60*, Oxford, 2004, pp. 13–14.

27 Christopher Daniell, *Atlas of Early Modern Britain*, London, 2014, Map 90; Campbell, 'North–South dichotomies', p. 161.

28 Fernand Braudel, *Civilization and Capitalism, 15th–18th Century*, vol. 3: *The Perspective of the World*, trans. Siân Reynolds, London, 2002, p. 365.

29 Thomas Platter, *Travels in England in 1599*, quoted in Jeremy Boulton, 'London 1540–1700', in Peter Clark, ed., *The Cambridge Urban History of Britain*, vol. 2: *1540–1840*, Cambridge, 2000, p. 315.

30 Campbell, 'North–South dichotomies', pp. 146–7. The progenitor of Lollardism, John Wycliffe, hailed from Richmondshire but Oxford supplied him with his intellectual training.

31 Aske told his interrogators that he mourned the demise of northern abbeys because they 'gave great alms to poor men and laudably served God'. The appropriation of monastic land meant that 'the profits of these abbeys yearly goeth out of the country to the King's Highness, so that in short space little money ... shall be left in the same country in consideration of the absence of the king's highness in those parts, want of his law and the frequentation of merchandise.' R. W. Hoyle, *The Pilgrimage of Grace and the Politics of the 1530s*, Oxford, 2009, p. 47.

32 Hoyle, *The Pilgrimage of Grace*, p. 9; Michael Bush and David Bownes, *The Defeat of the Pilgrimage of Grace: A Study of the Postpardon Revolts of December 1536 to March 1537 and Their Effect*, Hull, 1999, p. 1.

33 Bush and Bownes, *The Defeat of the Pilgrimage of Grace*, pp. 290–3.

34 J. J. Scarisbrick, *Henry VIII*, new edn, New Haven, 1997, p. xvii.

35 Diarmaid MacCulloch, *Thomas Cranmer: A Life*, New Haven, 1996, p. 178.

36 Anthony Fletcher and Diarmaid MacCulloch, eds, *Tudor Rebellions*, rev. 5th edn, Harlow, 2008, p. 51.

37 Fletcher and MacCulloch, *Tudor Rebellions*, p. 163.

38 'And to rejoice in ancient blood, what can be more vain? Do we not all come from Adam our earthly father?' quoted in Fletcher, *Tudor Rebellions*, p. 110.

39 H. N. Birt, *The Elizabethan Religious Settlement: A Study of Contemporary Documents*, London, 1907, p. 306.

40 M. E. James, 'The concept of order and the Northern Rising 1569', *Past & Present*, 60, August 1973, pp. 49–83.

41 Lawrence Stone, *The Crisis of the Aristocracy 1558–1641*, abridged edn, Oxford, 1971, p. 121.

42 Hastings Robinson, ed., *The Zurich Letters, or The Correspondence of Several English Bishops and Others, with Some of the Helvetian Reformers during the Reign of Queen Elizabeth*, 2nd edn, Cambridge, 1846, p. 337.

43 Diana Newton, *North-East England, 1569–1625: Governance, Culture and Identity*, Woodbridge, 2006, p. 66; S. J. Watts, 'Tenant-right in early seventeenth-century Northumberland', *Northern History*, 6, 1971, pp. 64–87; Watts, *From Border to Middle Shire: Northumberland 1586–1625*, Leicester, 1975, p. 134.

44 Brian Manning, *The English People and the English Revolution*, 2nd edn, London, 1991, p. 281.

45 Musgrove, *The North of England*, pp. 121–2, 132–40, 228–36.

46 Norman McCord and Richard Thompson, *The Northern Counties from AD 1000*, London, 1998, pp. 173–8.

47 Joyce Lee Malcolm, *Caesar's Due: Loyalty and King Charles, 1642–1646*, London, 1983, pp. 64–5.

48 The parochial structure of the established church was especially weak in Lancashire. Many Justices of the Peace and officers of the palatinate had Catholic sympathies, and the Stanleys themselves were ambivalent. The county had the highest proportion of recusant households in England (90 per 1,000 households), followed by Durham (25 per 1,000), despite the Protestant leanings of the textile towns who sold their wares via London, a major European centre of the New Learning. John Bossy, *The English Catholic Community 1570–1850*, London, 1979, Chap. 5 and Map 1; Christopher Haigh, *Reformation and Resistance in Tudor Lancashire*, Cambridge, 1975.

49 Woolrych, *Britain in Revolution*, p. 250.

50 Woolrych, *Britain in Revolution*, p. 250; Musgrove, *The North of England*, p. 236.

51 Andrew Hopper, *'Black Tom': Sir Thomas Fairfax and the English Revolution*, Manchester, 2007, p. 37.

52 Ian J. Gentles, 'Fairfax, Thomas, third Lord Fairfax of Cameron (1612–1671)', *ODNB*, online edn, January 2008; Michael Schoenfeldt, 'Marvell and the designs of art', in Derek Hirst and Steven N. Zwicker, eds, *The Cambridge Companion to Andrew Marvell*, Cambridge, 2010, p. 93.

53 David Farr, *John Lambert, Parliamentary Soldier and Cromwellian Major-General*, Woodbridge, 2003, p. 211; A. H. Woolrych, 'Yorkshire and the Restoration', *Yorkshire Archaeological Journal*, 39, 1956–8, pp. 483–507.

54 Woolrych, *Britain in Revolution*, p. 14.

55 Belying his family name, North was born just off Piccadilly and sat for Banbury in Oxfordshire.

56 Eugene Charlton Black, *The Association: British Extraparliamentary Political Organisation*, Cambridge, MA, 1963, p. 33.

57 Donald Read, *The English Provinces c.1760 to 1960: A Study in Influence*, London, 1964, p. 14; John Morley, *The Life of Richard Cobden*, vol. 1, Cambridge, 2010 [1881], p. 392.

3. Industrialisation and Revolt

1 'The Manchester election', *Manchester Times*, 31 July 1847; Asa Briggs, *Victorian People*, Harmondsworth, 1977, p. 212.

2 Read, *The English Provinces*, pp. 148–9.

3 It implied 'the assumption of political power' by the masses of the people 'as a means of meeting their social requirements.' Karl Marx, 'The Association for Administrative Reform – People's Charter', 5 June 1855, in *Karl Marx and Frederick Engels on Britain*, pp. 431–2.

4 Friedrich Engels, *The Condition of the Working Class in England*, trans. Florence Kelley-Wischnewetsky, Oxford, 2009, p. 21.

5 Léon Faucher, *Manchester in 1844: Its Present Condition and Future Prospects*, London, 1844, p. 16.

6 Asa Briggs, *The Age of Improvement 1783–1867*, 2nd edn, Harlow, 2000, pp. 21–2.

7 *Royal Commission on the Condition of the Poorer Classes in Ireland. Appendix G: Report on the State of the Irish Poor in Great Britain*, PP 1836, 40, p. 68.

8 Defoe, *A Tour through the Whole Island of Great Britain*, pp. 491–2.

9 Jennifer Tann, 'The employment of power in the West of England wool textile industry, 1790–1840', in N. B. Harte and K. G. Ponting, eds, *Textile History and Economic History*, Manchester, 1973, p. 218; Jones, *Locating the Industrial Revolution*, p. 66.

10 Fernand Braudel, *Civilisation and Capitalism 15th–18th Century*, vol. 2: *The Wheels of Commerce*, trans. Siân Reynolds, London, 2002, p. 601.

11 Kenneth Morgan, 'Liverpool's dominance in the British slave trade, 1740–1807', in David Richardson, Suzanne Schwarz and Anthony Tibbles, eds, *Liverpool and Transatlantic Slavery*, Liverpool, 2007, pp. 14–5.

12 S. G. Checkland, *The Gladstones: A Family Biography 1764–1851*, Cambridge, 1971, p. 198.

13 *The Debates in Parliament – Session 1833 – on the Resolutions and Bill for the Abolition of Slavery in the British Colonies*, London, 1834, pp. 268–79.

14 E. J. Hobsbawm, 'The machine breakers', *Past & Present*, 1, February 1952, pp. 65–6. Lancashire hand-spinners 'pining for want of Employment' petitioned in vain for a tax on factory machinery, which they labelled 'a mere Monopoly for the immense Profits and Advantages of the Patentees and Proprietors, to the great Loss and Detriment of the Public'. *House of Commons Journal*, 37, 27 April 1780, pp. 804–5.

15 David Spring, 'English landowners and nineteenth-century industrialism' and J. T. Ward, 'Landowners and mining', in J. T. Ward and R. G. Wilson, eds, *Land and Industry: The Landed Estate and the Industrial Revolution*, Newton Abbot, 1971.

16 Industrialisation of cotton spinning swelled the number of handworkers in ancillary sectors slower to mechanise. Handloom weavers, comprising up to a quarter of Lancashire's working population, were totally reliant on business from mill owners and putters-out who cut wages when times were hard and held them low when trade recovered. MPs rejected their pleas for a statutory minimum wage, instead stripping away their welfare entitlements through revisions to the Poor Law. The *Manchester Times*, a mouthpiece of the mill owners, hammered the point home: the weavers' pleas were 'founded in utter ignorance of the circumstances which regulate the wages of labour, which it is as impossible for Parliament to control as it is for it to regulate the price of cotton or any other article'. Not until the 1840s did an

improved power loom convert weaving into a factory process and oust this low-cost, desperately impoverished community of outworkers. 'The hand-loom weavers and the bread tax', *Manchester Times*, 16 December 1837, quoted by Donald Read, 'Chartism in Manchester', in Asa Briggs, ed., *Chartist Studies*, London, 1959, p. 32.

17 Michael Bentley, *Politics without Democracy, 1815–1914*, 2nd edn, London, 1996, pp. 33, 38.

18 Thompson, *The Making of the English Working Class*, p. 217.

19 Marx, 'Parliamentary debates', 25 February 1853, in *Karl Marx and Frederick Engels on Britain*, p. 381.

20 Charlotte Brontë, *Shirley*, Oxford, 1979, p. 300; Elizabeth Gaskell, *Mary Barton*, Oxford, 1987, p. 203.

21 Gaskell, *Mary Barton*, p. 458; Benjamin Disraeli, *Sybil, or The Two Nations*, Oxford, 2008, p. 183. Disraeli would vote against public-health legislation.

22 Parlt. Hist. 30, p. 495.

23 *The Times*, 18 June 1799; Parlt. Reg. 8, p. 323; J. L. Hammond and Barbara Hammond, *The Town Labourer 1760–1832*, London, 1917, pp. 117–24.

24 Thompson, *The Making of the English Working Class*, p. 514.

25 Lord Palmerston as War Secretary observed that there was 'sufficient protection for the constitution' in the make-up of Britain's standing army, its officers 'identified by their property, their connexions and general interests, with the civil prosperity of the state'. HC Deb 8 March 1816, vol. 33, p. 108.

26 Kevin Binfield, ed., *Writings of the Luddites*, Baltimore, 2004, p. 210.

27 Brontë, *Shirley*, pp. 391, 431; Binfield, *Writings of the Luddites*, p. 209.

28 D. F. E. Sykes and Geo. Henry Walker, *Ben o' Bills, the Luddite*, London, 1898, pp. 165–9; Binfield, *Writings of the Luddites*, p. 200.

29 Binfield, *Writings of the Luddites*, pp. 179–81.

30 The Tory prime minister's father Charles, an Oxfordshire baronet and a long-serving president of the Board of Trade, was created Earl of Liverpool in 1796 after being awarded the freedom of the city 'in gratitude for the essential services rendered to the town of Liverpool by his Lordship's late exertion in Parliament in support of the African Slave Trade'. Peter Fryer, *Staying Power: The History of Black People in Britain*, London, 1984, p. 57.

31 Archibald Prentice, *Historical Sketches and Personal Recollections of Manchester*, London, 1851, pp. 52–8; George Pellew,

The Life and Correspondence of the Right Hon. Henry Adding-ton, First Viscount Sidmouth, vol. 3, London, 1847, pp. 78–93; Annual Register 55, pp. 348–9.

32 Robert Walmsley, *Peterloo: The Case Reopened*, Manchester, 1969, p. 16 – an apologia for Hulton.

33 Robert Poole, '"By the law or the sword": Peterloo revisited', *History*, 91, 302, 2006, pp. 254–76; Joyce Marlow, 'The day of Peterloo', *Manchester Region History Review*, 3, 1, pp. 3–7; M. L. Bush, *The Casualties of Peterloo*, Lancaster, 2005, p. vii and Table 1; Pellew, *Sidmouth*, pp. 261–2, 269–71; Prentice, *Historical Sketches*, chap. 11.

34 John Belchem, 'Manchester, Peterloo and the radical challenge', *Manchester Region History Review*, 3, 1, pp. 12–14.

35 Musgrove, *The North of England*, pp. 274, 293; Bush, *The Casualties of Peterloo*, pp. 25, 55.

36 William Benbow, *Grand National Holiday and Congress of the Productive Classes*, London, 1977 [1832].

37 John A. Hargeaves, 'Introduction', in John A. Hargeaves and E. A. H. Haigh, eds, *Slavery in Yorkshire: Richard Oastler and the Campaign against Child Labour in the Industrial Revolution*, Huddersfield, 2012, p. 30.

38 *Cobbett's Weekly Political Register*, 9 August 1823.

39 Nassau W. Senior, *Letters on the Factory Act, as It Affects the Cotton Manufacture*, London, 1837, pp. 14–15. 'The manufacturers chose him as their prize-fighter', explains Marx. 'With their usual practical acuteness they had realised that the learned professor "wanted a good deal of finishing"; that is why they invited him to Manchester.' Karl Marx, *Capital*, vol. 1, trans. Ben Fowkes, London, 1990, p. 333.

40 Edward Baines Junior, *History of the Cotton Manufacture in Great Britain*, London, 1835, p. 457.

41 *Cobbett's Weekly Political Register*, 24 November 1832.

42 *Leeds Mercury*, 16 October 1830, reprinted in Hargeaves, 'Introduction', p. 3. Emphasis in original.

43 Thompson, *The Making of the English Working Class*, pp. 376–81. For Oastler's career: Cecil Driver, *Tory Radical: The Life of Richard Oastler*, Oxford, 1946; Hargeaves, 'Introduction'.

44 Resolutions of the Master Worsted Spinners of Halifax, 5 March 1831, reprinted in Driver, *Tory Radical*, Appendix A. Emphasis in original.

45 Geoffrey B. A. M. Finlayson, *The Seventh Earl of Shaftesbury*, Vancouver, 2004, p. 300; Marx, 'Parliamentary debates', p. 382.

46 Marx, *Capital*, vol. 1, pp. 533–3; Harriet Martineau, *The Factory*

Controversy; A Warning against Meddling Legislation, Manchester, 1855.

47 Michael Brock, *The Great Reform Act*, London, 1973, pp. 105–6.

48 E. A. Smith, *Lord Grey 1764–1845*, Oxford, 1990, pp. 10–11, 327.

49 Bentley, *Politics without Democracy*, p. 33.

50 Stephen M. Lee, '"The pride of my publick life": George Canning and the representation of Liverpool, 1812–1823', *Transactions of the Historic Society of Lancashire and Cheshire*, 149, 1999, pp. 73–98.

51 Anthony Howe, *The Cotton Masters 1830–1860*, Oxford, 1984, p. 92.

52 Nancy D. LoPatin, *Political Unions, Popular Politics and the Great Reform Act of 1832*, Houndmills, 1999, p. 17.

53 LoPatin, *Political Unions*, pp. 78–9, 135–6.

54 Read, *The English Provinces*, p. 156.

55 HC Deb 17 December 1831, 3rd series, vol. 9, pp. 497–500.

56 HC Deb 17 December 1831, 3rd series, vol. 9, pp. 497–500; Edward Baines [Junior], *The Life of Edward Baines*, 2nd edn, London, 1859, pp. 129–30; Thompson, *The Making of the English Working Class*, pp. 899–900.

57 *Return of Population of Counties and Towns That Have Returned, and Will Continue to Return, Members to Parliament*, PP 1831–2, 442; Norman Gash, *Politics in the Age of Peel*, 2nd edn, Hassocks, 1977, pp. 73–85; HC Deb 27 July 1831, 3rd series, vol. 5, p. 420.

58 Howe, *The Cotton Masters*, Table 3.2; Brock, *Great Reform Act*, p. 334; Asa Briggs, 'National bearings', in Briggs, *Chartist Studies*, p. 295.

59 After receiving a fright in the build-up to the Kennington Common rally of 10 April 1848, 'Lord John observed that action might bring on a revolution, but that in the long run inaction must.' John Prest, *Lord John Russell*, London, 1972, p. 303. Among Tories, Disraeli concurred: 'I, for one, am no advocate of finality'. Roland Quinault, '1848 and parliamentary reform', *Historical Journal*, 31, 4, 1988, p. 845.

60 Michael S. Edwards, *Purge This Realm: A Life of Joseph Rayner Stephens*, London, 1994, pp. 44–5.

61 Engels, *Condition of the Working Class*, p. 247; Briggs, 'The local background of Chartism', in Briggs, *Chartist Studies*, p. 3.

62 Chase, *Chartism*, pp. 162–4.

63 Edwards, *Purge This Realm*, p. 44–5.

64 W. Napier, *The Life and Opinions [of] General Sir Charles James Napier*, vol. 2, 2nd edn, London, 1857, pp. 3–4, 32–3; Malcolm Chase, *Chartism: A New History*, Manchester, 2007, pp. 84–7, 94–106.

65 Edwards, *Purge This Realm*, p. 54.

66 In the event, only the miners of Monmouthshire went beyond strike action into armed insurrection in 1839. Around twenty of their number were shot dead by infantrymen, and ringleader John Frost, a Newport tailor, was convicted of high treason – 'levying war against her Majesty in her realm' – and sentenced to be hung, drawn and quartered. He survived thanks to popular agitation for clemency. Wary of provoking further unrest, the Crown brought a reduced charge of seditious conspiracy against Samuel Holberry, an unemployed labourer in charge of aborted revolutionary preparations in Sheffield. Holberry was sentenced to four years in Northallerton prison, chosen by prosecutors on the basis that inmates there were 'worse fed & hardest worked'. One of Holberry's associates, fifty-two-year-old John Clayton – rheumatic, asthmatic, suffering from kidney stones – lasted ten months. Holberry died a year later at York Castle of tuberculosis, aged twenty-seven. Chase, *Chartism*, pp. 134, 140, 152–7.

67 Carlyle, *Past and Present*, chap. 3.

68 Mather, 'The government and the Chartists', pp. 386–94; Chase, *Chartism*, chap. 7.

69 Brock, *Great Reform Act*, p. 322. Chase, *Chartism*, pp. 220, 225.

70 David Goodway, *London Chartism 1838–1848*, Cambridge, 1982, p. 223.

71 *The Times*, 11 April 1848; Saville, *1848*, chaps 4, 5; Chase, *Chartism*, pp. 300–3.

72 Saville, *1848*, pp. 121–2, 140–1; A. J. Arbuthnot, 'Arbuthnot, Sir Thomas', rev. S. Kinross, *ODNB*, 2004; Chase, *Chartism*, pp. 343–7.

73 Cf. Nicholas C. Edsall, *Richard Cobden: Independent Radical*, Cambridge, MA, 1986, pp. 26–8.

74 Morley, *Cobden*, vol. 1, pp. 96–7; Marx, 'The Chartists', 10 August 1852, in *Karl Marx and Frederick Engels on Britain*, p. 358.

75 R. Robson, *The Cotton Industry in Britain*, London, 1957, Statistical Appendix A2.

76 J. T. Ward and R. G. Wilson, 'Introduction', in Ward and Wilson, *Land and Industry*, p. 8.

77 Read, *The English Provinces*, p. 141; David Ayerst, *The Manchester Guardian: Biography of a Newspaper*, Ithaca, NY, 1971,

p. 72; Howe, *The Cotton Masters*, pp. 204–5, 213; Anthony Howe, *Free Trade and Liberal England 1846–1946*, Oxford, 1997, p. 12–7; Norman McCord, *The Anti-Corn Law League 1838–1846*, Abingdon, 2006, p. 48.

78 McCord, *The Anti-Corn Law League*, p. 204.

79 For relations between the *Economist* and the ACLL see Alexander Zevin, *Liberalism at Large: The World According to the Economist*, London and New York, 2019, chap. 1.

80 HC Deb 29 June 1846, 3rd series, vol. 87, pp. 1053–4; McCord, *The Anti-Corn Law League*, pp. 203–4; Benjamin Disraeli, *Lord George Bentinck: A Political Biography*, London, 1852, pp. 211–16; Howe, *Free Trade*, pp. 8–12;

81 Morley, *Cobden*, vol. 1, pp. 390–401.

82 'The peace party is nothing but the *Free-Trade party in disguise*. No exploitation of peoples by medieval wars but only by means of trade wars – such is the peace party.' Marx to Ferdinand Freiligrath, 31 July 1849, in *Karl Marx and Frederick Engels on Britain*, p. 534.

83 Cobden to Henry Ashworth, 8 January 1848, in *The Letters of Richard Cobden*, vol. 2: *1848–1853*, ed. Anthony Howe, Oxford, 2010, pp. 6–7; Howe, *The Cotton Masters*, p. 238; Read, *The English Provinces*, pp. 151–7; Edsall, *Cobden*, p. 311.

84 John Morley, *The Life of Richard Cobden*, vol. 2, London, 1881, p. 396.

85 D. T. Jenkins and K. G. Ponting, *The British Wool Textile Industry 1770–1914*, London, 1982, p. 303. See also Howe, *The Cotton Masters*, chap. 7.

86 Brock, *The Great Reform Act*, p. 322; Howe, *The Cotton Masters*, p. 234; Briggs, *Victorian Cities*, p. 100.

87 W. D. Rubinstein, *Men of Property: The Very Wealthy in Britain since the Industrial Revolution*, 2nd edn, London, 2006, pp. 79, 128–38. See also Perry Anderson, 'The figures of descent', *New Left Review*, I/161, January–February 1987, pp. 34–5.

88 McCord, *The Anti-Corn Law League*, pp. 29–30; P. J. Cain and A. G. Hopkins, *British Imperialism 1688–2015*, 3rd edn, London, 2016, pp. 55–8; Morley, *Cobden*, vol. 1, p. 134.

89 Gaskell, *North and South*, p. 40. Gaskell softens the blow by then marrying off her protagonists. 'This land of long chimneys': a phrase of Hyde mill owner Thomas Ashton, quoted by Sven Beckert, *Empire of Cotton: A Global History*, London, 2014, p. 80.

4. The Tide Turns

1 Eric Hobsbawm, *Worlds of Labour*, London, 1984, p. 182.

2 *The Times*, 4 September 1874.

3 Anthony Slaven, *British Shipbuilding 1500–2010*, Lancaster, 2013, pp. 62–4; Eric Hobsbawm, *The Age of Empire 1875–1914*, London, 1989, p. 308.

4 Kenneth Warren, *Chemical Foundations: The Alkali Industry in Britain to 1926*, Oxford, 1980, chaps 8, 9; Matthew Arnold, 'The future of Liberalism', in Matthew Arnold, *Complete Prose Works*, vol. 9, ed. R. H. Super, Ann Arbor, MI, 1973, p. 145.

5 Combined totals for the North, North West and Yorkshire–Humberside standard statistical regions. Frank Geary and Tom Stark, 'Regional GDP in the UK, 1861–1911: new estimates', *Economic History Review*, 68, 1, 2015, Table 3.

6 Slaven, *British Shipbuilding*, Tables 2.2, 3.2; D. A. Farnie, 'The textile machine-making industry and the world market, 1870–1960', in Mary B. Rose, ed., *International Competition and Strategic Response in the Textile Industries since 1870*, London, 1991, pp. 150–3.

7 Geary and Stark, 'Regional GDP', Table 3; C. H. Lee, 'Regional growth and structural change in Victorian Britain', *Economic History Review*, 34, 3, 1981, pp. 438–52.

8 P. J. Cain and A. G. Hopkins, *British Imperialism 1688–2015*, 3rd edn, London, 2016, chap. 6.

9 Morley, *Cobden*, vol. 2, pp. 221, 224.

10 D. A. Farnie, *The English Cotton Industry and the World Market 1815–1896*, Oxford, 1979, pp. 171–5; Lance E. Davis and Robert A. Huttenback, *Mammon and the Pursuit of Empire: The Political Economy of British Imperialism, 1860–1912*, Cambridge, 1986, pp. 209–11.

11 Cain and Hopkins, *British Imperialism*, chap. 6.

12 More precisely, 36 per cent in Lancashire, 43 per cent in the West Riding (grouped with Nottinghamshire and Derbyshire), and 49 per cent in Northumberland and Durham as of July 1923. *Report of the Royal Commission on the Distribution of the Industrial Population*, 1940, Cmd 6153, p. 268.

13 *St James's Gazette*, 18 December 1893.

14 Walter Greenwood, *Love on the Dole*, London, 1993 [1933], p. 158.

15 F. A. McKenzie, *The American Invaders*, London, 1902, p. 157–8, 164; Brian Bowen, 'The building of the British Westinghouse electric and manufacturing plant, Trafford Park, Manchester,

1901–2', *Construction History*, 25, 2010, p. 86–7; D. A. Farnie, *The Manchester Ship Canal and the Rise of the Port of Manchester 1894–1975*, Manchester, 1980, chaps 1, 6.

16 John Galsworthy, *In Chancery*, New York, 1920, p. 333.

17 B. R. Mitchell, *British Historical Statistics*, Cambridge, 2011, 'Population and vital statistics', Table 6; Galsworthy, *In Chancery*, p. 333; W. D. Rubinstein, 'The Victorian middle classes: wealth, occupation and geography', *Economic History Review*, 30, 4, 1977, pp. 617–8.

18 J. A. Hobson, *Imperialism: A Study*, London, 1902, p. 159.

19 Briggs, *Victorian Cities*, p. 96; R. Robson, *The Cotton Industry in Britain*, London, 1957, Statistical Appendix A2.

20 *The Times*, 7 January 1864; Farnie, *The English Cotton Industry and the World Market*, chap. 4.

21 'Why Lancashire is less Liberal than Yorkshire', *Spectator*, 26 July 1884. Thomas Milner Gibson: Anti-Corn Law Leaguer who accepted office from Russell in 1846, lost Ashton in 1868 under an enlarged borough franchise, just as Gladstone was defeated in South West Lancashire.

22 Neville Kirk, *Change, Continuity and Class: Labour in British Society 1850–1920*, Manchester, 1998, chaps 2, 3; Sidney Pollard, 'Nineteenth-century cooperation: from community building to shopkeeping', in Asa Briggs and John Saville, eds, *Essays in Labour History*, London, 1960, pp. 74–112; Angus Hawkins, *The Forgotten Prime Minister: The 14th Earl of Derby*, vol. 2, Oxford, 2008, p. 271.

23 See Royden Harrison's excellent discussion in *Before the Socialists: Studies in Labour and Politics 1861–1881*, 2nd edn, Aldershot, 1994, pp. xxxii–xlvi, and chap. 3, on which this account draws.

24 HC Deb 12 March 1866, vol. 182, cc37–8.

25 HC Deb 23 April 1866, vol. 182, c1897.

26 J. R. Vincent, *The Formation of the British Liberal Party 1857–1868*, 2nd edn, Hassocks, 1976, p. 171.

27 Lucy Brown, 'Chartists and the Anti-Corn Law League', in Briggs, *Chartist Studies*, p. 348; Gustav Meyer, *The Era of the Reform League*, Mannheim, 1995, p. 17; Vincent, *Liberal Party*, p. 174.

28 Marx to Engels, 1 May 1865, in *Karl Marx and Frederick Engels on Britain*, p. 540.

29 'Great meeting of the working classes in Leeds', *The Times*, 9 October 1866; Vincent, *Liberal Party*, pp. 183, 192.

30 Angus Hawkins, *The Forgotten Prime Minister: The 14th Earl of Derby*, vol. 1, Oxford, 2007, pp. 6, 304, and vol. 2, p. 321. Emphasis in original.

31 HC Deb 17 May 1867, vol. 187, cc717, 725–6; Hawkins, *The Forgotten Prime Minister*, vol. 2, pp. 321, 356–7; *The Times*, 18 October 1867.

32 Lord Cranborne, 'The Conservative surrender', *Quarterly Review*, October 1867, quoted in Harrison, *Before the Socialists*, pp. 107–8.

33 Kirk, *Change, Continuity and Class*, p. 27; Henry Pelling, *Social Geography of British Elections 1885–1910*, London, 1967, pp. 232–3.

34 'Why Lancashire is less Liberal than Yorkshire'.

35 L. J. Satre, 'Thomas Burt and the crisis of late-Victorian Liberalism in the North East, *Northern History*, 23, 1987, pp. 174–193; H. A. Clegg, *A History of British Trade Unions since 1889*, vol. 1, Oxford 1964, p. 105.

36 Eugenio F. Biagini, *Liberty, Retrenchment and Reform: Popular Liberalism in the Age of Gladstone, 1860–1880*, Cambridge, 1992.

37 H. C. G. Matthew, *Gladstone 1809–1898*, Oxford, 2001, p. 509; Richard Shannon, *Gladstone: Peel's Inheritor, 1809–1865*, London, 1999, p. 473.

38 Shannon, *Gladstone*, pp. 31–2, 468; Briggs, *Victorian People*, pp. 234–5; HC Deb 11 May 1864, vol. 175 c324.

39 John Ramsden, *An Appetite for Power: A History of the Conservative Party since 1830*, London, 1998, pp. 102–4; H. J. Hanham, *Elections and Party Management*, Hassocks, 1978, chap. 14.

40 18 November 1868, in *Karl Marx and Frederick Engels on Britain*, p. 545.

41 'Defeat in South Lancashire was irritating, considering the cult Gladstone had made of its civic virtues since his expulsion from Oxford. But the ignominy of retreating to the second Greenwich seat was more than compensated for by the enlarged Liberal majority overall.' Richard Shannon, *Gladstone: Heroic Minister 1865–1898*, London, 1999, p. 56.

42 D. G. Paz, *Popular Anti-Catholicism in Mid-Victorian England*, Stanford, 1992, pp. 18, 222–3.

43 John Belchem, *Irish, Catholic and Scouse: The History of the Liverpool-Irish, 1800–1939*, Liverpool, 2007, pp. 1, 9; John Belchem, 'The peculiarities of Liverpool', in his edited volume *Popular Politics, Riot and Labour: Essays in Liverpool History 1790–1940*, Liverpool, 1992, pp. 10–11; Pelling, *Social Geography*, pp. 247–52; Philip Waller, *Democracy and Sectarianism: A Political and Social History of Liverpool 1868–1939*, Liverpool, 1981, p. 60.

44 Waller, *Democracy and Sectarianism*, p. 134; Waller, 'Forwood, Sir Arthur Bower', *ODNB*, 2004.

45 Asquith made Lever a baronet in 1911, just as the soap king began producing palm oil in the Belgian Congo using the murderous system of forced labour fashioned under Leopold II. Lever is lauded as a philanthropist for his clean-edged industrial colony in Cheshire, Port Sunlight, and because his trustees used his immense wealth to establish a major grant-making body. At home he was 'a benevolent despot', writes Davenport-Hines. Away from Western eyes the benevolence could be dispensed with. Richard Davenport-Hines, 'Lever, William Hesketh, first Viscount Leverhulme', *ODNB*, online edn, January 2011; Jules Marchal, *Lord Leverhulme's Ghosts: Colonial Exploitation in the Congo*, trans. Martin Thom, London, 2008.

46 'National Liberal Federation', *Leeds Mercury*, 4 November 1886; A. W. Roberts, 'Leeds Liberalism and late-Victorian politics', *Northern History*, 5, 1970, pp. 152–3.

47 John Scott and Catherine Griff, *Directors of Industry: The British Corporate Network 1904–76*, Cambridge, 1984, Table 3.5.

48 Clive Trebilcock, *The Vickers Brothers: Armaments and Enterprise 1854–1914*, London, 1977; R. P. T. Davenport-Hines, 'Vickers as a multinational before 1945', in Geoffrey Jones, ed., *British Multinationals: Origins, Management and Performance*, Aldershot, 1986, pp. 43–74.

49 Sidney Webb and Beatrice Webb, *The History of Trade Unionism*, London, 1894, pp. 228, 284.

50 Hanham, *Elections and Party Management*, pp. 326–7.

51 A. E. Musson, *The Congress of 1868*, London, 1982; the Webbs, arch Fabian centralisers, were sceptical of the TUC's capacities to coordinate the movement. Webb and Webb, *The History of Trade Unionism*, pp. 464–74.

52 John Morrill, *Revolt in the Provinces*, 2nd edn, London, 1999, p. 56.

53 Cain and Hopkins, *British Imperialism*, pp. 155–6; Peter Harnetty, *Imperialism and Free Trade: Lancashire and India in the Mid-Nineteenth Century*, Manchester, 1972, chap. 2.

54 Max Egremont, *Balfour: A Life of Arthur James Balfour*, London, 1980, p. 71; Blanche E. C. Dugdale, *Arthur James Balfour*, vol. 1, London, 1936, p. 104; *The Times*, 6 January 1906.

55 Egremont, *Balfour*, p. 206.

56 HC Deb 25 April 1910, vol. 17, cc100–1.

57 Musgrove, *The North of England*, p. 298.

58 'Labour has so associated itself that even defeat must be victory,'

commented the *Yorkshire Factory Times*: Keith Laybourn, *Philip Snowden: A Biography*, Aldershot, 1988, p. 18. Manningham was owned by a Conservative, Samuel Cunliffe Lister, but the Liberals in charge of policing in Bradford had come down heavily against the locked-out workers. James Hinton, *Labour and Socialism: A History of the British Labour Movement 1867–1974*, Brighton, 1986, pp. 56–7; Derek Barker, 'The Manningham Mills strike, 1890–91', *Northern History*, 50, 1, 2013, pp. 93–114.

59 Engels to F. A. Sorge, 18 January 1893, in *Karl Marx and Frederick Engels on Britain*, p. 577; E. P. Thompson, 'Homage to Tom Maguire', in Briggs and Saville, *Essays in Labour History*, p. 277 n.

60 Alan Fowler and Terry Wyke, eds, *The Barefoot Aristocrats*, Littleborough, 1987, pp. 93, 129–30; Clegg, *British Trade Unions*, p. 324.

61 Fowler and Wyke, *The Barefoot Aristocrats*, p. 119.

62 The Marxist Social Democratic Federation grew out of London's radical clubs but developed a secondary concentration of support in north-east Lancashire, its leader Henry Hyndman fighting several general elections in Burnley. Alan Fowler, *Lancashire Cotton Operatives and Work, 1900–1950*, Aldershot, 2003, pp. 15–23.

63 HC Deb 31 January 1913, vol. 47, c1704; Fowler and Wyke, *The Barefoot Aristocrats*, p. 131; Brian Iddon, 'Alfred Gill', in Alan Haworth and Dianne Hayter, eds, *The Men Who Made Labour*, London, 2007, pp. 61–5.

64 Webb and Webb, *The History of Trade Unionism*, pp. 411–4 and Appendix 4. For the geography of strikes see Humphrey Southall and David Gilbert's contributions to Andrew Charlesworth, David Gilbert, Adrian Randall, Humphrey Southall and Chris Wrigley, eds, *An Atlas of Industrial Protest in Britain 1750–1990*, Basingstoke, 1996.

65 Born into the Leeds woollen trade in 1852, Asquith attended the City of London School. 'From that time onwards', he wrote, 'with the exception of my terms at Oxford, I have been to all intents and purposes a Londoner'. He blotted his copy book in the North while Home Secretary under Gladstone in 1893, when two striking miners were shot dead at Featherstone, not far from his boyhood home in Morley, by soldiers whose despatch he had authorised. H. H. Asquith, *Memories and Reflections*, vol. 1, Toronto, 1928, p. 9; Robert G. Neville, 'The Yorkshire miners and the 1893 lockout', *International Review of Social History*, 21, 3, 1976, pp. 337–57.

66 Roger Geary, *Policing Industrial Disputes: 1893 to 1985*, Cambridge, 1985, pp. 31–3; Waller, *Democracy and Sectarianism*, pp. 251–8; 'Fierce riots in Liverpool', *Manchester Guardian*, 14 August 1911.

67 Eric Wigham, *Strikes and the Government 1893–1981*, London, 1982, pp. 25–7; HC Deb 22 August 1911, vol. 29, c2326.

68 Bentley, *Politics without Democracy*, p. 328.

69 'The Working Men's Association to the Radical Reformers of Great Britain and Ireland', 8 May 1838, reprinted in *The People's Charter*, London, 1848, p. 9.

70 'Reform conference in Manchester', *Manchester Guardian*, 1 June 1867.

71 Margaret M. Jensen, 'Roper, Esther Gertrude', *ODNB*, 2004. An important example of the older bourgeois tradition is Barbara Bodichon's *Reasons for the Enfranchisement of Women*, London, 1866.

72 Bentley, *Politics without Democracy*, p. 335.

73 The WSPU gained more traction among politically active women workers in the West Riding than in south-east Lancashire. Trade unionism was weaker in the Yorkshire textile trades, creating less scope for Roper's constitutionalist approach to working-class suffragism: Jill Liddington, *Rebel Girls: Their Vote for the Vote*, London, 2006, pp. 318–20.

74 Randolph Churchill, *Lord Derby: 'King of Lancashire'*, London, 1959, chap. 9; Peter Simkins, *Kitchener's Army: The Raising of the New Armies 1914–16*, Barnsley, 2014, pp. 57, 71, 83–5; Brock Millman, *Managing Domestic Dissent in First World War Britain*, London, 2000, pp. 105–6; Graham Maddocks, *Liverpool Pals*, London, 1991.

75 Antonio Gramsci, 'Notes on the Southern Problem', p. 20.

76 Farnie, *The English Cotton Industry and the World Market*, p. 81.

5. Dereliction

1 B. Bowker, *Lancashire under the Hammer*, London, 1928, pp. 32–42.

2 Stefanie Diaper, 'The Sperling combine and the shipbuilding industry', in J. J. van Helten and Y. Cassis, eds, *Capitalism in a Mature Economy: Financial Institutions, Capital Exports and British Industry, 1870–1939*, Aldershot, 1990, pp. 71–94.

3 HC Deb 8 November 1928, vol. 222, cc353–4; Robert W. D.

Boyce, *British Capitalism at the Crossroads 1919–1932*, Cambridge, 1987, pp. 172–3.

4 Combined total for the North, North West and Yorkshire–Humberside standard statistical regions. Frank Geary and Tom Stark, 'What happened to regional inequality in Britain in the twentieth century?', *Economic History Review*, 69, 1, 2016, Table 1.

5 'The distribution of industry', *Economist*, 3 March 1945.

6 Peter Scott, *Triumph of the South*, Aldershot, 2007, pp. 54–5.

7 J. B. Priestley, *English Journey*, Harmondsworth, 1977 [1934], p. 10.

8 Martin Pugh, *We Danced All Night: A Social History of Britain between the Wars*, London, 2009.

9 'Bad trade: its cause and cure. A lecture by Mr Philip Snowden', *Todmorden & District News*, 29 January 1904; Philip Snowden, *The Christ That Is to Be*, Keighley, 1903, p. 8.

10 HC Deb 30 July 1924, vol. 176, cc2091–2. 'He might have stepped out of the frame of a portrait of a handsome courtier of the Middle Ages', Snowden marvelled on first sight of Norman. 'I never hear uninformed remarks about the callousness of international finance but I think of the injustice done through ignorance to the high and unselfish motives of the governor of the Bank.' Philip Viscount Snowden, *An Autobiography*, vol. 2, London, 1934, p. 614.

11 HC Deb 26 March 1924, vol. 171, c1452.

12 Even the cotton unions, however, were caught up in the strike wave of 1919. Fowler and Wyke, *The Barefoot Aristocrats*, chap. 8.

13 John McIlroy and Alan Campbell, 'Fighting the legions of hell', in McIlroy, et al., eds, *Industrial Politics and the 1926 Mining Lockout*, Cardiff, 2004, Table 2.5.

14 Jack Lawson, *The Man in the Cap: The Life of Herbert Smith*, London, 1941, pp. 203, 253.

15 Cab 23/15, 7 August 1919; John Campbell, *F. E. Smith, First Earl of Birkenhead*, London, 1983, pp. 34, 777.

16 John Maynard Keynes, *The Economic Consequences of Mr Churchill*, London, 1925, p. 23. Emphasis in original.

17 Hester Barron, *The 1926 Miners' Lockout*, Oxford, 2010, Table 1.1.

18 Frank McLynn, *The Road Not Taken*, London, 2012, p. 379.

19 *Report of the Royal Commission on the Coal Industry* (1925) 1926, Cmd 2600, pp. 228, 235; M. W. Kirby, *The British Coalmining Industry 1870–1946*, London, 1977, pp. 75–7.

20 'The trade unions' decision', *Manchester Guardian*, 3 May 1926.

21 Diary of Beatrice Webb, 28 July 1927, typewritten transcript, vol. 41, pp. 4503–5, LSE digital library.

22 Lord Citrine, *Two Careers*, London, 1967, pp. 371–2; Lord Citrine, *ABC of Chairmanship*, London, 1948.

23 Quoted in Edmund Frow and Ruth Frow, 'Manchester diary', in Jeffrey Skelley, ed, *The General Strike 1926*, London, 1976, pp. 164–5.

24 Margaret Morris, *The General Strike*, London, 1980, p. 236.

25 Lord Citrine, *Men and Work: An Autobiography*, London, 1964, pp. 188, 196. See also Perry Anderson, 'Origins of the present crisis', *New Left Review*, I/23, January–February 1964, pp. 45–6.

26 'The peace news in Manchester', *Manchester Guardian*, 13 May 1926; Frow and Frow, 'Manchester diary', pp. 168–9.

27 A. J. Cook, *The Nine Days*, London, 1926 p. 21, emphasis in original; Citrine, *Two Careers*, p. 262.

28 David Gilbert, 'The miners' lockout of 1926', in Charlesworth et al., *An Atlas of Industrial Protest in Britain*, pp. 146–7.

29 Martin Jacques, 'Consequences of the General Strike', in Skelley, *The General Strike*, p. 382; Robert Brenner, 'The dynamics of retreat', *Jacobin*, 3 March 2016.

30 Peter Scott, 'The state, internal migration, and the growth of new industrial communities in interwar Britain', *English Historical Review*, 115, 461, 2000, pp. 329–53.

31 Cunliffe-Lister: Hendon MP married to a Yorkshire coal heiress, the granddaughter of Samuel Cunliffe Lister of Manningham Mills. HC Deb 7 December 1927, vol. 211, c1423. Scott, 'Internal migration', p. 334, citing Alan E. Booth, 'The timing and content of government policies to assist the depressed areas, 1920–1939', University of Kent D.Phil. thesis, 1975, p. 97; *Report of the Industrial Transference Board 1928*, Cmd 3156, p. 18.

32 Scott, 'Internal migration', pp. 337–9.

33 Orwell, *The Road to Wigan Pier*, p. 81.

34 *Census of England and Wales 1931: General Report*, London, 1950, p. 162. The insured unemployment rate in London and the South East peaked at 14 per cent in 1932: serious, but only half the figure recorded in the North and in Scotland, and not nearly as stubborn. W. R. Garside, *British Unemployment 1919–1939*, Cambridge, 1990, Table 4.

35 P. J. Cain and A. G. Hopkins, *British Imperialism 1688–2015*, 3rd edn, London, 2016, pp. 589–97, 698; John Walton, *Lancashire: A Social History, 1558–1939*, Manchester, 1994, p. 329.

36 D. C. Coleman, *Courtaulds: An Economic and Social History*, vol. 2, Oxford, 1969, Figure 16.

37 Priestley, *English Journey*, p. 157.

38 John Jewkes and Allan Winterbottom, *An Industrial Survey of Cumberland and Furness: A Study of the Social Implications of Economic Dislocation*, Manchester, 1933, p. 9.

39 The North treated as Cheshire, Yorkshire and above. G. D. H. Cole, *A History of the Labour Party from 1914*, London, 1948, p. 222.

40 MacDonald to Joe Brown, 23 March 1928, in David Marquand, *Ramsay MacDonald*, London, 1977, p. 481.

41 MacDonald to Lady Londonderry, 29 December 1928, in Nicholas Owen, 'MacDonald's parties: the Labour party and the "aristocratic embrace", 1922–31', *Twentieth Century British History*, 18, 1, 2007, p. 48.

42 Boyce, *British Capitalism*, pp. 214–16, 230, 292.

43 Quoted in 'British fiscal policy', *Manchester Chamber of Commerce Monthly Record*, 41, 6, 1930, p. 173.

44 'The financial situation', CP 3 (31), 7 January 1931.

45 C. H. Feinstein, *Statistical Tables of National Income, Expenditure Output of the UK, 1855–1965*, Cambridge, 1976, Table 58; *British Labour Statistics Historical Abstract 1886–1968*, London, 1971, Table 162.

46 'The new government', *Economist*, 15 June 1929.

47 Cain and Hopkins, *British Imperialism*, p. 449.

48 Henry Clay, *Lord Norman*, London, 1957, p. 335.

49 Cain and Hopkins, *British Imperialism*, p. 451; Carol E. Heim, 'Limits to intervention: the Bank of England and industrial diversification in the depressed areas', *Economic History Review*, 37, 4, 1984, pp. 533–50.

50 'Mr J. H. Thomas in Manchester', *Manchester Chamber of Commerce Monthly Record*, 41, 1, 1930, p. 7; Morgan, *MacDonald*, p. 161.

51 Skidelsky, *Politicians and the Slump*, pp. 242–4; 'Notes on the problems of the depressed areas', CP 1 (31), 1 January 1931, p. 29.

52 'Mr J. H. Thomas in Manchester', p. 8.

53 Cab 43 (31), 21 August 1931.

54 Snowden, *An Autobiography*, vol. 2, p. 957.

55 Edmund Frow and Ruth Frow, *The Battle of Bexley Square*, Salford, 1994; *Manchester Guardian*, 2 October 1931, 8 October 1931.

56 Marquand, *Ramsay MacDonald*, pp. 669, 779; Hester Barron,

'Labour identities of the coalfield: the general election of 1931 in County Durham', *History*, 97, 326, 2012, pp. 204–229.

57 'Mr Clynes and the result', *The Times*, 29 October 1931.

58 Duncan Tanner, 'Snowden, Philip, Viscount Snowden', *ODNB*, online edn, January 2011.

59 Cab 89 (31), 14 December 1931; Philip Williamson, *National Crisis and National Government*, Cambridge, 2003, pp. 494–5.

60 'Unemployed disorder', *Manchester Guardian*, 8 October 1931; Richard Croucher, *We Refuse to Starve in Silence: A History of the National Unemployed Workers' Movement, 1920–46*, London, 1987, pp. 132–6.

61 'Puzzled and anxious House', *Manchester Guardian*, 30 January 1935.

62 Keith Middlemas, *Politics in Industrial Society*, London, 1979, p. 232.

63 Fredric Miller, 'The British Unemployment Assistance crisis of 1935', *Journal of Contemporary History*, 14, 2, 1979, pp. 329–52.

64 *The Times*, 20 March 1934.

65 Robert Self, *Neville Chamberlain: A Biography*, Aldershot, 2006, pp. 221–2.

66 Alan E. Booth, 'An administrative experiment in unemployment policy in the thirties', *Public Administration*, 56, 2, 1978, p. 144.

67 'Reports of the investigation into the industrial conditions in certain depressed areas', 1934, Cmd 4728, p. 107; 'Summary of investigators' recommendations and of departmental comments thereon', CP 220 (34), 2 October 1934, p. 18.

68 HC Deb 14 November 1934, vol. 293, c2002; Miller, 'Unemployment policy', p. 468.

69 *Second Report of the Commissioner for the Special Areas (England and Wales)*, 1936, Cmd 5090, p. 6.

70 Heim, 'Limits to intervention', pp. 536–9; Booth, 'An administrative experiment', p. 149.

71 Emphasis added. Fredric Miller, 'The unemployment policy of the National Government, 1931–1936', *Historical Journal*, 19, 2, 1976, p. 469.

72 Marquand, *Ramsay MacDonald*, p. 779.

73 Miller, 'Unemployment policy', p. 464.

74 Priestley, *English Journey*, p. 296.

75 Ellen Wilkinson, *The Town That Was Murdered: The Life Story of Jarrow*, London, 1939, pp. 155, 191–2.

76 Ellen Wilkinson, 'The Congress of 1921', *Communist*, 27 August 1921, Marxists Internet Archive.

77 Matt Perry, *The Jarrow Crusade: Protest and Legend*, Sunderland, 2005, p. 16.

78 Paula Bartley, *Ellen Wilkinson*, London, 2014, p. 91.

79 Perry, *The Jarrow Crusade*, pp. 66–7.

80 Herbert Dunelm, 'The methods of marches', *The Times*, 24 October 1936.

81 'Minister sees the hunger marchers', *Manchester Guardian*, 13 November 1936.

82 'The betrayal of the special areas', *Spectator*, 13 November 1936.

83 *Third Report of the Commissioner for the Special Areas (England and Wales)*, 1936, Cmd 5303, Part I and Appendix V.

84 Herbert Loebl, *Government Factories and the Origins of British Regional Policy 1934–1948*, Aldershot, 1988, p. 150 and Appendix 12; Peter Scott, 'The audit of regional policy: 1934–1939', *Regional Studies*, 34, 1, 2000, pp. 61, 63; Scott, *Triumph of the South*, p. 165; 'Special areas', *Economist*, 4 December 1943.

85 Self, *Chamberlain*, p. 231.

86 Orwell, *The Road to Wigan Pier*, p. 158.

87 Combined total for the North-Eastern, North-Western and Northern Ministry of Labour divisions. *British Labour Statistics Historical Abstract 1886–1968*, London, 1971, Table 162.

6. Forged in Yorkshire

1 Hilaire Belloc, *The Modern Traveller*, London, 1898, p. 41; David Kynaston, *The City of London*, vol. 4: *A Club No More, 1945–2000*, London, 2002, p. 43.

2 Kynaston, *The City of London*, vol. 4, p. 54.

3 *Report of the Royal Commission on the Distribution of the Industrial Population 1940*, Cmd 6153.

4 Ben Pimlott, *Hugh Dalton*, London, 1986, pp. 176, 236–7.

5 Ben Pimlott, ed., *The Second World War Diary of Hugh Dalton 1940–45*, London, 1986, p. 731; Alan Booth, 'The Second World War and the origins of modern regional policy', *Economy and Society*, 11, 1, 1982, p. 16.

6 The North Eastern area was extended northwards to include the port of Blyth and Ashington, and southwards over Teesside and Darlington. The Highlands, Merseyside, St Helens–Wigan and Wrexham were added to the roster by 1949, increasing the coverage of the development areas to 18 per cent of the national population.

7 'The distribution of industry', *Economist*, 3 March 1945.

Building licenses were phased out by the Churchill government in 1954.

8 Harold Wilson, *A Prime Minister on Prime Ministers*, London, 1977, p. 297.

9 Forrest Capie, *The Bank of England: 1950s to 1979*, Cambridge, 2010, p. 32; Kynaston, *The City of London*, vol. 4, p. 10.

10 'Mr Ellis Smith on his resignation', *The Times*, 14 January 1946.

11 Kynaston, *The City of London*, vol. 4, p. 10; Jim Tomlinson, 'The Attlee government and the balance of payments, 1945–51', *Twentieth Century British History*, 2, 1, 1991, pp. 59, 62.

12 CM (47) 16, 4 February 1947.

13 Tomlinson, 'The Attlee government', p. 50.

14 Kenneth O. Morgan, *Labour in Power, 1945–1951*, Oxford, 1985, p. 193.

15 'It comes out in the wash that the American loan is primarily required to meet the political and military expenditure overseas,' Keynes observed. 'If it were not for that, we could scrape through without excessive interruption of our domestic programme.' John Saville, *The Politics of Continuity: British Foreign Policy and the Labour Government 1945–6*, London, 1993, p. 152.

16 *Board of Trade Journal*, 5 August 1950, p. 290.

17 Scott, 'British regional policy', p. 380.

18 Scott, 'British regional policy', pp. 379–80; *Distribution of Industry 1948*, Cmd 7540, pp. 16–17.

19 CM (50) 36, 15 June 1950.

20 Production Committee minutes for 20 May 1949, quoted in Barnett, *The Lost Victory*, p. 342.

21 E. Allen, A. J. Odber and P. J. Bowden, *Development Area Policy in the North East of England*, Newcastle, 1957, p. 61.

22 'Revealed, 30 years after our first nuclear explosion', *The Times*, 30 September 1982.

23 Leonard Owen, managing director of AEA's industrial group. Lorna Arnold, *Windscale 1957: Anatomy of a Nuclear Accident*, 3rd edn, Basingstoke, 2007, p. 102.

24 Arnold, *Windscale*, Table A5.

25 Christopher Driver, *The Disarmers: A Study in Protest*, London, 1964, pp. 12–13; Matthew Brown, 'Bob Edwards: a lifetime on the left', Independent Labour Publications, 13 December 2013.

26 'Windscale atom plant overheats', *The Times*, 12 October 1957; J. B. Priestley, 'Britain and the nuclear bombs', *New Statesman*, 2 November 1957.

27 Peter Scott, 'The worst of both worlds: British regional policy, 1951–64', *Business History*, 38, 4, 1996, p. 44.

28 '"Senseless" strikes', *The Times*, 31 July 1950; 'Obituary: Lord Williamson', *The Times*, 1 March 1983.
29 Martin Upham, *Tempered – Not Quenched: The History of the ISTC*, London, 1997, p. 25.
30 Russell, *Looking North*, p. 268.
31 Richard Hoggart, *The Uses of Literacy*, Harmondsworth, 1973 [1957], p. 325.
32 John Braine, *Room at the Top*, Harmonsworth, 1959 [1957], pp. 24, 29.
33 David Ayerst, *Guardian: Biography of a Newspaper*, London, 1971, p. 96.
34 Ayerst, *Guardian*, p. 601.
35 'The press', *Spectator*, 7 February 1964.
36 Russell, *Looking North*, pp. 89–90, 268–71, citing Philip Dodd, 'Lowryscapes: recent writings about "the North"', *Critical Quarterly*, 32, 2, 1990, pp. 17–28.
37 Geoffrey Moorhouse, *Britain in the Sixties: The Other England*, Harmondsworth, 1964, pp. 14–15.
38 Unemployment figures for 1949–64: H. W. Armstrong, 'Regional problems and policies', in N. F. R. Crafts and N. W. C. Woodward, *The British Economy since 1945*, Oxford, 1991, Table 10.4. Manufacturing employment figures for 1953–63: Department for Economic Affairs, *The North West: A Regional Study*, HMSO, 1965, p. 25.
39 'The City's markets operated with devastating efficiency in draining capital out of the country on the slightest pretext': Geoffrey Ingham, *Capitalism Divided? The City and Industry in British Social Development*, Basingstoke, 1984, p. 283 n.
40 Scott, 'The worst of both worlds', p. 52.
41 From an average of 0.93 percentage points in 1955–7 to 1.4 points in 1958: Scott, 'The worst of both worlds', p. 52.
42 'Cotton industry', C (55) 76, 19 March 1955, Annex A, 'Memorandum from the Cotton Board'; John Singleton, 'Showing the white flag: the Lancashire cotton industry, 1945–65', in Mary B. Rose, ed., *International Competition and Strategic Response in the Textile Industries since 1870*, London, 1991, p. 137.
43 Any resort to trade barriers, Thorneycroft warned the Cabinet, would 'precipitate embarrassing demands for similar protection over a wide range of goods' and give rise to 'political complications in relation to the Commonwealth'. 'Cotton industry', C (55) 76, 19 March 1955.
44 'Lancashire', C (55) 42, 14 February 1955.
45 'The Rochdale by-election', *Rochdale Observer*, 25 January 1958.

46 Harold Macmillan, *The Macmillan Diaries*, vol. 2: *Prime Minister and After, 1957–66*, ed. Peter Catterall, Basingstoke, 2011, pp. 94, 100.

47 Emphasis added. 'Local unemployment', C (58) 69, 28 March 1958; Macmillan, *The Macmillan Diaries*, p. 233.

48 Scott, 'The worst of both worlds', p. 54.

49 'Industrial development on Merseyside', C (60) 16, 5 February 1960. The new arrivals had transformed the declining port-city of Liverpool into the 'Detroit of Great Britain', boasted a delighted lord mayor. Given what lay in store for both towns once the auto trade plunged into crisis in the early seventies, he couldn't have hit upon a better comparison. Brian Marren, *We Shall Not Be Moved: How Liverpool's Working Class Fought Redundancies, Closures and Cuts in the Age of Thatcher*, Manchester, 2016, p. 24.

50 Andrew Taylor, *The NUM and British Politics*, vol. 1: *1944–1968*, Aldershot, 2003, pp. 126, 179–80.

51 'Reappraisal of the coal industry', C (62) 104, 3 July 1962.

52 D. R. Thorpe, *Supermac: The Life of Harold Macmillan*, London, 2010, p. 474.

53 'Although nobody should underestimate the short-term shock of deflation that probably lies ahead, the hope of real regeneration can reasonably be pitched just a little higher than seemed likely before the Chancellor spoke on Tuesday.' 'The great deflation', *Economist*, 29 July 1961.

54 'New discomforts for the North East', *The Times*, 28 August 1962.

55 'Dry-eyed farewell in the North-East to a "black" 1962', *Newcastle Journal*, 2 January 1963.

56 'Borough's shock for the Tories', *Evening Gazette*, 7 June 1962.

57 HC Deb 9 July 1935, vol. 304, c232.

58 Macmillan, *The Macmillan Diaries*, p. 374.

59 CC (62) 63, 29 October 1962.

60 'Special help for NE urged', *The Times*, 15 September 1962.

61 'The four tough years', *Newcastle Journal*, 16 November 1963.

62 *The North East: A Programme for Regional Development and Growth 1963*, Cmd 2206, pp. 10, 15; 'Hailsham: "all a bit long-term"', *Newcastle Journal*, 15 November 1963.

63 *Sunderland Echo*, 13 October 1964.

64 Singleton, 'Showing the white flag', p. 141; Mary B. Rose, 'The politics of protection: an institutional approach to government–industry relations in the British and United States cotton industries', *Business History*, 39, 4, 1997, Table 2.

65 'Mr Wilson promises New Deal', *The Times*, 9 March 1964; 'Let's go with Labour for the New Britain', in F. W. S. Craig, ed., *British General-Election Manifestos, 1900–1974*, London, 1975, p. 261.

66 Harold Wilson, *Memoirs: The Making of a Prime Minister, 1916–1964*, p. 10.

67 Harold Wilson, *Memoirs*, p. 75.

68 Wilson, *Memoirs*, p. 82.

69 Henry Brandon, *In the Red: The Struggle for Sterling 1964–66*, London, 1966, p. 56. 'Wilson completely accepted sterling's international role and in so doing endorsed the existing structure of London's commercial markets; their integration with the world economy; and, above all, the City's hegemony'. Ingham, *Capitalism Divided?*, p. 285 n.

70 George Ball, 'Some thoughts on the British crisis', 28 July 1965, *Foreign Relations of the United States 1964–1968*, vol. 8: *International Monetary and Trade Policy*, doc. 65.

71 Glen O'Hara, 'The limits of US power: transatlantic financial diplomacy under the Johnson and Wilson administrations', *Contemporary European History*, 12, 3, 2003, p. 263; Jim Tomlinson, *The Labour Governments 1964–1970*, vol. 3: *Economic Policy*, Manchester, 2004, p. 231.

72 'Furthermore, the government has endorsed not only the City's priorities, but also, to a considerable extent, its remedies. It is true that it postponed deflation for a long as it could – thus aggravating the situation further. But, at the pinch, in July 1966, it was prepared to be as ruthless in curbing demand as any Tory government, and to sacrifice the National Plan and many other dear schemes besides in the attempt to cut imports by deflation.' *Banker*, October 1967, quoted in Frank Longstreth, 'The City, industry and the state', in Colin Crouch, ed., *State and Economy in Contemporary Capitalism*, London, 1979, p. 183.

73 'Mr Wilson promises New Deal', *The Times*, 9 March 1964.

74 Jeremy Bray, *Decision in Government*, London, 1970, p. 149.

75 Colin Wren, *Industrial Subsidies: The UK Experience*, Basingstoke, 1996, Table 5.3.

76 Ian J. Smith, 'The effect of external takeovers on manufacturing employment change in the Northern region between 1963 and 1973', *Regional Studies*, 13, 5, 1979, pp. 421–37.

77 'Cotton leaves the Royal Exchange', *Guardian*, 30 December 1968.

78 Taylor, *The NUM*, p. 239.

79 Richard Crossman, *The Diaries of a Cabinet Minister*, vol. 2,

London, 1976, pp. 431–2; Taylor, *The NUM*, pp. 204, 221.

80 Taylor, *The NUM*, p. 250.

81 'The changing North: promise born of problems', *The Times*, 22 January 1971.

82 HC Deb 2 July 1970, vol. 803, c56.

83 Combined total for the North, North West and Yorkshire–Humberside standard statistical regions. Frank Geary and Tom Stark, 'What happened to regional inequality in Britain in the twentieth century?', *Economic History Review*, 69, 1, 2016, Table 1.

7. Freedom of the City

1 *The Times*, 6 January 1972. The following account draws on Tony Eccles, *Under New Management: The Story of Britain's Largest Worker Cooperative*, London, 1981.

2 Ken Coates, *Work-Ins, Sit-Ins, and Industrial Democracy*, Nottingham, 1981, p. 63.

3 Coates, *Work-Ins*, p. 72 n.

4 'How Ivor made a million', *Liverpool Free Press*, May 1974.

5 'Deep in the aftergrowth', *Economist*, 30 October 1976.

6 HC Deb 17 May 1977, vol. 932, c341.

7 M. W. Kirby, *The Decline of British Economic Power since 1870*, London, 1981, Table 24; Ron Martin, 'Regional imbalance as consequence and constraint in national economic renewals', in Francis Green, ed., *The Restructuring of the UK Economy*, Hemel Hempstead, 1989, Table 4.1. Employment figures are for 1971–9.

8 CM (64) 12, 18 February 1964.

9 Adrian Williamson, *Conservative Economic Policymaking and the Birth of Thatcherism, 1964–1979*, Basingstoke, 2015, p. 141.

10 J. D. McCallum, 'The development of British regional policy', in Duncan Maclennan and John B. Parr, eds, *Regional Policy: Past Experience and New Directions*, Oxford, 1979, pp. 19–20.

11 HC Deb 18 February 1971, vol. 811, cc2162–3.

12 Mark Metcalf, *Benny Rothman: A Fighter for the Right to Roam, Workers' Rights and Socialism*, London, 2016, p. 44; 'Factory cannot be saved', *Guardian*, 4 February 1972.

13 HC Deb 21 March 1972, vol. 833, c1369.

14 McCallum, 'The development of British regional policy', Table 1.6; J. R. L. Howells, 'The location of research and development: some observations and evidence from Britain', *Regional*

Studies, 18, 1, 1984, Table 1; 'Britain's sunrise strip', *Economist*, 30 January 1982.

15 The number of jobs generated by inter-regional moves fell from an annual average of 25,000 in 1966–71 to 18,000 in 1972–5. Stuart Nunn, 'The opening and closure of manufacturing units in the United Kingdom 1966–75', Government Economic Service, Working Paper 36, November 1980, Table 4.

16 *Industrial and Regional Development 1972*, Cmd 4942, p. 7.

17 Ingham, *Capitalism Divided?*, p. 220.

18 CP (72) 155, 13 December 1972.

19 CM (72) 59, 20 December 1972.

20 Joe Gormley, *Battered Cherub*, London, 1982, pp. 57, 185.

21 Gormley, *Battered Cherub*, pp. 61–2, 193.

22 Arthur Scargill, 'The new unionism', *New Left Review*, I/92, July–August 1975, p 13.

23 Gormley, *Battered Cherub*, pp. 141, 196, emphasis in original; meeting of ministers on 5 February 1974, CAB 128/48.

24 Andrew Taylor, *The NUM and British Politics*, vol. 2: *1969–1995*, Aldershot, 2005, p. 77.

25 'Causes of the recent improvement in the rate of unemployment in the Northern region relative to Great Britain', Northern Region Strategy Team, Technical Report 11, 1976.

26 *Labour's Programme for Britain*, London, 1972, p. 12.

27 'Boost to hopes of saving steelworks', *Hartlepool Mail*, 5 September 1974.

28 H. W. Richardson and E. G. West, 'Must we always take work to the workers?', *Lloyds Bank Review*, January 1964, p. 41; John Wood, *A Nation Not Afraid: The Thinking of Enoch Powell*, London, 1965, p. 88.

29 Graham Hallett et al., 'Regional policy forever?', Institute of Economic Affairs, 1973; Gerald Manners, 'Reinterpreting the regional problem', *Three Banks Review*, September 1976, p. 39.

30 Denis Healey, *The Time of My Life*, London, 2006, p. 34; Edward Pearce, *Denis Healey: A Life in Our Times*, London, 2002, p. 54.

31 Healey, *The Time of My Life*, p. 101; Hugh Wilford, *The CIA, the British Left and the Cold War: Calling the Tune?*, Abingdon, 2013, p. 55; Harold Wilson, *Memoirs: The Making of a Prime Minister 1916–64*, London, 1986.

32 Wilson, *Memoirs*, p. 205.

33 Pearce, *Healey*, p. 155.

34 Healey, *The Time of My Life*, p. 67.

35 Pearce, *Healey*, p. 406; Healey, *The Time of My Life*, p. 393.

36 Peter Jay, 'Into battle with Mr Healey', *The Times*, 16 January 1975.

37 Tony Benn, *Against the Tide: Diaries 1973–76*, London, 1989, p. 593.

38 CM (76) 30, 4 November 1976. Regional policy is credited with creating 268,000 manufacturing jobs in the development areas between 1971 and 1981, compared to 336,000 in the previous decade. Barry Moore, John Rhodes and Peter Tyler, *The Effects of Government Regional Economic Policy*, HMSO, 1986, p. 10.

39 *West Cumberland Times and Star*, 30 October 1976, 6 November 1976; Healey, *The Time of My Life*, p. 383; *Leeds Weekly Citizen*, 3 December 1976, 17 December 1976.

40 'Public spending to be cut by £2,500m and indirect taxes up', *The Times*, 16 December 1976.

41 John Bowers, 'Regional policy', in Michael Artis, ed., *Labour's Economic Policies, 1974–79*, Manchester, 1991, p. 257.

42 *Devolution: The English Dimension*, HMSO, 1976, p. 19.

43 'Unions accept loss of 1,500 jobs in Hartlepool steel plant closure', *The Times*, 13 December 1977.

44 Andrew Gillespie and David Owen, 'The relationship between national and local unemployment: a case study of the Northern region, 1971–80', Centre for Urban and Regional Studies, University of Newcastle upon Tyne, Discussion Paper No. 34, January 1981, pp. 13–15.

45 Healey, *The Time of My Life*, pp. 432, 437.

46 Philip Ziegler, *Wilson: The Authorised Life*, London, 1995, pp. 482, 504.

47 Eccles, *Under New Management*, p. 62.

48 Leo Panitch and Colin Leys, *The End of Parliamentary Socialism*, 2nd edn, London, 2001, p. 99.

49 'Tories may challenge £4m Benn grant', *The Times*, 23 December 1974.

50 'Secret takeover bid angers workers' co-op', *Sunday Times*, 17 September 1978.

51 Tony Benn, *Conflicts of Interest: Diaries 1977–80*, London, 1990, pp. 119–20.

52 Benn, *Conflicts of Interest*, p. 300.

53 H. G. Overman and L. A. Winters, 'The port geography of UK international trade', *Environment and Planning A*, 37, 10, 2005, Table 2.

54 CM (78) 18, 11 May 1978.

55 Peter Jenkins, *The Battle of Downing Street*, London, 1970, p. 61.

56 'Speke now, pay later', *The Times*, 22 February 1978.

57 'It is frequently the Merseyside factories of big companies which turn out not to have been receiving a continued updating of investment or a share of growing activity to compensate for declining areas.' 'Why Mersey sound is off key', *Financial Times*, 2 February 1979.

58 Jack Jones, *Union Man*, London, 1986, pp. 295, 305, 307.

59 'Ministers in secret deal to sack leaders of workers' co-operative', *Sunday Times*, 26 November 1978.

60 'Kirkby co-op to seek fresh aid', *Guardian*, 12 December 1978.

61 'Mersey mourns more lost jobs', *Sunday Times*, 19 November 1978.

62 *Liverpool Daily Post*, 20 January 1979.

63 P. E. Lloyd and D. E. Reeve, 'North West England 1971–1977: a study in industrial decline and economic restructuring', *Regional Studies*, 16, 5, 1982, Table 4; Peter Lloyd and John Shutt, 'Recession and re-structuring in the North West region, 1975–82: the implications of recent events', in Doreen Massey and Richard Meegan, eds, *Politics and Method: Contrasting Studies in Industrial Geography*, London, 1985, Table 2.2.

64 HC Deb 22 February 1979, vol. 963, c618.

65 *Liverpool Echo*, 28 March 1979; *Liverpool Daily Post*, 28 March 1979.

66 HC Deb 12 December 1978, vol. 960, c369.

67 Henry Friedman and Sander Meredeen, *The Dynamics of Industrial Conflict: Lessons from Ford*, London, 1980, p. 206.

68 *Liverpool Echo*, 28 March 1979, 30 March 1979; Eccles, *Under New Management*, p. 342.

8. Enemy Damage

1 J. R. Lowerson, 'Editorial preface', *Southern History*, 1, 1979, p. 9.

2 'Divided kingdom', *Economist*, 18 September 2013.

3 Arthur Scargill speech to the 1985 NUM conference, printed in a Socialist Action pamphlet, *In Defence of the NUM*, undated, p. 20.

4 HC Deb 12 June 1979, vol. 968, c240. Howe was born in Port Talbot to a Liverpudlian mother, but self-identified as a 'London-living, Winchester- and Cambridge-educated and apparently uncymric Conservative'. Geoffrey Howe, *Conflict of Loyalty*, London, 1995, p. 3.

5 Bank of England external finance director Kit McMahon, in whom Healey placed a great deal of trust, proposed to colleagues on 26 September 1975, 'If we can establish internally, with the Treasury, the principle of keeping the growth in money supply down and taking any necessary measures to that end, we will in due course get an extra lever on the chancellor to attack public expenditure itself ... *A fortiori*, if we could get a public statement of a target for the growth of money supply, we should have a tighter rope round the chancellor's neck.' Duncan Needham, *UK Monetary Policy from Devaluation to Thatcher, 1967–82*, Basingstoke, 2014, pp. 90–1, 98–9.

6 'State and industry closer on curbing inflation', *The Times*, 11 January 1975.

7 'The intention had always been to attack wage inflation by using tight monetary policy to bear down on company profits': Duncan Needham, 'The 1981 budget', in Duncan Needham and Anthony Hotson, eds, *Expansionary Fiscal Contraction: The Thatcher Government's 1981 Budget in Perspective*, Cambridge, 2014, p. 171. Such was also the CBI's view: Adrian Williamson, *Conservative Economic Policymaking and the Birth of Thatcherism, 1964–79*, Basingstoke, 2016, p. 236.

8 Morrison Halcrow, *Keith Joseph: A Single Mind*, London, 1989, p. 11.

9 HC Deb 4 December 1963, vol. 685, c1273.

10 'Getting to grips with the catastrophic effects of inflation', *The Times*, 6 September 1974.

11 David Smith, *The Rise and Fall of Monetarism*, London, 1987, p. 82.

12 Charles Moore, *Margaret Thatcher: The Authorised Biography*, vol. 1: *Not for Turning*, London, 2013, pp. 480, 504.

13 Sidney Pollard, *The Wasting of the British Economy*, 2nd edn, Beckenham, 1984, p. 183.

14 Ron Martin, 'Thatcherism and the Britain's industrial landscape', in Ron Martin and Bob Rowthorn, eds, *The Geography of Deindustrialisation*, Basingstoke, 1988, pp. 264–7.

15 Howe, *Conflict of Loyalty*, p. 141; Martin, 'Thatcherism', p. 264.

16 Total FDI outflow from the UK: \$46.1 billion in 1981–5 rising to \$140.5 billion in 1986–90. Total FDI inflow to the UK: \$21.6 billion in 1981–5 rising to \$108.7 billion in 1986–90. Ray Barrell and Nigel Pain, 'Foreign direct investment, innovation and economic growth within Europe', in Ciaran Driver and Paul Temple, eds, *Investment, Growth and Employment: Perspectives for Policy*, London, 1999, Table 9.2.

17 Ian Stone, 'East Asian FDI and the UK periphery', in Philip Garrahan and John Ritchie, eds, *East Asian Direct Investment in Britain*, London, 1999, pp. 75, 84.

18 Shielded from Conservative cuts to the higher-education budget, Cranfield was on its own telling 'a model Thatcherite university': 'Cranfield College of Aeronautics history', 2006.

19 Lewis Johnman and Hugh Murphy, *British Shipbuilding and the State since 1918: A Political Economy of Decline*, Ithaca, NY, 2002, pp. 235–6. 'Despite Nissan being a considerable consumer of state funds, local media and political opinion have continuously portrayed the company as the donor of public goods, and not as private capital sponsored by the public exchequer': Philip Garrahan and Paul Stewart, *The Nissan Enigma: Flexibility at Work in a Local Economy*, London, 1992, p. 77.

20 HC Deb 7 November 1979, vol. 973, c449.

21 'The too noisy walkabout', *Newcastle Journal*, 12 July 1980.

22 Margaret Thatcher, *The Downing Street Years*, London, 1993, p. 112. Ministers were privately aware that 'the unions had already agreed to substantial reductions in the total workforce, and their resistance to the management's insistence that the whole of any pay increase must be financed from higher productivity (which would necessitate further job losses) was perhaps understandable'. CC (80) 1, 10 January 1980.

23 Martin, 'Thatcherism', Table 8.3.

24 Peter Hall et al., *Western Sunrise: The Genesis and Growth of Britain's Major High-Tech Corridor*, London, 1987, pp. 3, 127; J. Mohan, 'Public expenditure, public employment and the regions,' in Peter Townroe and Ron Martin, *Regional Development in the 1990s*, London, 1992, p. 222.

25 Beryl Bainbridge, *English Journey*, London, 1985, pp. 40, 120–4.

26 *Newcastle Journal*, 6 September 1980, 27 September 1980.

27 Ron Martin and Peter Townroe, 'Changing trends and pressures in regional development', in Townroe and Martin, *Regional Development in the 1990s*, Table 1.1.1.

28 HC Deb 17 July 1979, vol. 970, c1307; 24 July 1979, vol. 971, c373; 21 January 1980, vol. 977, c35. The IDC process was already basically inoperative: in the previous six years, only twenty-eight out of some 7,000 applications for new industrial floor space had been knocked back. HC Deb 4 December 1981, vol. 14, c523.

29 *North–South: A Programme for Survival*, London, 1980, p. 31; 'Increased awareness of North–South divide', *The Times*, 21 November 1980.

30 'Across the North–South divide', *Business*, September 1987.

31 'The nonsense of North–South', *Sunday Times*, 11 January 1987. 'England, for me, is London, my home for all my working life, bar periodic stints in America. The rest of England is for flying over, north to the land of my birth, west to New York, my second favourite city, south to the Côte d'Azur, my preference for a home in the country.' Andrew Neil, 'So what is England?', *Spectator*, 16 April 2008.

32 David Smith, *North and South: Britain's Economic, Social and Political Divide*, London, 1989, pp. 6, 275, and *passim*.

33 Heseltine minute to Thatcher, 'It took a riot', 13 August 1981, PREM19/578.

34 Anthony Steen: Conservative MP for Liverpool Wavertree. 'Who needs Merseyside?', *Economist*, 14 October 1978; Joseph to Thatcher, 21 December 1978, Churchill Archive Centre: Thatcher MSS (2/1/1/39).

35 'Merseyside – a regional policy case study: report by the Central Policy Review Staff', June 1981, PREM 19/576. Social inadequacy is a sinister term in government usage, deployed by American eugenicists a century ago to justify the incarceration and sterilisation of people dependent on state welfare. Joseph had himself dabbled in these noxious waters, hinting in a speech to the Edgbaston Conservative Association in October 1974 at support for compulsory birth control for young unmarried women from the lowest social classes 'until we are able to remoralise whole groups and classes of people'. He shrilly declared, 'The balance of our population, our human stock, is threatened.' Halcrow, *Keith Joseph*, p. 83.

36 'Unlike most other EZs, Speke contained only a limited amount of dereliction and offered potential investors immediately developable land. Despite this advantage the area attracted only a modest amount of development. By the end of the decade the only major development was that carried out by a government agency: English Industrial Estates, whose programme of advance factory construction had actually begun prior to designation.' Chris Couch, *City of Change and Challenge: Urban Planning and Regeneration in Liverpool*, Abingdon, 2003, p. 113.

37 Rob Imrie and Huw Thomas, 'Assessing urban policy and the urban development corporations', in their edited volume *British Urban Policy*, 2nd edn, London, 1999, Table 1.11.

38 Marren, *We Shall Not Be Moved*, p. 113.

39 'Police open fire on civilians', *New Statesman*, 17 July 1981.

40 'A law unto themselves', *New Statesman*, 7 August 1981.

41 Moore, *Not for Turning*, p. 637; Heseltine, 'It took a riot', pp. 14, 18. The housing charity Shelter pointed to 'something ludicrous in Mr Heseltine's professions of concern about the problems he has seen on Merseyside, when it was he who savaged the Housing Investment Programme and re-calculated the Rate Support Grant to favour the shire counties at the expense of inner cities': Peter Taaffe and Tony Mulhearn, *Liverpool: A City That Dared to Fight*, London, 1988, p. 53.

42 Howe minute to Thatcher, 'Liverpool', 11 August 1981, PREM 19/578.

43 Howe minute to Thatcher, 'Merseyside', 4 September 1981, PREM19/578.

44 'Merseyside: note by the Central Policy Review staff', March 1981, PREM 19/576.

45 Thatcher, *Downing Street Years*, p. 144.

46 Paul N. Balchin, *Regional Policy in Britain: The North–South Divide*, London, 1990, Table 2.25.

47 Thatcher, *Downing Street Years*, p. 339.

48 Moore, *Not for Turning*, p. 539.

49 Arthur Scargill, 'The new unionism', *New Left Review*, I/92, July–August 1975, pp. 31–2.

50 John Saville, 'An open conspiracy: Conservative politics and the miners' strike 1984–5', *Socialist Register*, 22, 1985–6, p. 306.

51 Taaffe and Mulhearn, *Liverpool*, p. 136.

52 Letwin to Thatcher, 'Rate capping: Misc 109', 25 March 1985, PREM19/1616.

53 'Enemy within' was a Methodist phrase previously used by Attlee in relation to the communist left: Charles Moore, *Margaret Thatcher: The Authorised Biography*, vol 2: *Everything She Wants*, London, 2015, pp. 163–4.

54 Ian MacGregor, *The Enemies Within: The Story of the Miners' Strike, 1984–5*, London, 1986, p. 196; Frank Ledger and Howard Sallis, *Crisis Management in the Power Industry: An Inside Story*, London, 1995, pp. 125–7, 172–5.

55 Taaffe and Mulhearn, *Liverpool*, p. 203.

56 Marren, *We Shall Not Be Moved*, p. 168.

57 Geoffrey Smith, 'Commentary', *The Times*, 27 November 1985.

58 Massey, 'Heartlands of defeat', p. 23.

59 Steve Quilley, 'Entrepreneurial turns: municipal socialism and after', in Jamie Peck and Kevin Ward, eds, *City of Revolution: Restructuring Manchester*, Manchester, 2002, pp. 82, 88.

60 Ecotec, 'Ex-post evaluation of objective 1, 1994–99: national report – UK', draft final report, 27 February 2003, p. 17, 85.

61 Kynaston, *The City of London*, vol. 4, p. 625.

62 Tom Nairn, *The Break-Up of Britain*, 2nd edn, London, 1981 [1977], p. 388.

63 Jan Toporowski, 'The financial system and capital accumulation in the 1980s', in Francis Green, ed., *The Restructuring of the UK Economy*, Hemel Hempstead, 1989, p. 251.

64 Emma Duncan, 'The new North', *Sunday Times*, 6 May 1990.

65 'The recession did not suddenly produce a sharp shift in population, or in company head offices, or even in relative shares of gross domestic product, from South to North.' David Smith, *North and South: Britain's Economic, Social and Political Divide*, 2nd edn, London, 1994, pp. 167, 336. In a *Sunday Times* column of 2018, Smith would reflect, 'I wrote a book about North–South divisions as long ago as the 1980s, which I will not be as vulgar as to plug here, to be told by some at the time that any such imbalances were fast disappearing, and that it was all old hat. Well, that hat may be old, but it is still being worn.' 'We need to talk about the growing North–South divide', *Sunday Times*, 25 November 2018.

9. The Bank of South East England

1 Tony Metcalf, 'Blair's Britain', *Northern Echo*, 2 May 1997.

2 Conor Burns, 'Margaret Thatcher's greatest achievement: New Labour', ConservativeHome.com, 11 April 2008; Peter Mandelson and Roger Liddle, *The Blair Revolution: Can New Labour Deliver?*, London, 1996, p. 1.

3 Kevin Maguire, 'In Blair's backyard, the natives stir', *New Statesman*, 15 May 2000.

4 HC Deb 25 January 1988, vol. 126, cc60–1.

5 HM Treasury, 'Productivity in the UK 3: the regional dimension', November 2001, p. 39; Office of the Deputy Prime Minister Committee, 'Reducing regional disparities in prosperity', 24 June 2003, HC 492-I 2002–03, Ev 827.

6 Regional Policy Commission, *Renewing the Regions: Strategies for Regional Economic Development*, Sheffield, 1996, p. vii.

7 'North jobs go to save South', *Newcastle Journal*, 21 October 1998.

8 'The Bank of South East England', *Newcastle Journal*, 22 October 1998; Anthony Browne, 'Southern comfort stings North', *Observer*, 12 September 1999; 'Governor tries to douse North's fire', BBC, 22 October 1998.

9 'Made in Morocco for Marks & Spencer', *Sunday Mirror*, 14 March 1999.

10 'Our jobs are not dispensable', *Newcastle Journal*, 2 October 1998; 'Flying squads to help jobless', *The Times*, 17 September 1998.

11 Stephen Burgess, 'Measuring financial sector output and its contribution to UK GDP', *Bank of England Quarterly Bulletin*, 2011, Q3, p. 234; ONS data set, 'Regional GVA NUTS1', 10 December 2014, Table 1.3.

12 Alastair Campbell, *The Alastair Campbell Diaries*, vol. 3: *Power and Responsibility*, *1999–2001*, ed. Alastair Campbell and Bill Hagerty, London, 2011, p. 171.

13 'I'll fight to bridge the gap, promises Blair', *Northern Echo*, 27 November 1999.

14 The 'observation that there are rich northerners and poor southerners is not very enlightening', retorted the *Economist*. 'Mr Blair's argument is in danger of resting on anecdotes, rather than averages.' 'Straddling the great divide', *Economist*, 9 December 1999.

15 George Monbiot, 'Move the capital', *Guardian*, 2 September 1999.

16 'Move the capital?', *Prospect*, December 2002.

17 Robert Chote, Rowena Crawford, Carl Emmerson and Gemma Tetlow, 'Public spending under Labour', IFS 2010 Election Briefing Note No. 5, p. 5; Andrew Grice, 'Brown denies spending plans are a "huge gamble"', *Independent*, 16 July 2002; Blair, *A Journey*, pp. 282–3.

18 Ismail Erturk, Julie Froud, Sukhdev Johal, Adam Leaver and Karel Williams, 'Accounting for national success and failure: rethinking the UK case', *Accounting Forum*, 36, 2012, Table 3.

19 ONS, 'North of England economic indicators', 5 November 2014, Figure 3.

20 'North East "winning war against unemployment"', *Newcastle Journal*, 15 October 1998.

21 Jasper Gerard, 'The rise and rise of London', *Telegraph*, 17 February 2007.

22 Doreen Massey, *World City*, Cambridge, 2007, pp. 12, 93; 'Interview: Ken Livingstone', *Prospect*, April 2007.

23 Richard Roberts, *The City: A Guide to London's Global Financial Centre*, London, 2008, Table 12.7; Philip Augar, *Reckless: The Rise and Fall of the City*, London, 2010, pp. 47–8, 122.

24 'Institutions that can encourage criminality and intensify irresponsibility are poor allies of social and civic regeneration',

cautioned the Archbishop of Canterbury, later confronted by Occupy protesters outside St Paul's levelling similar charges at the cathedral's banking associates.

25 Iain Dey, 'Why Northern Rock was doomed to fail', *Telegraph*, 16 September 2007; Treasury Committee, 'The run on the Rock', 24 January 2008, HC 56–I, 2007–08; J. Neill Marshall, 'A geographical political economy of banking crises', *Cambridge Journal of Regions, Economy and Society*, 6, 3, 2013, p. 468.

26 'After the fall', *Economist*, 29 November 2007.

27 Peter Kilfoyle, *Labour Pains: How the Party I Love Lost Its Soul*, London, 2010, p. 44.

28 Maguire, 'In Blair's backyard'.

29 Colin Rallings and Michael Thrasher, 'Why the North East said "No": the 2004 referendum on an elected Regional Assembly', ESRC Devolution Briefing No. 18, February 2005, p. 4.

30 In the aftermath of the 2010 general election defeat, Paul Salveson, a prominent Yorkshire Labour activist, with the backing of Blue Labour theorist Maurice Glasman, urged the party to rediscover a communitarian, values-led 'socialism with a northern accent'. He cited Bradford in the West Riding, birthplace of the ILP, where Labour had just bucked the national trend to recover municipal control, as an example of 'how Labour should be working across the country'. Within months, however, Labour was routed in a Bradford parliamentary by-election, and its council leader toppled, by George Galloway's left-wing Respect party, in what Galloway dubbed the 'Bradford Spring'. Salveson afterwards defected to the Yorkshire Party. Paul Salveson, *Socialism with a Northern Accent: Radical Traditions for Modern Times*, London, 2012, pp. 190–1.

31 David Cameron and George Osborne speeches to the Conservative Party conference, 2 October 2013 and 29 September 2014 respectively; Nick Clegg speech at Northern Futures Summit, 6 November 2014; 'The Coalition: our programme for government', May 2010, p. 7.

32 Tim Stanley, 'The age of Nick Clegg is drawing to an end', *Telegraph*, 28 April 2015.

33 James Reed and Kate Proctor, 'David Cameron "in off-camera jibe at Yorkshire"', *Yorkshire Evening Post*, 11 September 2015.

34 Richard Wellings, 'North to pay heavy price for dependence on public spending', IEA, 16 November 2009; National Audit Office, 'Taxpayer support for UK banks: FAQs', last updated July 2016.

35 Abul Taher, '"Soviet" Britain swells amid the recession', *Sunday Times*, 25 January 2009.

36 ONS data set, 'RPUB1 Regional labour market: regional public and private employment', 15 March 2017. Excluding effects of major reclassifications.

37 Tony Dolphin, 'The impact of the recession on northern city regions', IPPR North, October 2009, p. 16.

38 Antoine Bozio, 'European public finances and the Great Recession: France, Germany, Ireland, Italy, Spain and the United Kingdom compared', *Fiscal Studies*, 36, 4, p. 416.

39 Carl Emmerson and Gemma Tetlow, 'UK public finances: from crisis to recovery', *Fiscal Studies*, 36, 4, 2015, p. 574. David Innes and Gemma Tetlow, 'Central cuts, local decision-making: changes in local government spending and revenues in England, 2009–10 to 2014–15', IFS, March 2015, p. 9. Excludes transport spending.

40 Christina Beatty and Steve Fothergill, 'Jobs, welfare and austerity: how the destruction of industrial Britain casts a shadow over present-day public finances', CRESR, November 2016, p. 19; 'Hitting the poorest places hardest: the local and regional impact of welfare reform', CRESR, April 2013, p. 18.

41 'Economic evidence base for London 2016', Greater London Authority, November 2016, Figure 1.18 and Table 1.13.

42 'The distributional effects of asset purchases', Bank of England, 12 July 2012; Fraser Nelson, 'QE: the ultimate subsidy for the rich', *Spectator*, 23 August 2012.

43 ONS, 'UK House Price Index: data downloads January 2017', 21 March 2017, historical back series.

44 Dolphin, 'The impact of the recession', pp. 5–6; ONS, 'London's economy has outperformed other regions since 2007', 13 March 2013.

45 *Telegraph*, 19 November 2010. Young was ushered back into government within a year.

46 ONS, Regional GVA (income approach), Table 1. Deflated using the implied deflators in ONS data set, 'Regional gross value added (production approach) constrained data tables', Table 3.

47 'Fixing the foundations: creating a more prosperous nation', Cm 9098, July 2015, p. 70.

48 Grace Blakeley, 'Paying for our progress: how will the Northern Powerhouse be financed and funded?', IPPR North, February 2017, pp. 16–17.

49 Ian Gordon, 'Quantitative easing of an international financial centre: how central London came so well out of the post-2007 crisis', SERC Discussion Paper 193, September 2015.

50 ONS statistical bulletin, 'UK business register and employment survey (BRES): 2014 revised and 2015 provisional', 28 September 2016, Figure 1; ONS data set, 'RPUB1 Regional labour market'; Sarah O'Connor, 'London and the southeast see fewer public sector job losses', *Financial Times*, 19 February 2015.

51 David Blanchflower, 'The North is still not feeling this recovery – and the Conservatives are likely to pay for that at the polls', *Independent*, 24 February 2014; Andrew Haldane, 'Whose recovery?', text of speech given in Port Talbot, 30 June 2016, p. 9.

52 ONS statistical bulletin, 'Regional gross value added (income approach), UK: 1997 to 2015', 15 December 2016; ONS compendium, 'Wealth in Great Britain Wave 4: 2012 to 2014', 18 December 2015, pp. 7, 43–45.

53 *Independent*, 8 June 2016.

54 Christina Beatty, Steve Fothergill and Tony Gore, 'The real level of unemployment 2012', CRESR, September 2012; Department for Communities and Local Government, 'The English indices of deprivation 2015', 30 September 2015, p. 3 and Table 3.

55 The surprise referendum result left the *Guardian* no choice but to acknowledge a failure 'to reckon sufficiently early with all the towns and estates left behind by an international economic order which has not treated them well. Doncaster, Wakefield and Hull – to take three northern examples – have been abandoned for decades, by London far more than by Brussels.' Editorial, 'The vote is in, now we must face the consequences', *Guardian*, 24 June 2016.

56 'Theresa May's failed gamble', *Economist*, 10 June 2017.

57 Vernon Bogdanor, 'Cameron's English problem', *New York Times*, 3 October 2014.

58 Between 1997 and 2015, gross value added per head fell from 90 to 83 per cent of the UK average in the East Midlands and from 90 to 82 per cent in the West Midlands, the steepest drops on the mainland. Northern Ireland fell nine points to 73 per cent. Office for National Statistics data set, 'Regional gross value added (income approach), UK: 1997 to 2015', 15 December 2016, Table 3.

59 Kirby Swales, 'Understanding the Leave vote', NatCen Social Research, December 2016, p. 7; Michael Ashcroft, 'How the United Kingdom voted on Thursday … and why', Lord Ashcroft Polls, 24 June 2016. For opposing eve-of-poll views on 'Lexit', see the contributions of Neil Davidson, David Renton and Ed Rooksby to *Jacobin*, 22 June 2016.

60 Briggs, 'The local background of Chartism', p. 25.

61 'SSI Redcar steel plant mothballed', BBC, 28 September 2015.

62 ONS data set, 'Population of the United Kingdom by Country of Birth and Nationality', 25 August 2016, Table 1.1.

63 Chris Hanretty's estimated breakdown of the vote by Westminster constituency, accessed from his 'Ward level results from the EU referendum', medium.com, 6 February 2017.

64 Jonathan Walker, 'Labour will impose laws ensuring North East gets a fair share of spending', *Newcastle Chronicle*, 7 February 2017.

65 The site chosen, Dean Clough Mills, closed in Thatcher's recession to be redeveloped as a business park and arts complex by a Bolton-born textile and property magnate. Dean Clough is exceptional: of the 1,500 textile mills still standing in the West Riding, 1,350 remain underused or vacant: 'Engines of prosperity: new uses for old mills', Historic England (a state-sponsored quango), 30 June 2016, p. 2.

66 The only Conservative gains in the North other than Middlesbrough South were genteel Southport in the Merseyside suburbs, from the Lib Dems, and Copeland in west Cumberland, home to the Sellafield nuclear complex, already won from Labour in a by-election four months earlier.

67 Labour's popular vote in the three northern regions rose by 9–10 percentage points, in line with the national trend, giving it a majority (55 per cent) of the vote in the North East and North West, and 49 per cent in Yorkshire–Humber, where the Tories polled 41 per cent, except for the blip of 1983 their best showing since the 1950s.

68 Susan Watkins, 'Britain's decade of crisis', *New Left Review* 121, January–February 2020, p. 6; Neil Davidson, 'A Scottish Watershed', *New Left Review* 89, September–October 2014, p. 5.

10. Taking a Stand

1 HC Deb 6 March 1861, vol. 161, c1511. For John Saville, writing in *Socialist Register* a century later, Salisbury's words, spoken in opposition to the abolition of ecclesiastical taxes, offered 'a general proposition' for rearguard defence of the British status quo: Saville, 'Labour and income redistribution', *Socialist Register*, 1965, p. 148.

2 'Victory for Boris Johnson's all-new Tories', *Economist*, 13 December 2019.

3 The DUP rallied to the defence of universal welfare entitlements

and the state pension in its 2017 manifesto, but had previously sided with Osborne against Sinn Féin in a standoff over implementation of the Westminster coalition's benefit cuts. Cash transfers extracted from May had more to do with backroom clientelism than with anti-austerity politics.

4 For its trajectory: Wolfgang Streeck, 'Progressive regression: metamorphoses of European social policy', *New Left Review*, 118, July–August 2019.

5 Tim Bale, Paul Webb and Monica Poletti, *Footsoldiers: Political Party Membership in the 21st Century*, London and New York, 2020, Tables 3.1, 3.4, and Figure 3.1. In the population at large, 57 per cent of heads of households are ABC1s and 42 per cent of people aged between twenty-one and sixty-four have a degree.

6 Around 80 per cent of Labour members in the Midlands, the North and Wales wanted a manifesto pledge for a second referendum, higher figures than in the Remain strongholds of London (72 per cent) and Scotland (59 per cent), where more were undecided: 'Labour members polling', YouGov/People's Vote, fieldwork dates 13–18 September 2018.

7 *Independent*, 25 July 2018; *Observer*, 16 December 2018; *Financial Times*, 23 January 2019. The *Guardian* advocated in the first instance a citizen's assembly (8 January 2019) while offering a platform to People's Vote grandees: 'Blair, Clegg and Heseltine: why we need another EU referendum', 17 October 2018. The pro-Labour *Daily Mirror* tabloid, anxious not to alienate its northern working-class readership, kept clear of the fray.

8 Daniel Finn, 'The antisemitism controversy', *Jacobin*, 16 September 2018; Susan Watkins, 'Britain's decade of crisis', *New Left Review* 121, January–February 2020, pp. 11–15.

9 'Labour could gain more than 60 seats and 1.5 million votes if it backs EU referendum – poll', *Politics Home*, 20 September 2018.

10 'Brexit shift', *Best for Britain*, 14 August 2018, pp. 4 and 8.

11 Paul Mason, 'Brexit is a failed project. Labour must oppose it', *Guardian*, 11 December 2018. In the same newspaper, Polly Toynbee argued in high Whiggish terms that Labour MPs in Leave seats 'would earn more respect from constituents by taking a principled stand, explaining why they are determined to protect them from a bad Brexit': *Guardian*, 31 January 2017. For the polling: John Curtice, 'Is there a new geography of Brexit?', What UK Thinks, 17 August 2018.

12 Speech at the Centre for European Reform, 17 June 2019. Watson's manoeuvring was too much for his West Bromwich voters, who had voted 68:32 to leave the EU. He decided against

contesting the seat at the 12 December general election and it fell to the Conservatives on a 12 per cent swing.

13 'Brexit shift', *Best for Britain*, p. 4.

14 '26 Labour MPs: "We urge the party to back a deal before 31 October"', *Labour List*, 19 June 2019. Signatories included two east London MPs, Jon Cruddas and Jim Fitzpatrick – the latter the sole representative of a majority Remain constituency – and Stephen Kinnock, son of the former party leader, representing steel-making Aberavon in south Wales.

15 'Chancellor ends austerity for public services – but risks breaching current fiscal rules', Institute for Fiscal Studies, 4 September 2019.

16 Chris Curtis, 'The public oppose prorogation, but Boris won't care', YouGov, 10 September 2019.

17 Lisa Nandy, Labour MP for Leave-voting Wigan, joined the rebels in the division lobbies.

18 The *Financial Times* judged McDonnell's economic programme 'a one-way bet' likely to 'destroy investor confidence and usher in economic disaster': Editorial, 'Labour's agenda is not the answer for Britain', *Financial Times*, 5 September 2019. The City's best hope, observed a former chairman of Barclays, was to force a 'backtracking on some of the more extreme solutions': 'Corbyn's existential threat to the City', *Sunday Times*, 8 December 2019. Cf. Joe Guinan and Thomas Hanna, for whom the loss of passporting rights for UK-based finance houses presented a historic opportunity to reduce speculative trading and the asset-price inflation that accompanies it: 'Forbidden fruit', *IPPR Progressive Review*, 24, 1, 2017, p. 23.

19 Matthew Smith, 'Labour economic policies are popular, so why aren't Labour?', YouGov, 12 November 2019.

20 'Tory landslide, progressives split: a datapraxis analysis of the UK general election', Datapraxis, 14 December 2019, pp. 7 and 25.

21 'Tory landslide, progressives split', pp. 3 and 7. Turnout fell 3 percentage points in very pro-Leave Labour seats compared to 0.6 per cent in constituencies that had voted Remain in 2016: Matthew Goodwin, 'Nine lessons from the election', *Spectator*, 24 December 2019.

22 'How Britain voted in the 2019 general election', YouGov, 17 December 2019.

23 Chris Lloyd, 'A tidal wave of Toryism', *Northern Echo*, 14 December 2019.

24 'In Leigh, my hometown, far-right propaganda and hostility to

Jeremy Corbyn could unseat Labour', *i* newspaper, 2 December 2019. After the election, Mason averred that 'we lost because part of the former industrial working class in the Midlands and the North has detached itself from the values that are now core to our party': Paul Mason, 'After Corbynism: where next for Labour', 15 December 2019.

25 'Northern Tories have designs on old Labour heartlands', *Financial Times*, 11 June 2019. Two samples of voter opinion: 'I voted to leave, but Leave voters are being called racist and far right, which is not how it is. We have a local Labour MP in Helen Goodman who should be standing up for democracy. It shouldn't matter that she voted Remain'; 'The Brexit issue has been very bad. If I'd have voted for Brexit I'd be angry with Labour. They've dillied and dallied on it. It's been weak. A Labour leader should have said: "People have voted to leave and that's it whether you like it or not"': *Guardian*, 4 December 2019.

26 ONS Table WD613EW, Census 2011 approximated social grade (workday population); House of Commons Library constituency data; ONS Nomis area reports; HC Deb 25 April 1996, vol. 276, c663.

27 ONS data set, 'Population estimates: median ages for administrative, electoral and census geographies', 15 November 2018; House of Commons Library Statistics, 'KS402: tenure, by constituency, region and UK, Census 2011'.

28 Gross property wealth per family averages £77,000 in constituencies the Conservatives gained in 2019 in northern England, the West Midlands and Wales compared to £69,000 in seats that Labour held on to in these heartlands: Charlie McCurdy, et al., 'Painting the towns blue', Resolution Foundation, February 2020.

29 Engels, *The Condition of the Working Class in England*, p. 37.

30 Duncan Thomas, 'Sifting through the ruins', *Jacobin*, 15 December 2019. I'm grateful to Huw Beynon and Ray Hudson for their suggestions on the Bishop–Gorton divergence; see their *The Shadow of the Mine: Coal and the End of Industrial Britain*, forthcoming, 2021.

31 Peter Kellner, Patrick Loughran and Deltapoll UK, 'Northern discomfort: why Labour lost the general election', Tony Blair Institute for Global Change, 18 December 2019, p. 4. The authors go on to concede that Labour's crisis 'has been brewing for some years'.

32 'Corbyn still plays the crowds – but spirit of 2017 remains elusive', *Guardian*, 6 December 2019.

33 'There can be no socialist radicalism today within the European Union', insisted Costas Lapavitsas. Varoufakis's Democracy in Europe Movement 2025, which McDonnell endorsed, was merely the 'failed Syriza strategy writ large', oblivious to the class interests and national-hegemonic structures that 'Europe' actually stands for: Lapavitsas, 'Boris's deal is no left exit', *Tribune*, 21 October 2019; and Lapavitsas, *The Left Case against the EU*, Cambridge, 2019, p. 121.

34 HC Deb, 22 October 2019, cc842–4.

35 On the campaign trail, Johnson even stole the chief argument of Leave supporters on the left that EU withdrawal would free up the Westminster government to provide more state aid to industry.

36 Rare defeats on the margins: Norway voted twice to stay out of the Union; Danish and Swedish voters opposed adopting the euro. In 2016 the Dutch threw out the EU–Ukraine Association Agreement but were overruled by their States General.

37 Valéry Giscard d'Estaing, 'The EU Treaty is the same as the Constitution', *Independent*, 30 October 2007; *The Times*, 19 January 2019.

38 Lloyd, 'A tidal wave of Toryism'.

39 'To help England's north, link it up', *Economist*, 18 December 2019.

Conclusion

1 John Le Patourel, 'Is northern history a subject?', *Northern History*, 12, 1, 1976, p. 11.

2 Nairn, *The Break-Up of Britain*, pp. 13, 369, 388 and *passim*.

3 'Why a Labour government might mean a fall in sterling', *Economist*, 27 September 2017.

4 Nairn, *The Enchanted Glass*, p. 243.

5 Wang Chaohua, 'A tale of two nationalisms', *New Left Review*, 32, March–April 2005, pp. 83–103.

6 'The pragmatic case for moving Britain's capital to Manchester', *Economist*, 23 February 2017. Amazon opened a corporate headquarters in Manchester in January 2020, but London still accounted for three quarters of tech-sector investment: *Business Insider*, 16 January 2020. The *Economist* had previously floated the idea of a change of capital city in 1962, as Macmillan got into hot water over regional unemployment. 'There is now the threat of a pattern of unemployment that takes minds back irresistibly

to the thirties – a predominantly prosperous South and a basically regressive North', it observed. Regional policy couldn't be expected to solve this. 'It means trying to cajole private commercial enterprises to go to one part of the country when they know in their hearts that they would make bigger profits if they operated somewhere else.' To decongest central London and restore efficiency to its commerce and port, a new administrative capital should be built on the green-belt between York and Harrogate, to be called Elizabetha. The choice of name was presumably that of associate editor Alastair Burnet, a royalist sycophant. 'Anatomy of unemployment' and 'North to Elizabetha', *Economist*, 8 December 1962.

7 Mary Wollstonecraft, *An Historical and Moral View of the Origin and Progress of the French Revolution*, London, 1794, p. 508.

8 Londonism: 'a commitment to relentless growth and openness'. London has accomplished 'the transition from mere capital to global hub. Now it has a political philosophy to match': 'The capital's creed', *Economist*, 3 February 2011.

9 ONS, 'Total wealth in Great Britain: April 2016 to March 2018', 5 December 2019; Oxford Covid-19 Impact Monitor, 18 April 2020. London had a Gini coefficient of 0.7 in 2018 compared to 0.58 for the rest of the South East, the highest and lowest ratings in the country.

10 'The wheel turns', *Economist*, 23 May 2020.

11 ONS, 'Total wealth in Great Britain'; Geoffrey Ingham, *Capitalism Divided? The City and Industry in British Social Development*, Basingstoke, 1984, passim.

Index